CW00567448

"This innovative text for professionals and st_ psychology provides readers with a rare, in-dept ground to assessments and interventions usec recommend these engaging case studies for those who wish to see how to apply peer-reviewed research in practice."
— Jay P. Singh, PhD, Visiting Scholar,
Institute of Criminology,
University of Cambridge, UK

"This book very helpfully explores the work and role of forensic psychologists in a variety of settings using a series of case-studies. Adopting this approach enables the reader to gain a deeper understanding of how forensic psychologists assess and formulate treatment options when assisting young people, those with personality or neurodevelopment disorders, learning disabilities or sexual de-viancies. Organisational considerations are usefully factored into each chapter."
— Professor Michael Brookes OBE,
Professor of Forensic Psychology,
Chartered and Registered Forensic Psychologist, UK

"This book provides key insights into the variety of work undertaken by foren-sic psychologists. The case studies provided are interesting to read and clearly presented. This book is a great read for those developing their assessment and formulation skills in forensic psychology."
— Professor Theresa A. Gannon, Director of CORE-FP,
University of Kent and Consultant Forensic Psychologist,
Forensic Care Group, KMPT, UK

Case Studies in Forensic Psychology

Case Studies in Forensic Psychology offers the reader a unique insight into the often-hidden world of psychological assessment and intervention with people who have committed serious crimes. The book contains a breadth of forensic case studies, and each chapter details the real forensic work that psychologists do in their clinical practice in prison, psychiatric, and community settings. Assessment and therapeutic approaches used in each case study are discussed, as well as the state of the literature in each area (e.g. sexual violence risk assessment and schema therapy).

Each chapter will take the reader through a variety of offender profiles, their personal background, any relevant psychiatric or psychological diagnoses, and assessments and/or treatment completed. Case studies offer valuable insight into the clinical practice and day-to-day role of a forensic psychologist, demonstrating the work undertaken that empirical research does not offer. Uniquely, *Case Studies in Forensic Psychology* brings together treatment models *and* forensic research, demonstrating how theory translates into practice and considering whether it is effective at an individual level.

It is ideal for students of forensic psychology and forensic mental health, as well as practitioners at any stage of their career in this rapidly expanding field.

Dr. Ruth J. Tully is a Forensic Psychologist in the UK. She is a Registered Practitioner Psychologist with the Health and Care Professions Council (HCPC) and is a Chartered Psychologist with the British Psychological Society (BPS).

Dr. Jennifer Bamford is a Health & Care Professionals Council (HCPC) Registered and British Psychological Society (BPS) Chartered Forensic Psychologist in the UK.

Case Studies in Forensic Psychology

Clinical Assessment and Treatment

Edited by Ruth J. Tully and
Jennifer Bamford

Routledge
Taylor & Francis Group

LONDON AND NEW YORK

First published 2019
by Routledge
2 Park Square, Milton Park, Abingdon, Oxon OX14 4RN

and by Routledge
52 Vanderbilt Avenue, New York, NY 10017

Routledge is an imprint of the Taylor & Francis Group, an informa business

British Library Cataloguing-in-Publication Data
A catalogue record for this book is available from the British Library

Library of Congress Cataloging-in-Publication Data
Names: Tully, Ruth, editor. | Bamford, Jennifer, editor.
Title: Case studies in forensic psychology: clinical assessment and treatment / edited by Ruth Tully, Jennifer Bamford.
Description: Milton Park, Abingdon, Oxon;
New York, NY: Routledge, 2019. | Includes bilbiographical references.
Identifiers: LCCN 2018054128 (print) | LCCN 2018055130 (ebook) | ISBN 9780429013133 (Adobe) | ISBN 9780429013126 (ePub) | ISBN 9780429013119 (Mobipocket) | ISBN 9781138584815 (hardback) | ISBN 9781138584822 (pbk.) | ISBN 9780429505720 (ebook)
Subjects: LCSH: Forensic psychology—Case studies. | Forensic psychiatry—Case studies.
Classification: LCC RA1148 (ebook) | LCC RA1148 .C377 2019 (print) | DDC 614/.15—dc23
LC record available at https://lccn.loc.gov/2018054128

ISBN: 978-1-138-58481-5 (hbk)
ISBN: 978-1-138-58482-2 (pbk)
ISBN: 978-0-429-50572-0 (ebk)

Typeset in Garamond
by codeMantra

Printed and bound by CPI Group (UK) Ltd, Croydon, CR0 4YY

Contents

Figures

Tables

Acknowledgements

Special thanks go to each of the contributors to this book, who took the time out of busy practices to write chapters. We do not underestimate your contribution. We would also like to offer our sincere gratitude to those patients, prisoners, and service users who consented to have their stories told. If they did not allow others to hear their story, there would be no opportunity for practitioners to share experiences and learn from each other to contribute to the development of good practice.

Editors

Dr Ruth J. Tully (0000-0001-6477-6367)
BSc (Hons), MSc, DForenPsy, CPsychol, EuroPsy, AFBPsS, CSci, MAE, AFHEA.

Dr Ruth J. Tully is a Consultant Forensic Psychologist in the UK. She is a Registered Practitioner Psychologist with the Health and Care Professions Council (HCPC) and is a Chartered Psychologist with the British Psychological Society (BPS). She holds various postgraduate academic qualifications and a Professional Doctorate in Forensic Psychology, which is an academic and clinical practice qualification. Dr Tully is the Clinical Director of Tully Forensic Psychology Ltd, where she and her team of clinical and forensic psychologists, assistant psychologists, and speech and language therapists work nationwide in the provision of assessment, treatment/therapy, consultancy, and training across health and prison services, specialising in legal contexts. Dr Tully worked in Her Majesty's Prison and Probation Service for eight years, complemented by working in probation and psychiatric settings during and after this time, primarily with indeterminate/life-sentenced and 'high-risk' men and women. Dr Tully's wider experience includes working with adults and young people in the community and secure healthcare, prison, and community settings. She is experienced in various areas of assessment and intervention with a particular interest in violent offending, sexual offending, learning disability, developmental disorders, and personality disorders. Dr Tully is regularly involved in expert assessments in criminal, prison, immigration, and family law cases. She is an Associate Fellow of the BPS, and in 2013, she was given a BPS award for notable contribution to the field. Dr Tully is a recognised European Psychologist, Chartered Scientist, and a full practitioner member of the Academy of Experts. Dr Tully's ethos involves turning research into clinical practice, and she has published in peer-reviewed journals, being an invited peer reviewer for such journals. She is also an invited speaker and trainer at national and international events.

Dr Jennifer Bamford (0000-0003-3749-2507)
BSc (Hons), MSc, DForenPsy, CPsychol, AFBPsS, EuroPsy.

Dr Jennifer Bamford is an HCPC-Registered and BPS-Chartered Forensic Psychologist in the UK. She holds a BSc in Psychology, MSc in Applied Forensic Psychology, and a Professional Doctorate in Forensic Psychology. Alongside clinical placements, her doctoral-level study involved extensive research in the assessment and treatment of sexual offenders, complementing almost five years working for Her Majesty's Prison and Probation Service (HMPPS), specialising in the assessment and treatment of men who have committed sexual and/or violent offences. Dr Bamford's wider experience includes working with adult men and women in the community, secure healthcare, and prison settings, as well as with families and young people. She is experienced in various areas of assessment and intervention, including general offending behaviour, violent offending, sexual offending, learning disability, mental health, and personality disorders. Dr Bamford has published her research in sexual offending, and she has delivered lectures at several universities in the UK. She has also trained other professionals in ways of understanding and working with sexual offenders. Alongside her BPS Chartership, Dr Bamford is a Full Member of the Division of Forensic Psychology, an Associate Fellow of the BPS, and she was awarded the BPS Junior award in Forensic Psychology 2015 for 'outstanding quality and innovation'. Following her HMPPS employment, Dr Bamford moved to the private healthcare sector, and she currently works as a full-time independent forensic psychologist in private practice.

Contributors

Dr Sarah Ashworth (0000-0003-4054-358X)
BSc (Hons), DForenPsy, CPsychol, MFBPsS.

Dr Sarah Ashworth is a Forensic Psychologist in the UK. She specialises in working clinically with adults within secure psychiatric services with a range of complex needs. She has published academic and clinical papers, in addition to delivering national and international presentations. Dr Ashworth was awarded Winner of Outstanding Paper in the 2017 Emerald Literati Network Awards for Excellence and acts as an invited peer reviewer for academic journals. She provides training to a range of professionals and was awarded the Trainer Award at the National Learning Disability and Autism Awards 2018. She enjoys teaching on a variety of programmes across the country. Dr Ashworth also completes independent psychological assessments and provides consultancy to a specialist autism charity.

Dr Jennifer Bamford (0000-0003-3749-2507)
BSc (Hons), MSc, DForenPsy, CPsychol.

Dr Jennifer Bamford is a Forensic Psychologist in the UK. She has worked in a variety of forensic settings for almost ten years, including for Her Majesty's Prison and Probation Service, the NHS, and private hospitals. Dr Bamford specialises in the assessment of sexual offenders and has published her research in multiple-perpetrator sexual offending. Dr Bamford has worked in private practice for almost five years, assessing people with forensic histories in prison, hospital, and community for the purpose of parole, court hearings, family court assessments, and tribunals.

Dr Sara Northey (0000-0002-9610-2460)
BSc (Hons), MSc, PhD, CPsychol, AFBPsS, EuroPsy.

Dr Sara Northey is a Forensic Psychologist in the UK. She has worked in the field of forensic mental health for over 12 years, working with both male and female offenders in this time. She has worked in prisons and in secure mental health services and is currently the Principal Psychologist within a

Youth Offending Service. Dr Northey is also an experienced practitioner of Dialectical Behaviour Therapy, having used this model in her work with both adults and adolescents. Dr Northey has a special interest in working with complex psychological trauma and attachment difficulties in adolescents.

Lyn Shelton (0000-0001-9355-873X)
BSc (Hons), MSc, AFBPsS, CPsychol.

Lyn Shelton is a Senior Forensic Psychologist in the UK. She specialises in working clinically with adults in complex care settings. She has a history of working for HMPPS in England and Wales, as well as within secure psychiatric services. She also completes independent psychological assessments for court and parole board reviews. Ms Shelton's areas of specialism are working with clients with intellectual difficulties and forensic clients with a history of sexual offending; she has published her research on attitudes towards men who sexually offend. She is also an Eye Movement Desensitisation Reprocessing (EMDR) therapist.

Dr Ruth J. Tully (0000-0001-6477-6367)
BSc (Hons), MSc, DForenPsy, CPsychol, EuroPsy, AFBPsS, CSci, MAE, AFHEA.

Dr Ruth J. Tully is a Consultant Forensic Psychologist in the UK. She is the Clinical Lead of Tully Forensic Psychology Ltd, where she and her team of Forensic and Clinical Psychologists work throughout the UK in the provision of psychological assessment, treatment/therapy, consultancy, and training. Dr Tully's wider experience includes working with adults and young people in secure healthcare, social care, prison, and community settings. Dr Tully has an active research, publication, and public -speaking profile. She is considered a leading authority on violence and sex offender risk assessment in relation to research, clinical work, and training professionals.

Dr Jamie Yapp (0000-0002-8038-888X)
BSc (Hons), ForenPsyD, CPsychol.

Dr Jamie Yapp has been practising as a Forensic Psychologist in the UK for ten years, having worked in secure forensic services for women and in male autism spectrum disorder forensic inpatient services. He has also published within the academic field in the area of offender profiling. Dr Yapp currently works in private psychological practice, completing independent risk assessment reports for Court and parole board reviews, including assessment of risk, personality, mental health, and intellectual functioning. He is also a schema therapist and is a certified member of the International Society of Schema Therapy (ISST).

Chapter 1

Introduction

Ruth J. Tully and Jennifer Bamford

Forensic psychology practice

Forensic psychologists practice psychology in the field of crime and law. They typically work with people who have committed a crime (or may be at risk of doing so), victims of crime, and organisations involved in the criminal justice system. It would therefore be easy to assume that the range of work undertaken, or settings worked in, by a forensic psychologist is somewhat limited. However, this is not the case. In the UK, forensic psychologists work within varied settings alongside other applied psychologists, such as clinical and counselling psychologists. Examples of the types of environments forensic psychologists work in include:

- Prisons
- Secure psychiatric hospitals
- Community forensic healthcare settings
- Community probation settings
- Children's residential care homes
- Court settings
- Research settings
- Private practice
- Academia

Given these varied settings, it is clear that the client groups worked with can vary. Depending on their skills, training, and expertise, forensic psychologists can work with client groups such as:

- Any person posing a risk to other people and/or themselves
- People with mental health difficulties
- People with personality disorders
- People who have a learning disability
- People who pose a risk to those within their family
- People who have committed a crime, including sexual and violent crimes

- Victims and/or witnesses of crime
- Those who find themselves subjects of Court proceedings or initiating Court proceedings
- Prisoners
- Patients detained in secure psychiatric hospitals
- Adults, young people, and children (male or female)
- Professionals working in the criminal justice system

In the UK, there used to be a stereotype of forensic psychologists as all being criminal profilers, as was portrayed in a 1990s popular crime drama *Cracker*. However, in reality, there are very few psychologists directly employed by the police in the UK. It was also considered in the past that forensic psychologists work primarily in prisons and with offenders, rather than in the wide range of settings that they actually work in. However, much valuable work is undertaken by forensic psychologists with victims. Although in the UK, Her Majesty's Prison and Probation Services (HMPPS) are the largest employer of forensic psychologists, a growing number are employed in forensic mental health care and other settings. In the UK, forensic psychiatric hospitals are run either by the National Health Service (NHS) or by private healthcare providers, which are funded by the NHS to deliver services. There is a steadily growing number of forensic psychologists working in private healthcare settings, which pose different organisational strengths and challenges when compared to publicly funded NHS settings. In healthcare settings, it is also very common that a forensic psychologist would be working alongside other applied psychologists such as clinical or counselling psychologists, each complementing the other with a different range of skills and expertise.

The training route for forensic psychology in the UK, and internationally, is intensive and takes years of study, research, and supervised clinical practice. In our experience, this rigorous and challenging process produces psychologists who are very passionate about the work they do. Due to the complex, sensitive, and confidential nature of the work completed by forensic psychologists, it is often difficult to get an insight into their day-to-day practice. This case study book therefore not only aims to provide insight into what works in the assessment, treatment, and management of those individuals whom forensic psychologists work with, but it also aims to provide the reader with a rare insight into the type of assessments and interventions undertaken by forensic psychologists.

Any psychologist working in a forensic environment will be aware that there is always more than one 'client' in any given case. This is because the patient being worked with, the general public (whose risk protection is crucial), and the organisation responsible for the treatment and assessment of the patient can all be considered as relevant 'clients' or stakeholders. This poses ethical and legal challenges because to detain a person who poses a high risk of harm to others deprives them of their liberty yet to not detain them may place other people (or the patient themselves) at an unacceptable risk of serious harm. The forensic psychologist therefore has a difficult balance to maintain, and defensible decision-making is paramount at every stage of working with individuals in this context. The typical expectations of seeing a psychologist or therapist, such as confidentiality, therefore do not apply in forensic contexts, and psychologists have to ensure that the patient is engaging with them on the basis of understanding the limits to confidentiality and the multiple roles of the psychologist.

These are not the only ethical issues and dilemmas faced in this area. Psychologists are often involved in forensic risk assessment, such as when contributing to the parole process and making recommendations for the progression (or otherwise) of a person to open prison or the community, or when involved in mental health review tribunals and giving opinion on the safe discharge of the patient into the community or other lower secure services. This can, at times, lead to the psychologist's recommendations being unpopular with one party or another; for example, an individual who wants to be released from prison or discharged from hospital will not be happy if the psychologist's recommendation is for them to remain in a secure setting. This can have a range of implications, such as client disengagement from services and a decline in their well-being. Alternatively, the recommendation may not be popular with the general public or the offender's victim(s) if the recommendation is to progress, for example, to an open prison where potentially the offender could access victims. This demonstrates the importance of a joined-up approach to working with forensic clients, where other professionals involved also consider this range of issues, and between professionals, appropriate plans can be actioned that keep the right people informed of the right issues, and which ultimately minimise risk. The chapters of this book will serve to highlight the importance of involving a range of professionals alongside the psychologist.

Lessons learned from case studies

Case studies offer valuable insight into the clinical practice and day-to-day role of a forensic psychologist, and the work undertaken, that empirical research does not offer. There are many textbooks available that relate to this specific field, many treatment model handbooks, and much research into forensic issues. However, there is little available that draws this all together, demonstrating how this translates into practice, and considering if this is effective at an individual level. This book will provide a varied overview of assessment and treatment across some of the settings already mentioned in this chapter and will consider the impact of the work completed by the forensic psychologist in each case.

The patients we work with are not defined by their offence or client group (e.g. offender with mental health problems), although how we treat and assess patients does link back to what research has demonstrated as being effective with people with certain difficulties. For example, it has long been debated as to 'what works?' with sex offenders, with contemporary treatment being based on years of individual studies and meta-analyses to address this specific question. Therefore, whilst as psychologists we do not wish to define people by 'client group' or the setting in which we assessed or treated them, we have to offer the reader some distinction by making reference to these issues so that insight can be gained into what informed the work completed with these individuals.

The primary settings of these case studies are legal (Court), secure psychiatric services, and prisons, with each chapter offering a different theme such as sexual deviance, psychopathy, and mental health. Each case we work with is different. For example, one female forensic patient with a diagnosis of schizophrenia is significantly different from another female forensic patient with the same diagnosis, and whilst we have to look at the literature and evidence base as to 'what works' with this particular group of people, we also have to consider what have commonly been referred to as 'RNR' principles, meaning *risk*, *needs*, and *responsivity*. These principles assist in prioritising treatment appropriately and provide the most suitable intensity or level of service for a patient based on the level of 'risk', as well as helping psychologists consider the type of treatment required, based on treatment and risk-related 'needs'. The 'responsivity' principle allows us to consider the sometimes clear and sometimes subtle issues that apply to a patient and which might impact their ability to engage in assessment and treatment. These issues can link to learning needs, or triggers for distress, and personality style. By being aware of these issues, psychologists can then plan so as to attempt to maximise the impact of treatment for that individual. This RNR model was first put forward in 1990 by Andrews, Bonta and Hoge (1990), although has since been expanded upon and discussed in the context of cognitive social learning theory and personality (e.g. Andrews & Bonta, 2006). Other principles are commonly discussed in the literature alongside the RNR model, such as the therapeutic relationship between client and therapist/supervisor, and organisational issues that can facilitate the provision of services designed to assist change. Ultimately, the RNR principles operate on the premise that risk reduction is possible, and the literature over time about what works and for whom has been mixed, although positively these mixed findings have resulted in more methodologically sound research in this area, and researchers have also developed hypotheses as to why some treatments have been effective for some offenders and others have not been (Andrews et al., 1990).

In the forensic field, as in any area of healthcare, there is a focus on providing evidence-based assessment and interventions, underpinned by rigorous research. It is clear that a 'one size fits all' approach to working with offenders or victims is unlikely to be successful, based on the 'responsivity' principle when considering offenders, and the case studies within this book all demonstrate the importance of not just the individual's characteristics but also the context or environment in which they are being assessed and treated. It is one thing to consult the research, for instance, on effective risk-reduction treatment, but another to translate this into effective treatment in practice, with Andrews and Bonta (2006) discussing that 'real world' treatment effects are smaller than those found in research conditions. Despite this, the RNR principles have been considered successful, with organisations that apply RNR principles being found to more significantly reduce reoffending when compared to organisations that do not apply these principles (Lowenkamp, Latessa & Smith, 2006). Therefore, the RNR model tends to be considered and applied within contemporary forensic services alongside what can be varied modes of therapy. For instance, Cognitive Analytic Therapy (CAT), which considers reciprocal roles (Ryle, 1997) underpinned by psychoanalytic, cognitive, and personal construct theory, has been found to be useful for offenders (Pollock, 2006; Tully & Barrow, 2017). Additionally, within the field of sex-offender treatment, cognitive behavioural approaches have been considered to be effective in risk reduction (Moster, Wnuk & Jeglic, 2008), although this remains a controversial area with findings in the UK recently being less than promising (Mews, Di Bella & Purver, 2017). These approaches to treatment highlight that the RNR principles can be applied within and alongside other models, and the cases discussed in this book are good examples of the application of such principles in the assessment and treatment of individuals with a history of offending behaviour, or at risk of harming themselves and/or other people.

It is important to note that because of the very nature of the work completed by forensic psychologists, clinical judgement is a big part of the job. Structured tools may guide practice, and research may inform practice, but often clinical interpretation is how we make sense of all of that, balanced against what we know about our client. This means that sometimes clinicians can disagree about cases: how someone is defined, what their risks are, what treatment they may need, and how that treatment is delivered. There are lots of variables to consider and room for sometimes differing clinical viewpoints on each of them. The chapters in this book represent the clinical view and practice of each psychologist author in relation to that patient and the context of the assessment and treatment at that time. Whilst we will outline the theories and research that have underpinned our assessment, we accept that there may be a number of differing viewpoints from clinicians on an individual case. This, after all, is what sparks healthy, helpful debate amongst those working in forensic psychology, which ultimately helps ensure that treatment, assessment, and management recommendations fully consider the risk and needs of all concerned.

The structure of this book

This case study book presents one individual case per chapter. Each 'case' is a patient/client worked with by the author as part of their day-to-day role as a forensic psychologist.

Each of the patients discussed in this book gave informed consent to take part. Despite the careful anonymisation of the information in each case, where a circumstance or other information could potentially be recognisable, we have edited the work to protect both offenders' and victims' confidentiality. However, each case remains true to the themes and nature of the case as it was dealt with at the time and can be seen as an accurate portrayal of the cases worked with.

References

Andrews, D. A., & Bonta, J. (2006). *The psychology of criminal conduct* (4th ed.). Newark, NJ: LexisNexis.

Andrews, D. A., Bonta, J., & Hoge, R. D. (1990). Classification for effective rehabilitation: Rediscovering psychology. *Criminal Justice and Behavior, 17*, 19–52.

Andrews, D. A., Zinger, I., Hoge, R. D., Bonta, J., Gendreau, P., & Cullen, F. T. (1990). Does correctional treatment work? A psychologically informed meta-analysis. *Criminology, 28*, 369–404.

Lowenkamp, C. T., Latessa, E. J., & Smith, P. (2006). Does correctional program quality really matter? The impact of adhering to the principles of effective intervention. *Criminology & Public Policy, 5*, 575–594.

Mews, A., Di Bella, L., & Purver, M. (2017). *Impact evaluation of the prison-based core sex offender treatment programme.* London, UK: Ministry of Justice.

Moster, A., Wnuk, D. W., & Keglic, E. L. (2008). Cognitive behavioural therapy interventions with sex offenders. *Journal of Correctional Health Care, 14*(2), 109–121.

Pollock, P. H. (2006). Final thoughts: the way forward for cognitive analytic therapy in forensic settings. In P. H. Pollock, M. Stowell-Smith, & M. Gopfert (Eds.), *Cognitive Analytic Therapy for offenders: A new approach to forensic psychotherapy* (pp. 323–326). Hove: Routledge.

Ryle, A. (1997). The structure and development of borderline personality disorder: A proposed model. *British Journal of Psychiatry, 170*(1), 82–87.

Tully, R. J., & Barrow, A. (2017). Using an integrative, cognitive analytic therapy (CAT) approach to treat intimate partner violence risk. *Journal of Aggression, Conflict and Peace Research, 9*(2), 128–140.

Chapter 2

Young people

Offending behaviour and community services

Sara Northey

Overview

This chapter considers a case study involving psychological assessment and intervention with a young person who has committed a number of criminal offences. The referral, assessment, and initial intervention will be detailed, followed by a number of recommendations for future therapeutic intervention.

The needs of children and young people

Over the past 15 years, a number of policy documents have been published focusing on the mental health needs of children and adolescents. For example, in 2004, the Department of Health set out a plan for a comprehensive Child and Adolescent Mental Health Service (CAMHS), which is now being implemented (Department of Health, 2004). Voicing similar hopes to those in the document entitled 'Changing the Outlook' (Department of Health and HMPS, 2001), the National Service Framework insisted that children and young people in custody have the same right to access specific mental health services as do those in the general population. More recently, a government strategy document 'Healthy Children, Safer Communities' (Department of Health, Department of Children, Schools, and Families and Ministry of Justice, 2009) has highlighted the need for young people in contact with the criminal justice system to be viewed holistically. This document focused on the need for early identification of young people's mental health needs, whether directly related to their offending behaviour or not.

The Youth Offending Service (YOS) works with young people between the ages of 10 and 17 who have committed offences or are at risk of offending. The criminal age of responsibility in the UK is ten years. A fundamental goal of the YOS is to work with young people who present with increased risk of offending to reduce this risk and prevent young people from entering the custodial system. Typically, the YOS will become involved if a young person has committed an offence and had contact with the police following arrest, has been charged with a crime and has to attend Court, or has been convicted and given a sentence. Usually, the police are the first to make contact with YOS regarding a young person who has come to their attention. The YOS is part of the local council and is separate from the police and the Courts, but works very closely with these services.

The typical community sentences young people can receive include Youth Rehabilitation Orders (YRO), Referral Orders, and Reparation Orders. However, if a young person has committed a serious crime, including sexual or violent offences, they may receive a custodial sentence to be served within the secure estate. A YRO can last up to three years, and the Court will decide the number of requirements a young person will have to complete during the course of the YRO. This may include substance misuse and/or psychological intervention, voluntary community work, and offence-focused interventions, usually completed with a dedicated caseworker from the YOS. A Referral Order involves a programme of work devised by a panel of people from the local community alongside the YOS caseworker, which the young person must complete. A Referral Order may be short, lasting for a matter of months, or may be more comprehensive (depending on offence type and level of risk) and be over a year in duration. A Reparation Order requires the young person to complete a period of work where they 'make up' for the damage caused to the community resulting from their crime. This may include gardening, painting, or removing graffiti, for example. The Reparation Order will focus on a number of hours of work that the young person must complete. If a young person breaches any of these orders by not completing some or all of the requirements, then they may be returned to Court and re-sentenced. Published data shows that Referral Orders are consistently more effective than other sentences, in that young people given a Referral Order are less likely to reoffend than those given other types of sentence. This is the case even taking into account the fact that these orders are often given to young people for a first offence, and the offences are generally less serious (HM Inspectorate of Probation, 2016).

The YOS is focused on diverting young people away from crime and offending behaviour. In order to work with young people at risk of offending, they have developed a number of initiatives aimed at preventing crime. Examples include the development of a Prevention Team that specialises in working with young people at risk of offending who may have received a final warning; the YOS offers a specialist programme aimed at diverting them from further offending. This is delivered on a voluntary basis and requires the young person to self-motivate to attend. The YOS will also work with parents and carers, taking a whole family approach to reducing risk.

The mental health needs of children and young people within the criminal justice system have been well-documented (e.g. Harrington & Bailey, 2005). Prevalence rates of mental health problems vary from study to study, ranging between 50% and 100% (e.g. Fazel, Doll & Långström, 2008; Kroll et al., 2002). Kroll et al. (2002) studied boys aged 12 to 17 in secure care and found that **depression** and **anxiety** were the most frequent disorders, and psychological assessment and **Cognitive Behavioural Therapy** (CBT; Beck et al., 1979) the most frequently offered interventions. Harrington and Bailey's (2005) study of young offenders both in custody and the community found that 31% of their sample had an identifiable mental health issue. One-fifth of their participants were suffering from depression, and a tenth had engaged in self-harming behaviour in the month preceding the study. Similarly, around one in ten of their sample exhibited symptoms of anxiety. Conduct disorder, depression, and substance misuse were found to frequently co-occur. Therefore, research demonstrates that mental health needs are prevalent within the population of adolescents who offend and include anxiety, depression, self-harming behaviour, and substance misuse. CBT appears to be the most popular intervention offered to this population.

Young people in contact with the YOS may have had difficult childhoods. Research shows that young offenders are a particularly vulnerable group, frequently with a history of neglect, child protection intervention, social care placements, family breakdown, and school exclusions (Harrington et al., 2005; Jacobson et al., 2010). Official estimates suggest that a quarter of boys and two in five girls in custody report suffering violence at home (Youth Justice Board, 2007) and that 27% of young men and 45% of young women disclose having spent some time in care (HM Inspectorate of Prisons, 2011). Some of those in contact with YOS have been taken into care due to neglect or abuse and may not live with their biological parents whilst working with us. One or both parents may have offended and been taken into custody themselves, a parent may have had a significant illness, or the child may have been bereaved by the death of a parent. Such events are known as Adverse Childhood Experiences or ACEs. Research has found that a higher number of ACEs are linked to the increased likelihood of offending throughout the life cycle (e.g. Farrington, 2005).

Young people's traumatic childhoods may have impacted their ability to form secure attachments to others (Shillkret & Shillkret, 2011) and they may display challenging behaviours as a result of an inability to regulate their own emotions (Dvir et al., 2014). Secure attachments with caregivers play a vital role in aiding children to develop the ability to modulate physiological arousal. The inability to regulate the intensity of feelings and impulses may be the most far-reaching effect of trauma and neglect. Emotional dysregulation leads to a range of behaviours that are best understood as attempts at self-regulation. These include aggression, self-harming behaviours, eating disorders, and substance misuse (van der Kolk & Fisler, 1994).

Due to the increasing understanding of the impact of trauma and attachment difficulties on young people's risk of offending (for example, Patterson, DeBaryshe & Ramsey, 1990), there tends to be a psychologist or mental health practitioner within the YOS in each geographical area in England and Wales. If a caseworker is concerned that a child they are working with is experiencing mental health or emotional well-being difficulties, they can make a referral to a psychologist or mental health practitioner within their own service rather than having to make a referral to the National Health Service (NHS) CAMHS. This can reduce waiting times and ensure that a child within YOS can access mental health support and treatment as soon as possible. It can also provide the opportunity for a child to develop positive coping strategies, address trauma symptoms, and discuss attachment difficulties with a trained professional, hopefully having a positive impact on their risk of offending. However, it may sometimes be the case that a young person within the YOS requires medical intervention for a more serious mental health issue, such as psychosis, or more specific expertise, such as **autism** services. In this case, the YOS mental health practitioner or psychologist will conduct an assessment prior to making a referral to the relevant service.

The role of the psychologist within the YOS is wide-ranging and varied. They may be required to provide an assessment of a young person's general mental health functioning, including any symptoms of depression or anxiety, for example. They may also be tasked with more specific assessments such as tests for cognitive functioning or developmental disorders such as autism. A psychologist may assess for emerging symptoms of psychosis or complex issues such as trauma. Following assessment, a psychologist working within the YOS may then provide therapeutic intervention or it may be more appropriate to refer to another service for longer-term assessment followed by intervention.

In addition to individual assessment and intervention with a young person, the psychologist may provide input to pre-sentence reports to assist the Court or may provide additional consultation to a caseworker regarding their work with the young person. The work may not directly involve the young person but will often provide a psychological **formulation** of their difficulties, enabling the caseworker to work most effectively with the young person by developing a deeper understanding of their presentation. The psychologist may be able to signpost to relevant services within the community, such as counselling for emotional well-being or substance misuse services. Furthermore, one of the psychologist's roles is to facilitate a reflective practice forum for staff working within the service in order to prevent staff burnout and increase understanding of complex mental health issues.

The aim of this chapter is to provide an example of a forensic psychologist's work with a young person involved with the YOS. The process of referral, assessment, and intervention will be detailed.

Client background

Referral

The case being discussed within this chapter involves a young man who is being referred to as Mark (his true identity has been anonymised). Mark is 17 years old and had been known to the YOS for some time due to a history of minor offences. Concerns had been raised for some time regarding his emotional well-being and mental health functioning. Particular concerns were raised about Mark's low mood, anxiety, and lack of remorse regarding his offending behaviour alongside his substance misuse history. A mental health practitioner within the YOS referred Mark to CAMHS due to concerns about Mark's presentation. Mark and his father were offered an appointment for assessment, within which the young person is given the opportunity to discuss their concerns and hopes for the future, their risk of harm to self and others is assessed, and a plan is formulated with both the young person, their family, and the member of the CAMHS team. Following this initial assessment, the CAMHS worker recommended that Mark undergo a thorough assessment with the YOS psychologist and that therapeutic intervention be facilitated by the YOS. This initiated my contact with Mark and his family.

Family history

Mark's mother suffered from postnatal depression following his birth, and for the first few months after he was born, they resided together in a mother and baby unit for mental health and parenting support. Mark's maternal grandmother was extremely supportive during this time and continued to provide intensive support for the first two years of his life. His father was notably distant during his very early years and felt unable to provide much support for his wife's mental health issues due to his own alcohol dependence.

From around two years of age, Mark lived with both of his parents. However, the couple's relationship broke down when Mark was 11 years old and they divorced. Mark appears to have struggled to cope with the ending of his parents' marriage and engaged in some self-harming behaviour at this time, which involved scratching himself and superficial cutting. He did not require medical attention for his wounds. Mark also recalled experiencing some fleeting suicidal thoughts at this time. He presented as having difficulty in managing his emotions, particularly anger, and he experienced periods of low mood alongside what he reported as periods of **dissociation** (altered state of consciousness). During these periods where he appeared to be dissociating, he would describe a feeling of being outside of his own body, being disconnected from his actions.

Family dynamics were disrupted, and in the years following his parents' divorce, Mark maintained little contact with his father, electing to live with his mother. Mark's father had long-term difficulties relating to heavy alcohol use, which appears to have contributed to the distant relationship he and Mark had over the years. However, following a meal at his father's home, there had been a disagreement between Mark and his father, where Mark had threatened his father with a knife. They ceased contact with each other following this altercation. Mark had expressed deep anger and resentment towards his father, who remarried and had a young son, Mark's half-brother. Mark described feeling *"rejected and abandoned"* by his father despite him choosing to live with his mother. He had more recently chosen to cease all contact with his father and half-brother. Since this time, Mark expressed suicidal thoughts and had engaged in self-harming behaviour, cutting himself with a knife. He also reported that if he saw his father again, he would *"kill him"*. In addition, Mark's father reported that he believed Mark had stolen money from him in the past, which he had not reported to the police.

Although Mark had decided to stay with his mother following his parents' divorce, his relationship with her was strained. Mark reported that he had little respect for his mother, and they did not have a particularly close relationship. He appeared angry that his mother *"works all the time"*, and he felt she was unavailable to him, ignoring his phone calls whilst she was at work. Mark expressed that he felt a need to escalate his risk in order *"to get her attention"*. He stated that if the police telephoned her about him *"then she'll have to pay attention"*. Mark's mother worked full time as a nurse, often needing to work long hours leaving Mark at home alone. She found it difficult to reprimand or discipline her son, particularly as he became older, as she said that she felt *"frightened"* of him.

Education

Mark attended mainstream primary school and his attendance was good. He denied being bullied or bullying others. He went on to start mainstream secondary education; however, during his parents' divorce, he would frequently truant from school and began spending time with older peers who engaged in criminal behaviour.

Despite being an articulate and intelligent young man, Mark did not perform well in his GCSEs (exams taken aged 15 years) and was disappointed with his results. He was able to retake his exams and performed slightly better but continued to be disappointed by his results, believing that he could have done better.

Mark's behaviour at secondary school was disruptive and he was increasingly aggressive, towards both pupils and staff. He had been in trouble at school due to his violent behaviour and had been excluded several times. He self-reported to have broken a teacher's hand on one occasion, although this remained unconfirmed. Following this incident, Mark was permanently excluded at 15 and transferred to a local Pupil Referral Unit (PRU). He continued to demonstrate behavioural difficulties at the PRU and assaulted another pupil on one occasion, smashing windows and kicking down doors whilst chasing the pupil between classrooms. Mark described this event as an *"out of body experience"*, and although he claimed not to remember what happened due to what he described as being *"dissociated"*, he provided a clear and detailed account when questioned.

At the time of assessing Mark, he was not in education, employment, or training. He was initially motivated to attend college; however, he had been unable to obtain a place due to his forensic history and lack of qualifications. Mark expressed an interest in pursuing a career in the Armed Forces.

Substance misuse

Mark had long-standing substance abuse issues and had been drinking heavily since the age of 15. In addition, he used large amounts of cannabis on a daily basis and had been doing so since the age of 13. Mark reported that he relied on cannabis to *"slow down my thinking"*, and said that otherwise he can at times be distracted by racing thoughts. He was vague in his self-report about how he affords such a large amount of cannabis, and there were concerns that Mark was vulnerable to exploitation due to his drug use.

The use of alcohol and cannabis appear to have played a role in Mark's offending. He is reported to have drunk to excess on the night of the most recent offences (discussed below). Mark acknowledged that the use of alcohol caused him to become more verbally and physically aggressive.

Mark was referred to the substance misuse worker at the YOS and was encouraged to access substance misuse services after his assessment with CAMHS. At the time of assessing Mark, he did not present as motivated to address his use of alcohol or cannabis and continued to drink to excess on a regular basis. He also continued to use cannabis daily. Although he was offered drug counselling on several occasions, he did not engage with this intervention and expressed no interest in doing so.

Mental health

Mark complained of hearing voices and of *"seeing things that aren't there"*, including people in cars or passing him on bicycles. He said that he occasionally heard an alarm clock going off in his head and believed that he could tell the time without checking his watch. He told professionals involved in his case of his obsessional fantasies involving blood and faeces, and of experiencing an overwhelming desire to cause others pain. Mark reported fantasising about elaborate plans to kidnap someone and force them to perform dangerous tasks in order to escape. He explained that there was little preventing him from acting out his fantasies other than the legal processes resulting from likely arrest and criminal conviction.

Mark experienced poor sleep patterns, staying awake most of the night and sleeping during the day. This had been ongoing for several years by the time he was assessed. Although he reported finding it relatively easy to make friends, he tended to associate with other antisocial peers in his local area, all of whom were older than him.

During the assessment with Mark, he reported that he continued to have difficulty sleeping and was spending hours at night researching serial killers and mental health disorders on the Internet. He stated that he was fascinated by this material and it made him feel *"less alone"*. He would consume large amounts of alcohol throughout the night until he would eventually *"pass out"* in the early hours of the morning. He reported that he would then sleep for most of the day.

Forensic history

Mark had previously been referred to the YOS after he had been found in possession of indecent images of a younger female (aged 13) on his mobile telephone when he was 15. Mark had completed a short Youth Conditional Caution of three months with the YOS. He stated that he knew the female in the photographs and that she had shared images with a number of other young men. He did not view his possession of indecent images as an offence, a view that appeared to have been supported by his father, who dismissed Mark's behaviour. Mark continued to minimise this offence and demonstrated no remorse or victim empathy.

Following this previous conviction for a sexual offence, Mark was again involved with the YOS around a year later, at the age of 16. He received another caution for possession of cannabis and possession of a bladed weapon in a public place. Mark pleaded guilty to these offences. He engaged well with his caseworker from YOS on this occasion, completing sessions on weapon awareness, substance misuse, and emotion regulation. Mark was able to acknowledge that the use of alcohol could increase his risk and that there was an ongoing risk of reoffending if he continued to use cannabis. He reported that he had been carrying a knife for some time as a means of self-protection, as other young men that he associated with carried weapons and he did not want to be unarmed.

More recent to the assessment, Mark had been charged with a number of offences, including two counts of assault and perverting the course of justice. The victims of the assaults were adolescent males known to Mark and his friends. The details of the offence are that one evening, Mark and some of his associates were drinking in the woods near a local park. They had decided to camp overnight due to the warm weather and had erected tents and started a small campfire. Mark was drinking heavily on the night of the offence and had become angry with two or three of the other males there. He cannot remember what they had argued about. He had started to become verbally aggressive towards others in the group, and one of the young men had thrown a log from the campfire at Mark. Mark recalled picking up the log and throwing it at the other male. The log hit the victim in the chest, burning his t-shirt and causing minor injuries to the skin on his chest. Another member of the group became angry at Mark due to the injuries his friend had sustained and became involved in a physical fight with Mark. During the course of the fight, Mark had punched the other young man, splitting his lip and knocking a tooth from his mouth. Following the fights, Mark had left the group and returned home. The next morning, he is reported to have sent a text message to some members of the group, instructing them what to say if the offences were reported and if the police were to contact them, resulting in the perverting the course of justice charge.

Originally, Mark pleaded not guilty to these offences but changed his plea to guilty at Court. He was awaiting sentencing at the time of working with him.

Previous psychological history

As part of his first Youth Caution, Mark was required to complete six sessions of 'emotion management' focused intervention with the local healthcare-provided Assessment and Treatment Service. This involved a CBT approach to understanding and managing his anger, and although Mark is reported to have engaged well at the time, when questioned more recently, he disclosed that he had no recollection of any skills developed during the course of these sessions. He reported that they were *"unhelpful"* and a *"waste of time"*.

Following his caution for possession of cannabis and possession of a bladed weapon and his most recent arrest, the police had referred Mark's case to the YOS, as they were concerned about the level of risk of violence that he was presenting with. Mark had been working with his caseworker on a voluntary basis when concerns about his mental health and emotional well-being were raised again.

When a young person involved with the YOS in any capacity appears to have mental health or emotional well-being needs, then a referral for assessment is made to me as the team psychologist. In Mark's case, it was decided that a mental health assessment was warranted due to his presentation. He continued to present as emotionally dysregulated, struggling to contain his explosive anger at times, which had resulted in verbal aggression and/or physical violence. In addition, he was continuing to experience periods of low mood, low motivation, and poor sleep.

Assessment and analysis of Mark's case

Assessment

Adolescence is a period of change, and when assessing young people, it is important that this is kept in mind, as it can make the process of assessment more challenging (Smedley, 2017). The pattern of symptoms may be only just emerging and not yet well-established. Symptoms may change over time, and so careful and repeated assessment may be necessary. On a positive note, some of the cognitive developments that occur during adolescence may provide opportunities for young people in the criminal justice system to benefit from interventions that require skills such as perspective-taking and mentalisation.

Mark attended the assessment sessions as scheduled. He presented as engaged and motivated to discuss his current psychological difficulties. However, his description of his difficulties was somewhat superficial and appeared 'stage managed' at times. Mark appeared to want to present himself as suffering from psychological difficulties and as having a high risk of future violent offending, and in my view, he was exhibiting care-seeking behaviour. In order to inform my assessment of Mark's mental health issues, I administered a number of psychometric measures, which can be helpful in developing a picture of the young person's needs.

Paulhus Deception Scale (Paulhus, 1998)

In order to assess for impression management and self-deception, Mark was administered the Paulhus Deception Scale (PDS). This 40-item psychometric measure is designed to assess socially desirable responding both as a response set (impression management, which is a temporary tendency caused by situational demands) and as a response style (self-deception enhancement, which is a trait-like tendency apparent whenever an individual gives self-reports). The PDS is for use on those over 16 years of age, and at 17 years of age at the time of assessment, Mark fit the manual's guidance on use and application of the tool. The results of this assessment indicated a high level of impression management but a low level of self-deceptive enhancement. This type of profile tends to indicate an individual who is aware of their shortcomings but who wishes to appear publicly acceptable. It is likely that the implicit demands of the assessment had an influence on the way Mark presented during our meetings. Despite attempting to present as generally dysfunctional and 'risky', Mark also exhibited a need to establish attachments with professionals involved in his care. It is likely that his tendency to engage in positive impression management and socially desirable responding was linked to his need to make connections with those involved in his care.

Wechsler Adult Intelligence Scale-Fourth Edition (Wechsler, 2008)

Assessment of cognitive ability was completed to ensure that any ongoing intervention was designed to meet Mark's learning needs and also to inform other professionals working with him of his learning style. Despite exhibiting a degree of 'care-seeking behaviour', Mark also presented as very motivated to engage with psychometric testing and displayed a keen interest to learn more about his cognitive abilities. Mark had always presented as confident in his academic abilities and appeared to want to be able to demonstrate this during psychometric testing. He had been disappointed with his school performance and felt his exam results did not demonstrate his true capabilities. This assessment appeared to be an opportunity for him to demonstrate his true level of functioning. Therefore, it was not considered necessary to administer a tool for malingering (such as the Test of Memory and Malingering, Tombaugh, 1996) alongside the Wechsler Adult Intelligence Scale-Fourth Edition (WAIS-IV; Wechsler, 2008). A cognitive assessment was considered useful for inputting into the pre-sentence report to ensure that Mark understood the legal process and was able to engage with his legal team during his appearance at Court. Due to Mark's age at the time of assessment, the adult intelligence assessment was selected as being an appropriate assessment tool, rather than the Wechsler Intelligence Scale for Children-Fifth Edition (WISC-V; Wechsler, 2014). Mark's general cognitive ability, as estimated by the WAIS-IV (Wechsler, 2008), was found to be within in the 'low average' range. His general verbal comprehension abilities were in the 'average' range and his vocabulary was good. Mark's general perceptual reasoning abilities were in the 'low average' range. His ability to sustain attention, concentrate, and exert mental control was found to be within the 'low average' range. His ability to process simple or routine visual material without making errors was considered to be within the 'low average' range when compared to his peers. Due to Mark's relative strengths in verbal comprehension, it was concluded that he would not require the support of an intermediary in Court. However, due to lower cognitive functioning in the realm of working memory, it was considered that Mark may need some support in retaining information presented. This information was disseminated to the professionals involved in Mark's case to ensure that his cognitive functioning was supported on a day-to-day basis.

Beck Depression Inventory (Beck, Steer and Brown, 1990)

The Beck Depression Inventory (BDI-II) is a 21-item scale designed to assess the severity of depression in adolescents and adults. This measure was administered to Mark to assess his current mood and any current depressive symptoms. Both Mark and a number of professionals involved with his case had expressed concerns regarding low mood and depression. The results of the assessment indicated that Mark was experiencing severe levels of symptoms of depression, and this was an outstanding treatment need.

Beck Anxiety Inventory (Beck and Steer, 1990)

The Beck Anxiety Inventory (BAI) is a 21-item scale designed to assess the severity of anxiety in adolescents and adults. As Mark had reported anxiety symptoms and feelings of distress, the BAI was administered. Mark's score on the BAI indicated severe levels of symptoms of anxiety. Mark disclosed that his anxiety has been particularly focused on his upcoming trial and the possibility of receiving a custodial sentence.

Psychiatric evaluation

Over the course of my assessment, it became apparent to me that Mark's difficulties warranted a psychiatric assessment. This was due to his reported experience of unusual symptoms, such as visual hallucinations (e.g. seeing people sat in cars) and auditory hallucinations (e.g. hearing an alarm clock going off in his head). Therefore, I referred Mark to a Consultant Forensic Psychiatrist, and I completed a joint assessment of Mark with the psychiatrist to inform my work with him. Mark was not diagnosed with any significant mental health problems, although it was concluded that he was possibly at risk of developing mental health issues in the future and warranted monitoring. It was not concluded that Mark was presenting with any neurodevelopmental conditions, for example, Autistic Spectrum Condition (ASC). The psychiatric evaluation concluded that Mark's principal difficulties related to attachment alongside poor social development and interpersonal effectiveness. He appeared to be struggling with delayed social development and difficulties in establishing and maintaining healthy interpersonal relationships. Mark was described as struggling with prosocial assertiveness skills. No further psychiatric intervention was required, and Mark was not prescribed any medication for mental health issues. It was recommended that Mark and his family should be offered **Functional Family Therapy** (FFT; Alexander et al., 2013) and that Mark should be offered psychological support for his difficult experiences of family dynamics and the sense of rejection and abandonment he experienced in regard to his relationship with his father.

Intervention and case formulation

Intervention approach

Due to Mark engaging with the YOS on a voluntary (rather than mandatory) basis whilst awaiting trial and sentencing, there was a period of around three to four months in which to start therapeutic intervention. Mark was aware that this was to be an initial intervention that would then inform recommendations for future psychological intervention, which could be included in his pre-sentence report, to aid the Court's understanding of his needs. Having completed a psychometric and clinical assessment of Mark's presenting difficulties, it was then possible to plan the psychological intervention. Due to Mark's treatment needs being predominantly around anxiety and depression, it was thought that a CBT (Beck et al., 1979) approach would be most appropriate. This approach in essence considers that thoughts, feelings, and behaviour are all linked and that changing one's thinking can change behaviour (see Dobson, 2010).

The CBT approach is well-suited to young people within the criminal justice setting, as it can be tailored to the young person's needs; it can be practical and problem-focused, concentrating on the present, or it can be more in-depth, involving childhood experiences (Smedley, 2017). In this case, CBT created a format for a brief solution-focused approach to be taken within Mark's therapy. In addition, this also gave Mark the initial scope to focus on his current difficulties, with time to delve into earlier childhood issues depending on the outcome of his upcoming sentencing and longer-term involvement with YOS. A CBT approach enables the young person to develop the skills they need to manage symptoms of anxiety or depression, which can then pave the way for trauma or attachment-focused work in the future (Smedley, 2017). When working with young people who have offended, flexibility is fundamental in maintaining engagement (Smedley, 2017). A young person may agree to an intervention in order to complete the requirements of a legal order, such as a

YRO given by the Courts. They may find it helpful to engage with CBT to manage anxiety or depression better, but once they have established a trusting relationship with the therapist or psychologist, the young person may be able to progress to other types of intervention, such as trauma-focused therapy.

Case formulation

The first stage of Mark's intervention after completing initial assessment was to complete a formulation in collaboration with the psychologist. Mark was able to identify how his childhood environment, including a number of significant ACEs, had impacted his mood and development. He was able to begin to articulate how his strained and distant relationship with his father had led him to stifle his emotions. He acknowledged that he worried about his mother and how she was coping as a single parent but felt abandoned due to her having to work long hours. This was the start of his anxiety, which had escalated in recent times due to the fear of possibly receiving a custodial sentence as a result of his most recent offences. Mark also acknowledged that he used threatening behaviour as a means of attempting to control others around him, due to feeling out of control in many aspects of his life, including at home.

It was clear in this case how a collaborative approach to formulation provided the starting blocks for further therapeutic intervention. It can be a safe and containing way of starting therapy, particularly when working with younger people. The formulation is outlined below and helped to inform the intervention planning with Mark both for the short-term initial sessions, and in relation to the recommendations for the medium term. The formulation is a tentative hypothesis about the origins and maintenance of difficulties (Johnstone & Dallos, 2006) and was based on the analysis of all of the available information. This was a shared formulation, as Mark had contributed to the formulation, which can aid the validity of the formulation and can help increase patient insight.

- *Presenting problems*: The problem being examined was Mark's experience of intense and overwhelming anger that can result in verbal and physical aggression. Mark's difficulties have led him to become involved in the criminal justice system due to drug use and violence.
- *Predisposing factors (past issues that made Mark vulnerable to the problem)*: Mark experienced a number of ACEs, including his experience of his mother's mental health issues following his birth, his parents' divorce at the age of 12, and a distant relationship with his father, who had substance misuse issues relating to alcohol. Mark struggled with depression and anxiety and found it difficult to understand his emotions; these problems were present in the lead up to the offence (precipitating factors, discussed below) but could also be seen over time as predisposing factors. Due to behavioural difficulties exhibited at school, Mark was permanently excluded, which

may have reinforced his experience of rejection and not being 'good enough'. He would truant from school and spend time with older peers who were using drugs and engaging in criminal behaviours, such as shoplifting, pushing him towards antisocial others and an antisocial lifestyle, and away from prosocial influences and positive opportunities at school and in the community. He did not develop positive coping skills, as these were not consistently modelled to him.

- *Precipitating factors (what triggered the most recent difficulties)*: Following assessment, it was ascertained that Mark's difficulties related to his experience of symptoms of anxiety and depression. He struggled to regulate his emotions at times, and 'triggers' for the most recent episode of violence appeared to have been the use of alcohol and cannabis, low tolerance of frustration, and poor interpersonal relationships. Mark had not yet developed positive means of addressing difficulties within relationships and lacked appropriate assertiveness skills. It may be that disagreements with other young men in his social group triggered memories of difficulties in his relationship with his father and caused Mark to become emotionally dysregulated, resulting in violence.

- *Perpetuating factors (what maintains Mark's difficulties)*: Mark continued to attempt to regulate his emotions through substance misuse (namely alcohol and cannabis), and his aggression may have resulted in short-term emotional release for him. He continued to struggle with his relationship with his father and attempted to mask his distress through the use of verbal threats towards his father. Mark had not yet developed the ability to articulate his relationship needs nor to develop effective assertiveness and problem-solving skills. He continued to present with attachment difficulties, particularly with his father but also with his mother, who had mental health difficulties following his birth. Mark had not developed an understanding of his own emotions and how to manage them.

- *Protective factors*: These are factors that might help prevent future violence or that might help with some of Mark's problems. A significant protective factor was Mark's positive engagement with YOS on a voluntary basis. Support services were available to him via YOS, including psychological assessment, an education and employment specialist, and a dedicated caseworker. Mark's mother continued to be supportive of him and presented as keen to develop a positive and secure attachment with her son.

Now that professionals within the criminal justice system are beginning to understand more about the harmful impact on children of traumatic experiences in childhood (Bremner & Vermetten, 2001), it is possible to address the negative impact of ACEs by providing a safe, stable, and nurturing environment. The goal of any psychological intervention with children who have experienced a number of ACEs is to build social-emotional skills and resilience. This was a goal of the initial therapy with Mark, particularly as the psychiatric evaluation had indicated that his social-emotional skills were underdeveloped and that he was relying on aggression to manage his more difficult relationships.

There are a number of ways in which to promote resilience in young people within a CBT approach. First, it is important to acknowledge a child's experience of ACEs and consider how they may be affecting their behaviour. Therapists working with young people within the criminal justice system are reframing the question 'What's wrong with you?' to 'What happened to you?' The second question is less punitive and accusatory, freeing a young person to talk about their traumatic experiences. This shift has been in parallel with the Power Threat Meaning framework (PTM; British Psychological Society, 2018), which does not assume pathology but rather describes coping and survival strategies which have developed in response to particular conflicts and adversities, both past and present. Unlike the more traditional biopsychosocial models of mental distress, with the PTM Framework, there is no assumption of 'pathology', and the medical or biological models of functioning are not prioritised. In summary, this PTM Framework for the origins and maintenance of distress replaces the question at the heart of medicalisation, 'What is wrong with you?' with four others:

- 'What has happened to you?' (How has **Power** operated in your life?) 'How did it affect you?' (What kind of **Threats** does this pose?)
- 'What sense did you make of it?' (What is the **Meaning** of these situations and experiences to you?)
- 'What did you have to do to survive?' (What kinds of **Threat Response** are you using?)

Mark was able to identify a number of ACEs through the collaborative formulation. For Mark, one of the most important aspects of developing resilience was to enable him to identify his emotions, to talk about them, and to learn to express them appropriately. He needed help and support to develop problem-solving skills and assertiveness so that he would no longer need to rely on physical violence, or fantasies about violence, in order to cope. Furthermore, a goal of the therapeutic intervention with Mark was to promote healthy coping habits for times of distress, including **mindfulness** techniques, meaningful daily activities, and good sleep hygiene.

Through the sessions with him, it became apparent that Mark had difficulty in identifying his emotions and consistently rated his mood as *"five out of ten"* in every session, no matter the circumstances. In order to help Mark to begin to understand how he might be feeling, a list of emotions was provided to him, alongside a chart of facial expressions of emotions. At the beginning of the sessions, Mark was asked to pick three words and/or faces that best represented how he had been feeling the preceding week. He was then encouraged to talk about how these emotions felt in his body, how they affected his behaviour, and any methods he had for coping with his more difficult feelings. It was then possible to discuss coping strategies, other than use of alcohol or cannabis, for his more challenging and overwhelming feelings. Mark appeared to respond well to this approach, and this led me to be optimistic about the potential for him to gain from longer-term psychological interventions.

Future recommendations

Following Mark's sentencing at Court, a clearer understanding of the mandatory or voluntary requirements of his engagement with YOS will be gained, and it may be the case that he receives a custodial sentence. Based on whether Mark would be accessing continued treatment within a custodial environment or the community, there were a number of recommendations made for further treatment. These included the following:

- Continued psychological intervention focused on increasing resilience, managing anxiety and depression, and reducing the risk of reoffending was recommended. It was recommended that following this, Mark should work with a psychologist in order to address attachment difficulties and trauma resulting from ACEs.
- After reducing Mark's reliance on aggression and violence, particularly towards his father, he should be encouraged to engage in family therapy with both his mother and father.
- It was recommended that Mark be offered interventions and support in relation to his substance misuse in order to reduce his reliance on alcohol and cannabis. It was suggested that this could be done alongside his overarching therapy, and some psycho-education about the impact of substances on physical and mental health was recommended.
- Mark was recommended support to access further education, training, or employment. Engagement in meaningful activity is likely to improve psychological well-being and therefore may result in reduced violence risk as well as providing opportunities for prosocial interactions and building self-esteem.

Conclusions

This chapter aimed to provide an example of a forensic psychologist's work with a young person involved with the YOS. Mark was referred to the YOS psychologist on the basis of concerns of his caseworker regarding mental health and emotional well-being difficulties. In order to assess his difficulties, a thorough clinical interview was completed with Mark over a number of sessions, alongside the administration of a number of relevant psychometric tools. Despite Mark seeming to want to present as 'risky' and possibly exhibiting 'care-seeking' behaviour, psychometric testing demonstrated that he engaged in some socially desirable responding, wanting to be seen as publicly acceptable.

This seemed consistent with Mark's deep-rooted desire to be liked by others and a need for attachments despite his difficulties in establishing and maintaining relationships with peers and caregivers. His cognitive functioning was found to be in the 'low average' range, with his verbal comprehension abilities being 'average'; therefore, there were no concerns about his ability to engage with the legal process. Psychometric assessment indicated that Mark was experiencing severe anxiety and depressive symptoms, as professionals involved with him had believed was the case. A psychiatric evaluation determined that Mark was not diagnosed with ASC and that his difficulties were largely related to attachment problems.

Having established a picture of Mark's psychological difficulties, it was determined that a CBT approach (Beck et al., 1979) would be most appropriate due to his primary difficulties relating to anxiety and depression. Furthermore, due to the difficulties with family dynamics and Mark's attachment difficulties, it was recommended that FFT (Alexander et al., 2013) be offered.

References

Alexander, J. A., Waldron, H. B., & Robbins, M. S., & Neeb, A. (2013). *Functional family therapy for adolescent behavior problems.* Washington, DC: American Psychological Association.

Beck, A. T., Rush, A. J., Shaw, B. F., & Emery, G. (1979). *Cognitive therapy of depression.* New York, NY: The Guilford Press.

Beck, A. T. & Steer, R. A. (1990). *Beck Anxiety Inventory manual.* San Antonio, TX: The Psychological Corporation.

Beck, A. T., Steer, R. A., & Brown, G. K. (1990). *Beck Depression Inventory-II manual.* San Antonio, TX: The Psychological Corporation.

Bremner, J. D., & Vermetten, E. (2001). Stress and development: Behavioral and biological consequences. *Developmental Psychopathology, 13,* 473–489.

British Psychological Society (2018). *The Power Threat Meaning framework: An overview.* London, UK: Author.

Department of Health (2004). *National Service Framework for Children, Young People and Maternity Services.* London, UK: Department of Health.

Department of Health and HMPS (2001). *Changing the outlook: A strategy for developing and modernising mental health services in prison.* London, UK: Department of Health.

DoH, DCSF and MoJ and Home Office (2009). *Healthy children, safer communities: A strategy to promote the health and well-being of children and young people in contact with the youth justice system.* London: Department of Health, Department for Children, School and Families, Ministry of Justice and Home Office.

Dobson, K. S. (2010). *Handbook of cognitive-behavioural therapies* (3rd ed.). New York, NY: The Guilford Press.

Dvir, Y., Ford, J. D., Hill, M., & Frazier, J. A. (2014). Childhood maltreatment, emotional dysregulation and psychiatric comorbidities. *Harvard Review of Psychiatry, 22*(3), 149–161.

Farrington, D. P. (2005). Childhood origins of antisocial behaviour. *Clinical Psychology and Psychotherapy, 12*(3), 177–190.

Fazel, S., Doll, H., & Långström, N. (2008). Mental disorders among adolescents in juvenile detention and correctional facilities: A systematic review and metaregression analysis of 25 surveys. *Child and Adolescent Psychiatry, 47*(9), 1010–1019.

Harrington, R., Bailey, S., Chitsabesan, P., Kroll, L., Macdonald, W., Sneider, S., & Barrett, B. (2005). *Mental health needs and effectiveness of provision for young offenders in custody and in the community.* London, UK: Youth Justice Board for England and Wales.

HM Inspectorate of Prisons (2011). *The care of looked after children in custody, a short thematic review.* London, UK: HMIP.

HM Inspectorate of Probation (2016). *Referral orders – Do they achieve their potential?* London, UK: HMIP.

Jacobson, J., Bhardwa, B., Gyateng, T., Hunter, G., & Hough, M. (2010). *Punishing disadvantage: A profile of children in custody.* London, UK: Prison Reform Trust.

Johnstone, L., & Dallos, R. (2006) *Formulation in psychology and psychotherapy: Making sense of people's problems.* London, UK: Routledge.

Kroll, L., Rothwell, J., Bradley, D., Shah, P., Bailey, S., & Harrington, R. C. (2002). Mental health needs of boys in secure care for serious or persistent offending: A prospective longitudinal study. *The Lancet, 359,* 1975–1979.

Patterson, G. R., DeBaryshe, B. D., & Ramsey, E. (1990). A developmental perspective on antisocial behaviour. *American Psychologist, 44,* 329–335.

Paulhus, D. L. (1998). *Paulhus Deception Scales (PDS): The balanced inventory of desirable responding-7.* North Tonawanda, NY: Multi-Health Systems Inc.

Shillkret, R., & Shillkret, C. J. (2011). Attachment theory. In J. Berzoff, L. M. Flanagan, & P. Hertz (Eds.), *Inside out and outside in: Psychodynamic clinical theory and contemporary multicultural contexts* (3rd ed., pp. 186–207). Lanham, MD: Rowman & Littlefield.

Smedley, K. (2017). Cognitive behaviour therapy with adolescents in secure settings. In J. Harvey & K. Smedley (Eds.), *Psychological therapy in prisons and other secure settings* (pp. 71–101). London, UK: Routledge.

van der Kolk, B., & Fisler, R. E. (1994). Childhood abuse and neglect and loss of self-regulation. *Bulletin of the Menninger Clinic; Topeka, Kansas, 58*(2), 145.

Wechsler, D. (2008). *Wechsler Adult Intelligence Scale-Fourth Edition (WAIS-IV UK).* San Antonio, TX: Pearson Clinical.

Wechsler, D. (2014). *Wechsler Intelligence Scale for Children-Fifth Edition (WISC-V UK).* Bloomington, MN: Pearson.

Youth Justice Board (2007). *Accommodation needs and experiences of young people who offend.* London, UK: Youth Justice Board.

Chapter 3

Sexual deviancy
Assessment for court

Ruth J. Tully

Introduction

Forensic psychology in courts

An important role undertaken by forensic psychologists is that of an expert witness advising the Courts. Psychologists can give expert evidence on a variety of topics in this context, including learning disability, mental health, personality disorder, and risk issues. Importantly, a psychologist cannot give evidence as to guilt or innocence, as this is a matter for the Courts. However, their expert evidence can make a huge difference in relation to appropriate detention (e.g. in a psychiatric hospital or in a prison) and treatment/rehabilitation pathway.

In the field of sex offender risk assessment, it is generally accepted that unstructured clinical judgment is outperformed by structured risk assessment (e.g. Andrews, Bonta & Wormith, 2006; Janus & Prentky, 2003). A range of actuarial measures is now available for use, with meta-analysis concluding more accurate outcomes than unstructured judgment (Hanson & Morton-Bourgon, 2004). A limitation of actuarial measures is that they do not tell us much about current or changeable aspects of risk. Structured professional judgment assessments have been developed, which have been found in the research to be emerging as promising in their predictive ability (e.g. Tully, Chou & Browne, 2013). The current case involved the application of actuarial and structured professional judgment risk assessments, which will be detailed more fully later within this chapter. The benefit of combining this approach was the ability to formulate risk in a way that assisted me in developing plans for treatment to reduce the risk of sexual reoffending.

This case study details an adult male in his twenties who had been found guilty of several sexual offences. The patient, referred to as Jay to protect his confidentiality, was awaiting sentencing, and the Judge had directed for an expert psychologist to assess Jay's risk related to possible unusual sexual deviance.

Patient history

Childhood and education

Jay was brought up in the family home by his mother and father. He has two older half-sisters and a younger full sister. Jay described being closer to his younger sister. He reported that there was no domestic abuse in the home and that although his parents argued, this was not all the time. Jay said that he was not abused physically, sexually, or emotionally either inside or outside of his family. He added that his mother has **epilepsy**, which meant that as she could have a seizure at any time, his father was her full-time carer. Neither of them therefore worked, and the family relied on state benefits. He said that he was a quiet child for some of his childhood, although he felt a little jealous when his younger sister became more confident and outgoing than he was, adding that he did subsequently increase his own confidence. Jay described sometimes feeling as though his sisters were getting more attention than he was and that on one occasion, aged under ten, he took some of his mother's medication to get attention. He said that this feeling was particularly prominent as a child at Christmas, when he would worry that his sisters would get more presents than he did. Jay said that he wore night-time pull-up pants until around 11 years of age due to bed-wetting, although he denied that this got him extra attention or care from his mother.

Jay said that school was difficult for him as a child, as he had what he described as "*learning difficulties*", explaining that he struggled with reading, writing, and maths, although the school did not formally assess his additional educational or learning needs. He said that although he was able to make friends, the fact that he had epilepsy made it difficult, as these friends would worry he might have a fit when speaking with them. Jay said that after the first couple of years at secondary school, he settled in and made some friends. Jay would attend martial arts classes outside of school with two of his sisters, and he played for the school football team until he had an injury to his knee, meaning he could no longer engage in these activities. Jay said that he was not a bully at school. He reported that he was bullied by a boy who would physically assault him by kicking him and stamping on his legs. Jay said that he did not react to this, instead getting up and carrying on, which he said over time earned him the respect of the bully and the problems ceased. Jay denied engaging in any antisocial behaviour as a child and said that he did not associate with antisocial peers.

Jay reported that he would regularly attend school. He denied any physical punishments or abuse by staff. Jay said that he achieved several qualifications before leaving high school aged 16. He reported that he attended college full time for three years, successfully completing several technology-based qualifications.

Employment

Jay reported that following college, he was looking for work from around the age of 18 to 21. He said that he was actively looking for work, using a rota he made, whereby he would search for a job from 10 am to 3 pm every day;

he said he had a planned or structured day in this respect even though he was unemployed. Jay eventually achieved a seven-month contract working in a call centre. After this, he claimed state benefits and he would volunteer at a charity shop. He said he did this for around five years until he was arrested for the index offences. Jay described that whilst volunteering, he felt as though he was earning his benefit money, which was a feeling he liked. Jay said that in prison, he was working in a workshop. At the time of meeting Jay, he was located in a Vulnerable Prisoner (VP) wing, as he was at risk of harm from other prisoners due to his sexual offences.

Relationships and sexual history

Jay said that his first sexual relationship was with a female when he was aged 19 and she was aged 18. The couple were in a relationship for around 3 years, with them living together for most of this relationship. Jay said that his part-ner did not work as she had bipolar disorder, which is a disorder characterised by severe mood swings. She did not get along with Jay's parents. Jay described that after a couple of years together, his partner became violent and was reg-ularly violent towards him until the relationship ended. She hit him and also used items such as an iron pan to hit him on the head, and she attempted to hit his toes with a hammer. Jay said that she also cheated on him and became pregnant towards the end of the relationship, telling Jay that he had a *"one in ten chance of being the father"*. She was four months pregnant when Jay left the relationship. This female was Jay's first sexual partner. He said that the couple had sex around twice per week and he was satisfied with their sex life and that he did not tend to masturbate when in this relationship. He added that towards the end of the relationship, the frequency of sex had decreased, with him feeling as though the violence and relationship quality had put him off sex. Jay eventually left and went back to live with his parents. He said that after a couple of weeks, he was able to tell his mother about his victimisation by his ex-partner, which he had felt embarrassed about prior to getting his mother's support.

Jay was single for around five years, although after six months at his parents' home, he found independent accommodation. He said that when single, he would masturbate around one or two times per week to thoughts or online images of naked adult women. Jay was in a long-distance relationship with an adult female, who lived some distance away from him, at the time of the index offences. The couple would meet every couple of months and have sex. Jay had met this partner online on a social network. At the time of interviewing Jay, he said that he had written to her since his arrest, and as he had not had a reply, he assumed that the relationship had ended. He reported that this was difficult for him as he had her name tattooed on his body, and he also said that he missed her.

Jay denied ever having accessed indecent images of children, although he said that in the lead up to the offending, he had once searched for an image of a naked woman wearing a nappy. He admitted that he masturbated to this image around once per week for a period of about one month prior to the index offence.

Prior to coming to prison, Jay was close to his parents and his younger sister, who relatively recently had been diagnosed with a brain tumour. When he was residing in the community, Jay was not on speaking terms with his eldest sister, who he said is addicted to drugs. He said that she once asked him to lie to social services to say that she did not take drugs in front of her children, but that he refused to do so. He said that he has not spoken to this sister for several years. Jay said that he wrote to his parents from prison, but they contacted the prison and said that they do not want contact from him.

Mental health

The medical records did not detail any mental health diagnoses nor problems with drugs/alcohol. There was no indication of a past assessment for **personality disorder** nor for **psychopathy**. Jay denied any history of deliberate self-harm or attempted suicide, although he disclosed that once, as a child aged under ten, he took his mother's medication as a means of gaining others' attention. He did not present as **depressed** or overly **anxious** during my assessment of him, and he said that although he did not believe he could cope with prison initially, he said that he was finding life easier than he thought it would be in prison.

Offending history

Index offence

Jay had given a guilty plea to offences of attempting to engage in sexual communication with a child, attempting to meet a girl under the age of 16 following grooming, and attempting to cause/incite a female child under 13 to engage in sexual activity (penetration). The offences occurred over a period of four days and involved Jay communicating with a person whom he believed to be a 12-year-old female child, but the person in fact was part of a vigilante group who described themselves as *"sexual predator hunters"*. Jay had engaged in sexual discussion with the group over the internet, specifically via online chat applications available for mobile devices. The child profile created by the vigilante group was of a 12-year-old female child.

The online conversations with the child were sexual, with this being initiated by Jay. After the initial introduction, where the child clearly stated that she was aged 12, the content involved Jay asking her to come to live with him *"as friends"* when she said that she disliked living with her family. He asked if she had tried anything to comfort herself, suggesting she should wear a nappy (diaper). Following more chat, Jay made what appeared to be sexually motivated suggestions, asking to put the child in a nappy and to take pictures of her in the nappy, promising her that she would not get into trouble and that she had to promise that this would be their secret. Jay also asked her to "*have a wee in the nappy*". He then discussed touching her vaginal area, asking her if she would like him to touch it with his hand or his penis. He provided the child with his email address, offered to communicate via other applications, and discussed what seems to refer to penetrative sex and condoms. Jay then offered and arranged for the child to meet him by taking the bus. He offered to buy her sweets, said that he has some nappies, and said that the child could buy some sweets if he can have penetrative sex when she arrived at his house. Jay also asked the child about her underwear, suggesting that the child, whom he refers to as 'baby', should get pregnant and have a baby, with Jay saying he would help her to look after it. He said that he looks after babies in his family, but he does not sexually touch them as they are family. Jay also asked the child if she would perform oral sex on him, referring to this as being like sucking a lollipop for her. The conversation continued to arranging to meet, with Jay asking about her underwear. Jay was instead met and detained by the vigilante group at the bus station, and the Police then arrested him. Of note is that the vigilante group placed video recordings of Jay online, and these videos were viewed online several hundred thousand times in a matter of hours of his arrest. Community and media interest were therefore issues to consider.

When Jay's apartment was searched, several phone and storage devices were seized by Police. Also seized were condoms, unused nappies, used nappies, and female and male underwear.

Previous convictions

Jay had no previous convictions or cautions. Medical records from when he was aged 17 noted that he presented to his local doctor as being 'stressed' because his eight-year-old female cousin had accused him of sexually touching her. During interview, Jay denied inappropriately touching his cousin but said that she had accused him of asking to touch her genitals, which he also denied.

Psychometric assessment

Psychometric assessment was conducted with Jay to aid assessment of treatment need/change and response style. Psychometric assessments rely on self-report and are one way of considering change and treatment need. Psychometric tests that measure all attitudes and difficulties that link to risk of sexual offending do not exist; consequently, selected measures are used by clinicians to help 'build a picture' of the client and inform treatment recommendations. Psychometric assessments are selected based on client history, clinical presentation, and empirical research. In addition, the use of psychometric measures of response style/pattern can supplement and indicate the likely validity of other psychometric tests to some extent.

Several psychometric tests were utilised in Jay's case. The response style assessment (Paulhus, 1998) did not indicate distorted responding. The Beck Anxiety Inventory (BAI; Beck & Steer, 1990) indicated mild symptoms of anxiety, which alongside my clinical observations I considered were not at a level that would have impeded his performance on the remaining psychometric tests or in interview more generally. Self-esteem was not identified as an area of current treatment need using the Rosenberg measure (Rosenberg, 1965), although there were in my view aspects of self-esteem in relation specifically to his offending that may benefit from more exploration within future psychological treatment that Jay may engage with. Assessment of problem-solving patterns using the Social Problem-Solving Inventory-Revised (SPSI-R:L; D'Zurilla, Nezu & Maydeu-Olivares, 2002) identified strengths and weaker areas, although this was not identified as a particularly strong area of treatment need. These outcomes were considered as part of my overarching assessment of risk and my case formulation.

Static risk assessment

Risk Matrix 2000 (Thornton, 2010; Thornton et al., 2003)

The Risk Matrix 2000 is a static or actuarial risk measure which assesses the risk of sexual reconviction. It considers various static factors and compares an individual offender to groups of sex offenders and their reconviction rates. The Risk Matrix 2000 can be useful to assess the potential level of treatment need but can be less useful in making progression recommendations, as it is not amenable to change. This tool is widely used within prisons and probation in the UK and is used in prisons to help determine whether a sex offender has access to any psychological treatment. Although widely examined (Helmus, Babchishin & Hanson, 2013), the Risk Matrix 2000 tool is not widely validated on subgroups of sex offenders (Tully & Browne, 2013) such as those with the constraints and levels of supervision that apply to indeterminate or lengthy sentences.

The Risk Matrix 2000 tool relies on 'number of sentencing appearances' when considering offending history. As Jay had not had his sentencing hearing at the time of my assessment, this tool was only provisionally applied to his case on the basis that he appeared once for sentencing for the offences that he has pleaded guilty to. This did turn out to be the case.

Jay was assessed using the Risk Matrix 2000 Sexual Scale as having a *medium* risk of reconviction for a sexual crime. This meant that he had some of the characteristics that are associated with a raised risk of sexual recidivism in sexual offenders according to the Risk Matrix 2000 tool. In the Barnett, Wakeling and Howard (2010) study, which is a study relied upon by prisons and probation services in England and Wales, around 17% of sexual offenders were placed in lower-risk groups than Jay and around 33% in higher-risk groups. The same study found that around 1.5% of offenders in this risk group were reconvicted for a sexual offence within two years of being 'at risk' (either release from custody or start of community sentence). The sexual reconviction rate after four years for this group was around 2.8%. It is important to note that it is widely accepted that any rates of reconviction cited within research would underestimate the true rates of reoffending (Falshaw et al., 2003; Rice et al., 2006).

Importantly, the Risk Matrix 2000 does not consider treatment change and fluctuations in risk or manageability factors. A more dynamic assessment was therefore also required to assess the current risk. It is also important to recognise the research into the limitations of the tools we apply to sex offenders. The Barnett et al. (2010) paper resulted in statistics that are relied upon by prison and community services within their assessments, and this research was a revalidation of the Risk Matrix 2000 tool, because the original research that provided us with the 5-, 10-, and 15-year reconviction rates of the Risk Matrix 2000 was dated and not representative of modern offender management models. The newer research suffers from the same problem; the Barnett et al. (2010) paper is now several years old, and since then, there has been a change of government in the UK, and probation services have been restructured, meaning that offender management has further changed. Additionally, it is useful to be aware of a research paper by Cooke and Michie (2014) where the data used by Barnett et al. (2010) was reanalysed. This demonstrates that depending on which statistics one applies to the same reconviction and Risk Matrix item level data, outcomes vary as to how valid the items are in predicting reconviction. Thus, professionals who use the Risk Matrix 2000 to inform decisions regarding sentencing, progression, or treatment should be aware of the limitations of this method, above and beyond the fact that it is a static assessment, and decision-makers should not accept statistics like this uncritically.

The Risk Matrix 2000 therefore offers a useful filter whereby offenders who potentially need more treatment can be identified, but the application of the *exact* reconviction statistics from the Barnett et al. (2010) sample is difficult to apply at an *individual level*, such as Jay's case where clinical issues such as a possible specific sexual interest in nappies/urine and being caught offending by a vigilante group were relevant. Dynamic risk markers can be examined to explore individual risk, and overall, the 'medium' outcome on the sexual scale here relies on Jay's young age, because other than this he scored low on the static risk markers that have been found to link to sexual reconviction. Therefore, the Risk Matrix 2000 did not tell us much in relation to Jay's *current or outstanding treatment needs*. Importantly, the more changeable, and potentially acute, **risk factors** can be considered within dynamic risk assessment.

Dynamic risk assessment and case formulation

Risk for Sexual Violence Protocol (Hart et al., 2003)

The Risk for Sexual Violence Protocol (RSVP) is a structured professional judgment sexual violence risk assessment tool. It is the most widely used sex offender risk-assessment tool, available in seven different languages (Sutherland et al., 2012). It is a clinical assessment of risk factors for the assessment and management of the risk of sexual violence/offending; sexual violence is considered to be *actual, attempted, or threatened sexual contact with another person that is non-consensual*. Sexual contact may be construed broadly to include *acts such as sexual battery* (e.g. rape, sexual touching) or *communications of a sexual nature* (e.g. voyeurism, theft of fetish objects). This also includes other non-contact offences. Consent may be considered absent if the sexual contact was coerced (i.e. occurred without the victim's assent) or if the victim assented but was unable to appreciate the nature of the consequences of the sexual contact (e.g. immaturity or other vulnerability).

The risk factors included in the RSVP were determined from an extensive review of the literature on sexual violence. The tool itself was developed to increase the clinical utility of an older tool used for the same purpose, the Sexual Violence Risk-20 (SVR-20; Boer et al., 1997). The RSVP tool is not intended to be used as a *predictor* of sexual violence; rather, it is a method to structure clinical judgment in helping *to identify relevant risk factors, develop a formulation* for an individual's sexual violence, and *establish effective risk management plans* to prevent future sexual offending from occurring. This can then be used to consider overall risk and make appropriate recommendations. Risk factors of the RSVP are split into five domains: *sexual violence history, psychological development, mental disorder, social adjustment*, and *manageability*. There is an optional domain of *other* used to highlight other risk factors or other considerations that may impact risk, treatment, or management. Each risk factor's presence is assessed both in the past and recently (within the last 12 months). Scenarios are generated as part of this process in order to aid supervisors in being able to recognise and minimise risk indicators.

In administering the RSVP, clinicians are required to evaluate and document the presence of each risk factor and its relevance to violence. There are no cut-off scores to determine the nature or degree of risk posed; the presence of a single risk factor may suggest a high risk for future sexual violence. Each risk factor is defined, and users are encouraged to consider risk factors alone and as part of the bigger picture to evaluate and formulate risk.

It is important to recognise the limitations of dynamic or structured professional judgment risk tools. The literature supporting dynamic risk tools has not been evidenced as widely as that of static risk tools, which is likely to be linked to actuarial/static tools having been developed earlier than dynamic tools. Systematic review has evidenced that structured judgment tools are emerging within the literature (Tully et al., 2013; van den Berg et al., 2017), and this method is generally accepted within the field of forensic psychiatry and psychology as a valid and useful way of assessing risk at an individual level.

Sexual violence history

This domain of the RSVP considers five strong and specific risk markers for future sexual violence. The factors in this domain are primarily stable or static. Their status may change but may do so slowly. Opinions on changed status are more justifiable in worsening situations than where improvement is concerned. Table 3.1 summarises the findings in this domain.

Psychological adjustment

This domain comprises five dynamic factors reflecting aspects of psychological adjustment that have a strong and relatively specific conceptual link with decisions to commit sexual offences. These items are dynamic in nature and are important when considering a change in risk levels, for example, change over time or the impact of treatment. They are areas that can be targeted directly or indirectly through therapy and sex offender treatment. Table 3.2 summarises the findings in this domain.

Table 3.1 Summary of sexual violence history items

Item	Rating	
	Past	Recent
Chronicity of sexual violence	Not present	Not present
Diversity of sexual violence	Partially present	Partially present
Escalation of sexual violence	Present	Present
Physical coercion in sexual violence	Not present	Not present
Psychological coercion in sexual violence	Present	Present

Table 3.2 Summary of psychological adjustment items

Item	Rating	
	Past	Recently
Extreme minimisation or denial of sexual violence	Not present	Not present
Attitudes that support or condone sexual violence	Not present	Not present
Problems with self-awareness	Present	Present
Problems with stress or coping	Partially present	Partially present
Problems resulting from child abuse	Not present	Not present

Mental disorder

This domain comprises five dynamic factors that reflect the presence of significant psychopathology. The first of these factors considered, *sexual deviance*, is associated strongly and specifically with the risk of sexual violence. The remaining four factors in this domain are associated more generally with the risk of violence or criminality and so overlap with other risk assessment tools both in terms of concept and content of the items. They do, however, play indirect or predisposing roles within sexual offending. The findings in this domain are summarised in Table 3.3 below.

Social adjustment

This domain is made up of four dynamic risk factors that reflect problems relating to other people and fulfilling social roles or obligations. These risk markers may play indirect causal roles within sexual offending, and they are especially useful when considering the likelihood and imminence of future sexual violence. Table 3.4 summarises the social adjustment domain findings.

Table 3.3 Summary of mental disorder items

Item	Rating	
	Past	Recently
Sexual deviance	Present	Present
Psychopathic personality disorder	Not present	Not present
Major mental illness	Not present	Not present
Problems with substance use	Not present	Not present
Violent or suicidal ideation	Not present	Not present

Table 3.4 Summary of social adjustment items

Item	Rating	
	Past	Recently
Problems with intimate relationships	Present	Present
Problems with non-intimate relationships	Partially present	Partially present
Problems with employment	Present	Present
Non-sexual criminality	Not present	Not present

Manageability

The manageability domain comprises three factors that reflect problems managing the risk of sexual violence in the community. Each of these three factors is dynamic in nature, and they are associated more generally with the risk of violence or criminality. They are more likely to play an indirect role in sexual offending. These factors are useful when drawing conclusions about the likelihood, imminence, and frequency of future sexual offending. Table 3.5 summarises these findings.

Formulation of sexual offending

Prior to full consideration of manageability and overall risk, a narrative *formulation* of Jay's sexual offending was devised to aid understanding of his case and risk. Whilst there is no universally agreed definition of what formulation is, it can usefully be described as a summary of the patient's problems that aims to explain the development and maintenance of the problem on the basis of psychological theory. On the same basis, it can suggest how the client's difficulties relate to one another. Formulations are open to revision and reformulation, and importantly, they can aid treatment planning to help reduce the likelihood of the problem being maintained or reoccurring (see Johnstone & Dallos, 2006). Within psychological case formulation, the inclusion of causal factors from several different approaches or models is desirable; however, this does not necessarily result in the integration of the models with the case details, i.e. application of a specific model does not necessarily result in an ideographic case formulation.

Some well-known approaches to formulation advocate the use of templates for filling in lists of relevant factors from biological, social, interpersonal, and other domains (e.g. Weerasekera, 1996). Psychologists sometimes use a similar template known as '4P' (predisposing, precipitating, perpetuating, and protective) or 5P (with the fifth 'P' being the 'problem'). This format is not exclusively for use by psychologists and is relevant to other related disciplines; for example, this approach is also taught within psychiatric training in the UK (Royal College of Psychiatrists, 2010).

Table 3.5 Summary of manageability items

Item	Rating	
	Past	Recently
Problems with planning	Partially present	Partially present
Problems with treatment	Not present	Not present
Problems with supervision	Not present	Not present

Although these kinds of templates may be a useful starting point, they have two limitations: first, they do not require the various factors to be synthesised into a coherent narrative as opposed to simply being listed. In other words, these formulations are not necessarily integrated, even though they are sometimes described as such. Second, the approach does not necessarily include the personal meaning of the factors and life events. Psychological theory suggests that the impact of difficult circumstances or events is mediated through the meaning that they hold for the individual (Kinderman, Sellwood & Tai, 2008). Personal meaning can therefore be the integrating factor within a psychological formulation. One of the risks of the list-of-factors approach is that incompatible theoretical models can be merged. This is true of some versions of the widely used diathesis-stress or biopsychosocial model (British Psychological Society, 2011). Therefore, Jay's case formulation attempted to utilise the 5P approach to case formulation whilst considering the meaning of relevant events and circumstances for Jay.

In Jay's case, the area being considered as the 'problem' or 'presenting issue' was his sexual offence. The formulation was based on the analysis of all the available information, and importantly, the formulation is a shared formulation. Jay contributed to the formulation by joining in with discussion and answering questions about his life. He had a limited insight into the trajectory of his offending, but this is not uncommon with those with sexual convictions who have not yet engaged in any therapeutic interventions. The formulation is presented visually in Figure 3.1 below, and within the following narrative description.

Although Jay did not describe a history of abuse, his perception of not getting enough attention from his mother could have been a problem. Childhood attention-seeking (such as taking his mother's medication as a child) mirrored his reported experience in the lead up to the index offence, whereby he felt that his sister, who had a brain tumour, was getting his parents' attention more than he was. As a child, Jay experienced night-time bed-wetting, and so wore 'pull-up pants' (night-time nappy/diaper type products) until at least the age of 11. Jay did not attribute significance to this issue in relation to his offending and his later choice to wear a nappy for what he said were comfort reasons rather than sexual reasons. However, it appears reasonable to hypothesise that there was a link between this issue and the manifestation of a sexual interest in another person wearing a nappy, and his own use of nappies to urinate in for non-medical reasons as an adult. Perhaps as a child, the pull-ups brought him feelings of comfort, safety, and confidence. It may also be the case that his bed-wetting brought him extra attention from his mother, balancing his perception of attention between siblings. If Jay wore the nappies up to or beyond the age of 11, it is likely that his psychosexual development was influenced by this.

I formed the view that seeing his parents not working, as well as his first partner not working due to health reasons, normalised unemployment or perhaps the feeling of not being able to work and the need to depend on benefits/ other people. Jay was fit and able to work, without learning disability (although with some literacy issues), and so if he were working as hard as he said he was to

Pre-Disposing Factors (What made them Vulnerable?):

- Female dominate household > feeling 'different' and pushed out > craving attention or affection.
- Night-time bed wetting until at least the age of eleven > possibly gaining more care or attention from mother as a result > associating nappies or urine with care or comfort.
- Poor problem solving evident as a child.
- Possibly wearing pull-up pants/nappies/diapers during the age of sexual development and developing arousal to these, reinforced if masturbating wearing nappies.
- Mother unemployed, father her carer > normalised unemployment and reliance on others > unemployed as an adult with problems getting work.
- Got a relationship and spent a lot of time with partner as both unemployed > experienced domestic violence from his partner.
- Later got a long-distance relationship with partner > missed physical affection and feeling wanted because of distance.

Precipitating Factors (Triggers in relation to most recent episode):

- Sister's brain tumour > parents attending to her needs > feeling pushed out by family, relationship strained > feeling lonely, resentful.
- Long-distance relationship combined with limited intimacy skills > not feeling fulfilled emotionally or sexually.
- Poor problem solving and communication skills and could not deal with his feelings appropriately.
- Beginning to wear nappies as a comfort, although this may have started much before the direct lead up to the offence > sexual arousal or interest in urine/nappies.
- Unemployed and time on his hands.
- Masturbating to image of a woman in a nappy > reinforcing arousal and/or not being enough for him and desiring this in 'real life'.
- Use of online social networks to access victim.

Protective Factors:

- No learning disability diagnosis.
- Takes responsibility by admitting to offences.
- Motivated for employment.
- Motivated to engage in sex offender treatment.
- Detained in prison.
- Professional support available.

Problem/Presenting Issues:

Most recent sexual offences

Perpetuating Factors (what is/was/could keep the problem going):

- Sexual deviancy and acting on this by masturbation > reinforcing arousal.
- Poor problem solving.
- Lack of insight into risks posed.
- Limited social/family support.
- Complex family dynamic and perceived rejection.
- Feeling unloved/pushed out.
- Lack of constructive activity/employment > low self-esteem.

EXIT/DESISTANCE FROM OFFENDING

Figure 3.1 Clinical case formulation.

achieve employment, it was difficult to see how he was unable to find any form of work for so long, unless he was content with his life as it was and consciously or subconsciously did not want to work.

Jay experienced difficulties in his first relationship whereby he was violently victimised by his partner. After this relationship, he was single for some time before forming a long-distance relationship online with a woman he would meet up with every couple of months. Both relationships were sexual, and Jay reported that he was satisfied with the sex. Despite this, he offended whilst in the long-distance relationship that he was otherwise satisfied by, reporting that for him cuddling and physical touch was important for affection, and this was missing with the relationship being long-distance.

I hypothesised that the following factors appeared highly relevant to the lead up to the offence and the commission of it, meaning that these factors would need attention within any psychological treatment.

Deviant sexual interests

In the context of the RSVP tool, *sexual deviance* is sexual interest, preference, arousal, or behaviour that involves a focus on inappropriate persons or objects, i.e. those that fall outside the realm of what is considered legal or conventional in consenting adult relationships. Sexual deviance is a complex phenomenon, with this providing motivation for offending (e.g. Ward & Sorbello, 2003). There were two aspects to consider here: first, the fact that Jay attempted to meet, and had been communicating sexually with, someone whom he believed was a 12-year-old female child, and second, the (possibly related) aspect of his offending that involved him asking the child if she would wear a nappy, combined with there being used nappies (containing urine) found in Jay's home when it was searched. Jay strongly denied a sexual interest in children. He maintained that he was seeking company and comfort by contacting the victim, and he was unable to explain the sexual content of his messages. I did not believe he was wilfully holding back in this regard; rather, he did not fully understand his motivation for offending in this way. He was more able to discuss the nappies/diapers, although he also lacked insight into this aspect.

Jay discussed that he had himself been wearing nappies and urinating in them. He said that this was a reaction to feeling pushed out by his family for various reasons, and he said that he had approached a friend for advice with him saying he posed wearing nappies as a potential solution to his problem. He said that his friend had encouraged him. Jay did not acknowledge that to wear/urinate into a nappy may not be the first solution for most people facing a similar problem, seemingly oblivious to this or not wishing to admit to this being more than an attempt to feel comforted. He said that he would buy and wear adult nappies, using child nappies when he could not afford adult-sized nappies and holding these smaller nappies in place with his underpants over them. He denied any sexual arousal from wearing the nappy and said he had never masturbated whilst wearing a nappy / in possession of a nappy. Jay asked the 'child' decoy if she would urinate in a nappy, referred to her as 'baby' (which may or may not have been significant), and also discussed having a baby. Jay did admit to searching online for an image of a naked woman wearing a nappy and that he masturbated to this for around one month prior to the offences. He denied longer-term use of related pornographic material and denied accessing any illegal images of children to use for masturbatory purposes (there was no evidence to the contrary).

Assessment of sexual deviance requires a pattern of behaviour and not an isolated incident. A difficulty in assessing sexual deviance is that aside from observable behavioural evidence, assessment usually relies on self-report. Although there are methods that can be used to assess deviancy, such as **penile plethysmography** (PPG; a measure of blood flow to the penis, used as a proxy measure of sexual arousal) and visual reaction time tests, these methods are not routinely accessible to use in prisons due to expense and practical issues. Viewing time measures are easier to implement than the PPG and have some growing support as demonstrated within the meta-analysis in relation to sexual interest in children (Schmidt, Babchishin & Lehmann, 2017) although this does not necessarily help when considering other deviant interests such as a sexual interest in urine. As these methods were not used, sexual interests were discussed at length during the assessment with Jay. There was more evidence of sexual interest in nappies/diapers and possibly also urination than there was of a specific sexual interest in female children. However, it had to be considered for risk management purposes that there was a *possible* sexual interest in female children alongside the nappy interest. I formed the view that there was likely to have been some childhood trauma or other issues relevant to the development of these interests, which are likely to have been part of Jay's life for longer than he states. A starting point for psychological treatment was the fact that Jay acknowledged some form of sexual interest in nappies in him admitting to masturbating to an image of a woman wearing a nappy. Repeated masturbation could have contributed to increased, or at least maintained, arousal to this via conditioning, linking to him asking the online victim about nappy-wearing. It seemed probable that this interest in nappies was not exclusive to the one month prior to the index offence, and this would be important to be explored more within psychological treatment. The wearing of continence products at night as a child was likely to have had an influence on his sexual interests, especially if he was wearing these as his psychosexual identity developed during his adolescence. Related to this were issues such as Jay's poor problem-solving ability, deficits in his communication skills, and problems within relationships.

It is relatively easy to find others with similar interests online, whether this is a hobby or a sexual interest, and it would have been possible for Jay to search for others interested in nappies/urine without having to offend against a child. It was possible that he had a sexual attraction to children; I also considered it possible that he targeted a child because she was vulnerable, and therefore it was more likely that he could manipulate her to agree to his requests about nappies. With that said, his persistence in sexual communication and meeting the child, as well as sexual communication not being limited to the nappy/urination issue, did suggest, at the least, the capacity to be aroused by female children.

Intimacy

Jay was in his late twenties and had been in two relationships, with one of these being online/long-distance. He was in the online/long-distance relationship at the time of the offence yet did not discuss with his partner his feelings about life's problems, neither did he discuss the fact that he was not feeling emotionally supported in this relationship. Communication within intimate relationships and understanding intimacy were both in my view relevant treatment needs and a likely link to Jay's **attachment** problems which developed as a child and which manifested during adulthood.

Family dynamic/relationships

Jay reported few childhood and adult problems within his family, yet a theme of wanting his mother's attention seemed present as a child and indeed in the lead up to the offence as an adult. This dynamic would be important to explore further within treatment.

Protective factors

Rogers (2000) was one of the first to argue that risk assessment instruments only measure factors which increase the likelihood of recidivism; therefore, they are inherently and systematically skewed in their focus. Protective factors are variables that decrease the likelihood of recidivism. A balanced assessment report should give attention to risk factors and strengths. Jay had some tangible protective factors when assessed based on the Structured Assessment of Protective Factors (SAPROF 2nd Edition; de Vogel et al., 2012) model. These factors are highlighted in Table 3.6 below.

Table 3.6 Summary of protective factors for Jay

Domain	Protective factor
Internal	No diagnosis of learning disability
	Took responsibility for his actions
Motivational	Motivated for employment
	Motivated for psychological treatment
External	In custody with no victim group access
	Professional care and support available

Scenario planning

The RSVP is a particularly useful tool compared to other sex offender risk assessment tools, as it is structured to allow for scenario planning. These scenarios do not imply *prediction*, they merely allow for the case formulation to inform how future violence *could* manifest, so as to plan to reduce and manage the associated risks. The scenarios of the RSVP have been found within empirical research to be significant in identifying how future reoffending may manifest (Darjee et al., 2016).

A repeat type scenario was considered and could involve Jay using online or mobile communication to target a female child. The offence may involve sexual communication / inciting sexual acts, or it may diversify (i.e. a 'twist' scenario) to involve requesting photographs of the child. A repeat offence could involve attempting to meet the child, and if the person was not instead a vigilante group and an actual child attended, this could turn into an escalation scenario involving sexual assault of the child, taking photos of the child, encouraging her to engage in wearing nappies and/or urination-related acts, and could result in a rape offence. Further diversification of offending may involve targeting an adult woman who is vulnerable in some way, so as to target someone who may be considered easy to psychologically coerce into engaging in sexual acts related to nappies/urination.

The imminence of risk was considered to be low in closed prison (lack of victim access) but was considered to be moderate in the community. Observable warning signs of increased risk in community or prison conditions may be few because this case had sexual interests central to it, but these could include:

- evidence indicative of acting on sexual interest in nappies/urine or female children (in prison this may include accessing continence products via the healthcare department without appropriate need or via other prisoners or misuse of legitimate brochures/catalogues, and out of prison this may include online activity as well as purchases made in person),
- self-report of increased sexual thinking or of any offence-related fantasy,
- use of the Internet if not permitted to do so, being evasive about sites accessed if permitted to use the internet, or deleting internet history,
- purposefully attempting to access female children through employment or other means such as extended family or associations,
- having a relationship of poor quality or not meeting his needs but not addressing this through clear and open communication, and
- feeling pushed out by his family if he were to regain contact with them.

Based on the above, it was recommended that monitoring and supervision to manage risk (in prison or the community) could include regular searches of accommodation (looking for signs of Jay acting on his sexual interests), appropriate disclosure if he started an intimate relationship or his long-distance relationship continued (aimed at protecting any children associated with the relationship), support and therapeutic monitoring if he regained contact with his family, and support with developing employment-related skills/qualifications including improving literacy. Suggested treatment strategies are detailed further below.

Overall risk and manageability

The RSVP structured professional judgment assessment assisted in carefully examining 23 factors linked to sexual offending and aided a case formulation alongside scenario planning (warning signs, identification, and management) in Jay's case. The Risk Matrix 2000 assessment (completed provisionally) also informed the assessment of risk. It was my opinion that Jay posed at least a moderate level of risk of future sexual offending, meaning that specific risk management strategies would be required in order to keep the public safe.

Recommendations for the court

As it was likely that sexual deviance was a strong contributing factor to his risk, it was concluded that Jay's risk was likely to be chronic. Over time, meta-analyses have demonstrated that sexual deviancy/fantasy is one of the strongest predictors of sexual reoffending (e.g. Hanson & Morton-Bourgon, 1998), and evidence suggested that Jay lacked insight into his risk. It was therefore my recommendation to the Court, based on the assessments applied, that Jay's risk was not safely manageable in the community (e.g. if given a community sentence under the supervision of probation services). It was my opinion that he required specialist sex offender treatment in a prison/correctional setting. The specific recommendations in this case were as follows.

Sex offender treatment

Jay's (provisionally coded) Risk Matrix 2000 assessment screened him in to be considered for a prison-based sex offender treatment group. In the UK, men scoring 'medium' risk and above on the Risk Matrix 2000 were considered for psychological treatment, whereas those scoring 'low' were not eligible. It was recommended that Jay be transferred from his current prison location to a specialist sex offender treatment site to access psychological treatment. In the prisons within England and Wales, group-based sex offender treatment is routinely offered as opposed to individualised therapy. As part of the assessment process for this, it is routine for the prison to conduct intellectual functioning screening, to determine whether the person may require sex offender treatment that is adapted for lower-functioning offenders (usually $IQ < 80$). I was not convinced that Jay would require the adapted programme; although he had literacy difficulties, clinically he did not present as though he had a learning disability, although the prison psychologist would be able to determine this easily through routine assessment using a tool such as the Wechsler Adult

Intelligence Scale-Fourth Edition (WAIS-IV; Wechsler, 2008). Even if Jay was found to require the adapted group programme, he required this type of treatment prior to then engaging in more specialist treatment in the form of the Healthy Sex Programme, which is an individually delivered behaviour modification sex offender treatment programme available in the prisons of England and Wales that considers sexual interests in more depth. Jay did engage very well with me as a visiting psychologist, and so I had some optimism about his ability to gain from treatment and his ability to develop his insight and risk management strategies in the future.

Family relationships

During clinical interview, Jay mentioned that prison staff had informed him that his family had requested that he does not contact them. Their rejection played some role in Jay's pathway to offending, and so I recommended that this situation and his associated feelings be carefully monitored. Jay was very isolated with no friends or community contacts, although he did possess adequate social skills in relation to making new associations. Regardless, this isolation over time could contribute to him feeling very low, which would be unlikely to help his rehabilitation. It was recommended that if he did regain contact with his family, or indeed any other community support, community social services should be notified in relation to protecting any named children upon Jay's release. Jay mentioned having a baby with the victim in these offences, which, given the sexual interests that were considered relevant in his case, was of concern. Therefore, social services should be involved if Jay has a child in the future. He had disclosed that he may already be a father to a child with his ex-partner, although he was not certain that he was the father.

Risk to Jay from other prisoners

Jay was relatively young and he had not been in prison before. It was considered possible that this isolation and associated loneliness could be exploited by older or more seasoned prisoners who may seek to manipulate the weaknesses of others. It was recommended that this risk be monitored.

Risk to Jay due to offending being widely known about

Jay was apprehended by a vigilante group and images of this were shared online. It was therefore possible that other prisoners who may not take kindly to sex offenders could find out that Jay had sexual convictions and that he may be victimised because of this. It was recommended that if he remained in a mixed offence prison, he remained located in a VP wing. It was also recommended that as and when released from prison, any request by Jay that he resettle outside of his old area should be listened to. This was due to others knowing of his offences to not only aid his physical safety in case of vigilantes taking action to harm him but also to enhance the likelihood of success in relation to his eventual community reintegration.

Employment

It was recommended that Jay continue to develop his skills and education. He reported literacy difficulties and problems with numeracy, along with his belief that he had dyslexia. To further develop in this area, it was recommended that Jay apply to the education department to engage in literacy and numeracy courses and request that the education department complete an assessment of dyslexia so that they could best support him in his learning and vocational endeavours. When considering the case formulation, it was suggested that Jay should, within sex offender treatment, consider whether there were any psychological barriers to his ability to gain paid work in the past and how to overcome these barriers. Jay seemed able to maintain his prison work position in the workshop, and whilst it was considered that this could help with his continued socialisation and assist in him avoiding isolation, engaging in this type of work alone would not improve his learning and skills. Therefore, continuing to develop in this area through education and training was advised to aid the chances of successful community resettlement on his eventual release from prison.

Conclusions

The assessment described within this chapter was presented to the Court in the form of a written report. The sentencing Judge utilised the assessment to understand Jay's case and to assist in imposing an appropriate custodial sentence. He was sentenced to around four years in prison followed by several years under the supervision of community probation services. This was considered ample time to enable him to engage in the recommended sex offender treatment, although this sentence length is much lower than might be seen in other countries such as the USA, where the maximum sentence for an offence of a similar nature is 20 years.

The Court benefited from the risk assessment in order to help understand Jay's presentation and offending, and the treatment recommendations were particularly useful because this assessment was conducted at a time when prison-based offending behaviour programmes were undergoing significant changes that were not well-known within the criminal justice system more widely. Not all people with sexual deviance commit sexual offences, and not all people who sexually offend are sexually deviant; there is a multitude of factors that contribute to sex offending (e.g. Hart et al., 2003). However, as sexual deviance was relevant in this case, and literature does support that those with sexual deviance are at raised risk of reoffending (e.g. Hanson & Bussière, 1998), the assessment added significant value to the sentencing Judge. With the assistance of expert psychological evidence, the Judge was able to make an informed decision that was not solely based on sentencing guidelines (i.e. the law). Instead, the Judge based the sentence on sentencing guidelines alongside their knowledge of Jay's psychological treatment needs and a recommended treatment pathway.

Ultimately, this expert analysis of psychological risk assisted in providing a sentence that not only provides punishment for offending but also offers an optimal opportunity for rehabilitation and risk reduction, therefore assisting public protection. Given that sex offenders are not all sentenced to life in prison and the fact that they will therefore be released into the community in the UK, there is a common-sense argument to support the need for psychotherapeutic interventions to be provided for sex offenders, even if these are costly for correctional services to deliver. The evidence base for sex offender treatment is somewhat mixed, with the recent evaluation of group treatment programmes in England and Wales making for disappointing reading in relation to recidivism (Mews, Di Bella & Purver, 2017), with treatment significantly increasing the risk of reconviction rather than decreasing it as would be hoped for. In the evaluation of the effectiveness of sex offender treatment, there are many challenges, including the relatively low base rate of recidivism, and many studies in this area are of poor quality. Although meta-analysis has demonstrated some promising evidence of success in relation to the outcomes of treatment, the evidence base for sex offender treatment is not yet satisfactory (Schmucker & Lösel, 2015). Therefore, when evaluating offenders post-treatment, some caution needs to be applied, and it cannot be assumed that treatment completion has successfully reduced the risk of reoffending.

Clinicians have a wide choice of sex offender risk-assessment tools to choose from with developments in this field demonstrating support for both actuarial and structured professional judgment-based methods (Tully et al., 2013; van den Berg et al., 2017), and so knowledge of the actuarial/static and structured professional judgment approaches is essential for professionals working in this field. Selected tools should be appropriate for the assessment context and population under assessment. For instance, the static Risk Matrix 2000 (Thornton 2010; Thornton et al., 2003) is not recommended for use with sex offenders who have learning/intellectual disabilities because it is not well-validated on this population (Pryboda, Tully & Browne, 2015). Psychologists and other risk assessment professionals should therefore remain up to date with the literature in relation to this field so that their practice remains informed by the scientific literature. Only then can their input usefully assist the Court process.

References

Andrews, D. A., Bonta, J., & Wormith, S. J. (2006). The recent past and near future of risk and/or need assessment. *Crime and Delinquency, 52*, 7–27.

Barnett, G. D., Wakeling, H. C., & Howard, P. D. (2010). An examination of the predictive validity of the Risk Matrix 2000 in England and Wales. *Sexual Abuse: A Journal of Research and Treatment, 22*(4), 443–470.

Beck, A. T., & Steer, R. A. (1990). *Beck Anxiety Inventory manual.* San Antonio, TX: The Psychological Corporation.

Boer, D. P., Hart, S. D., Kropp, P. R., & Webster, C. D. (1997). *Manual for the Sexual Violence Risk-20: Professional guidelines for assessing risk of sexual violence.* Vancouver: British Columbia Institute Against Family Violence.

British Psychological Society (2011). *Good practice guidelines on the use of psychological formulation.* Leicester, UK: Author.

Cooke, D. J., & Michie, C. (2014). The generalizability of the Risk Matrix 2000: On model shrinkage and the misinterpretation of the area under the curve. *Journal of Threat Assessment and Management, 1*(1), 42–55.

Darjee, R., Russell, K, Forrest, L., Milton, E., Savoie, V., Baron, E., … Stobie, S. (2016). *Risk for Sexual Violence Protocol (RSVP): A real world study of the reliability, validity and utility of a structured professional judgment instrument in the assessment and management of sexual offenders in South East Scotland.* Scotland, UK: NHS Lothian Sex Offender Liaison Service.

de Vogel, V., de Ruiter, C., Bouman, Y., & de Vries Robbé, M. (2012). *SAPROF: Structured Assessment of PROtective Factors.* Utrecht, The Netherlands: Van Der Hoeven Stichting.

D'Zurilla, T. J., Nezu A. M., & Maydeu-Olivares, A. (2002). *Social Problem-Solving Inventory-Revised technical manual.* New York, NY: MHS.

Falshaw, L., Bates, A., Patel, V., Corbett, C., & Friendship, L. (2003). Assessing reconviction, reoffending and recidivism in a sample of UK sexual offenders. *Legal and Criminological Psychology, 8,* 207–215.

Hanson, R. K., & Bussière, M. T. (1998). Predicting relapse: A meta-analysis of sexual offender recidivism studies. *Journal of Consulting and Clinical Psychology, 66,* 348–362.

Hanson, R. K., & Morton-Bourgon, K. E. (2004). *Predictors of Sexual Recidivism: An Updated Meta-analysis* (Corrections Research User Report No. 2004–02). Ottawa, ON: Public Safety and Emergency Preparedness Canada.

Hart, S. D., Kropp, P. R., Laws, D. R., Klaver, J., Logan, C., & Watt, K. A. (2003). *The Risk for Sexual Violence Protocol (RSVP).* Burnaby, BC: The Mental Health, Law, and Policy Institute of Simon Fraser University.

Helmus, L., Babchishin, K. M., & Hanson R. K. (2013). The predictive accuracy of the Risk Matrix 2000: A meta-analysis. *Sexual Offender Treatment, 8*(2), 1–24 (online).

Janus, E. S., & Prentky, R. A. (2003). Forensic use of actuarial risk assessment with sex offenders: Accuracy, admissibility and accountability. *American Criminal Law Review, 40*(4), 1443–1499.

Johnstone, L., & Dallos, R. (2006). *Formulation in psychology and psychotherapy: Making sense of people's problems.* London, UK: Routledge.

Kinderman, P., Sellwood, W., & Tai, S. (2008). Policy implications of a psychological model of mental disorder. *Journal of Mental Health, 17*(1), 93–103.

Mews, A., Di Bella, L., & Purver, M. (2017). *Impact evaluation of the prison-based core sex offender treatment programme.* London, UK: Ministry of Justice.

Paulhus, D. L. (1998). *Paulhus Deception Scales (PDS): The balanced inventory of desirable responding-7.* North Tonawanda, NY: Multi-Health Systems Inc.

Pryboda, J., Tully, R. J., & Browne, K. D. (2015). Is the Risk Matrix 2000 applicable to intellectually disabled sex offenders? *Aggression and Violent Behavior, 25,* 184–190. doi:10.1016/j.avb.2015.08.002

Rice, M. E., Harris, G. T., Lang, C., & Cormier, C. (2006). Violent sex offenses: How are they best measured form official records. *Law & Human Behavior, 30*, 525–541. doi:10.1007/s10979-006-9022-3

Rogers, R. (2000). The uncritical acceptance of risk assessment in forensic practice. *Law and Human Behavior, 24*(5), 595–605.

Rosenberg, M. (1965). *Society and the adolescent self-image.* Princeton, NJ: Princeton University Press.

Royal College of Psychiatrists (2010). *A competency-based curriculum for specialist core training in psychiatry.* London, UK: Royal College of Psychiatrists.

Schmidt, A. F., Babchishin, K. M., & Lehmann, R. J. B. (2017). A meta-analysis of viewing time measures of sexual interest in children. *Archives of Sexual Behavior, 46*(1), 287–300.

Schmucker, M. & Lösel, F. (2015). The effects of sexual offender treatment on recidivism: An international meta-analysis of sound quality evaluations. *Journal of Experimental Criminology, 11*(4), 597–630. doi:10.1007/s11292-015-9241-z

Sutherland, A. A., Johnstone, L., Davidson, K. M., Hart, D. D., Cooke, D. J., Kropp, P. R., … Stocks, R. (2012). Sexual violence risk assessment: An investigation of the interrater reliability of professional judgements made using the risk for sexual violence protocol. *International Journal of Forensic Mental Health, 11*(2), 119–133.

Thornton, D. (2010). *Scoring guide for Risk Matrix 2000.10/SVC.* London, UK: Ministry of Justice.

Thornton, D., Mann, R., Webster, S., Blud, L., Travers, R., Friendship, C., & Erikson, M. (2003). Distinguishing and combining risks for sexual and violent recidivism. *Annals of the New York Academy of Sciences, 989*, 225–235.

Tully, R. J., & Browne, K. D. (2015). Appraising the Risk Matrix 2000 static sex offender risk assessment tool. *International Journal of Offender Therapy and Comparative Criminology, 59*(2), 211–224. doi:10.1177/0306624X13508928

Tully, R. J., Chou, S. C., & Browne, K. D. (2013). A systematic review on the effectiveness of sex offender risk assessment tools in predicting sexual recidivism of adult male sex offenders. *Clinical Psychology Review, 33*, 287–316. doi:10.1016/j.cpr.2012.12.002

van den Berg, J. W., Smid, W., Schepers, K., Wever, E., van Beek, D., Janssen, E., & Gijs, L. (2017). The predictive properties of dynamic sex offender risk assessment instruments: A meta-analysis. *Psychological Assessment.* Advance online publication. doi:10.1037.pas0000454

Ward, T., & Sorbello, L. (2003). Explaining child sexual abuse: Integration and elaboration. In T. Ward, D. R. Laws, & S. M. Hudson (Eds.). *Sexual deviance: Issues and controversies* (pp. 3–20). Thousand Oakes, CA: Sage.

Wechsler, D. (2008). *Wechsler Adult Intelligence Scale-Fourth Edition.* San Antonio, TX: Pearson Clinical.

Weerasekera, P. (1996). *Multiperspective case formulation: A step towards treatment integration.* Malabar, FL: Krieger.

Chapter 4

Male personality disorder

Treatment approaches within a secure mental health setting

Jamie Yapp

Introduction

Therapeutic approaches to working with personality difficulties

Schema Therapy (ST) is a treatment for complex psychological problems that has developed over a period of some 25 years. Founded by Jeffrey Young (1990; Young, Klosko & Weishaar, 2003), it combines aspects of cognitive-behavioural, interpersonal, psychodynamic, and experiential techniques. In comparison to **Cognitive Behavioural Therapy** (CBT; Beck, 1976), ST places a more intensive focus upon an individual's problematic emotions, childhood difficulties, and the therapeutic relationship.

Within the field of psychology, **schemas** work as filters through which individuals interpret, order, and predict the world and the behaviour of themselves and others. This mechanism of interpretation and prediction allows people to develop a self-image, an adaptive view of others, and solve problems. These schemas are comprised of bodily sensations, memories, emotions, and cognitions that have originated in childhood and are built upon during a person's life. Whilst schemas often have an adaptive role in childhood, such as a survival role within an abusive caregiving dynamic (whereby more hope is engendered if children believe that they are defective as opposed to the adult), by adulthood, these maladaptive schemas are dysfunctional, inaccurate, and limiting. Despite this, individuals are rarely consciously aware of their held schemas (Young et al., 2003).

People with personality difficulties have developed these maladaptive schemas and are less able to develop a positive self-image, to accurately interpret others' and their own behaviours, and to handle and resolve life's problems. According to Young et al. (2003), maladaptive schemas are developed at an early age as a result of the individual's exposure to parenting styles, early life events including trauma, and individual temperament.

These schemas are similar to the schema concept of Beck's cognitive model (Beck, Freeman & Davis, 2004), yet ST places greater importance on the origin of these schemas. Indeed, Young's model of personality and psychopathology mirrors that of Bowlby's (1969) **attachment** theory, in that a child's emotional needs need to be met by the primary caregiver. These core emotional needs that need to be met within childhood are identified as *secure attachment, autonomy and independence, limits and boundaries, validation of needs and feelings,* and *spontaneity and play* (Young et al., 2003).

When these needs are not consistently and adequately met, an individual develops early maladaptive schemas (EMS), which subsequently drive **personality disorder,** or elevated traits, within a person's developing personality profile. The impact of EMS can also include key components of psychosocial development, such as emotional regulation and the disturbance of this due to caregiver relationship dynamics (Cohen et al., 2005; Maughan & Cicchetti, 2002). Indeed, the development of personality pathology is related to both trauma and inconsistency/neglect from caregivers. Schemas are then often repeatedly endorsed due to playing an interfering role when completing tasks and subsequent repeated negative experiences, which serve to reinforce the maladaptive schema further. Each EMS implies a frustrated core emotional need from childhood experiences.

Young et al. (2003) postulated that there are 18 identified schemas that fall within five schema domains, as highlighted in Table 4.1 below:

Table 4.1 Early maladaptive schemas and schema domains

Schema domain	Schemas
Disconnection and rejection	Abandonment/Instability Mistrust/Abuse Emotional deprivation Defectiveness/Shame Social isolation/Alienation
Impaired autonomy and achievement	Dependency/Incompetency Vulnerability to harm and illness Enmeshment/Undeveloped self Failure
Impaired limits	Entitlement/Grandiosity Lack of self-control/self-discipline
Other-directedness	Subjugation Self-sacrifice Approval-seeking
Hypervigilance and inhibition	Negativity/Pessimism Emotional inhibition Unrelenting standards Punitiveness

Table 4.2 below evidences the link between these schema domains and the related core emotional needs that were missing for the person and led to the development of these schemas.

Individuals develop and maintain coping styles in order to protect themselves from re-experiencing these EMS (Young et al., 2005; Young & Brown, 2003). Young identifies three ways in which an individual copes with schemas: *surrender, avoidance,* and *overcompensation.*

- *Surrender* – the individual surrenders to their activated schema and adapts their thoughts, feelings, and behaviour in line with this schema. This leads individuals to repeat behavioural patterns from childhood and to re-experience and reinforce the emotional pain associated with each schema.
- *Avoidance* – the individual avoids situations that they know will activate the schema due to a desire to avoid the emotions that are associated with this schema activation. However, due to this avoidance, the schema and the associated emotional response is never challenged or corrected.
- *Overcompensation* – the individual acts in the opposite direction from the meaning of the schema, in an attempt to not be affected by it. This coping style can lead to the schema being underestimated, and to engagement in independent, assertive, and/or aggressive behaviour in response.

At the heart of the function of ST is the desire to help individuals to identify and meet their core emotional needs independently over time and thus change their dysfunctional life patterns by enacting a change of their schemas and modes.

The therapeutic relationship is deemed to be at the heart of this process, with the concepts of *limited reparenting* and *empathic confrontation* being central to the relationship. *Limited reparenting* is defined as the therapist acting as a good caregiver would in meeting child modes and core emotional needs within the boundaries of a therapeutic relationship, with the therapist needing to be able to respond to core needs as and when they present themselves (Young et al., 2003). *Empathic confrontation* involves the therapist confronting the

Table 4.2 Relationship between schema domains and basic needs

Schema domain	Related basic need
Disconnection and rejection	Safe attachment, acceptance, care
Impaired autonomy and achievement	Autonomy, competence, sense of identity
Impaired limits	Realistic limits, self-control
Other-directedness	Free expression of needs and emotions
Hypervigilance and inhibition	Spontaneity, playfulness

patient regarding their maladaptive behavioural patterns, both from therapy sessions and evidence from daily living. This is done in a compassionate and non-judgmental manner in order for the individual to gain insight into these behavioural patterns and enact change (Young et al., 2003). These two techniques form the basis of the therapeutic alliance, which grows throughout the intervention and through the consistent use of these techniques (Young et al., 2003, 2005). This is particularly important within forensic settings, as forensic patients are often more mistrustful and emotionally detached, making them more difficult to engage responsively within intervention (Kersten, 2015).

As stated, Young originally identified 18 different schemas, each of which was underlined by the implication that each schema implied a frustrated emotional need at its core. Through therapeutic experience and growing research evidence, these schemas have now become grouped into 'schema modes' when working with individuals with severe personality disorders, such as **borderline**, **antisocial**, or **narcissistic** personality disorders (Young et al., 2003). Schema modes (Young et al., 2005) help therapists to work with individuals whose mood and behaviours change frequently within a short period of time, with schema modes reflecting a group of schemas and coping styles that are activated at a given time (Lobbestael, van Vreeswijk & Arntz, 2007). As schema modes are largely dissociated from one another, they dominate an individual and their thoughts, feelings, and behaviour when they are activated (Young et al., 2003).

Schema modes are separated into *child modes, dysfunctional parent modes, dysfunctional coping modes,* and *healthy modes. Child modes* refer to feeling, thinking, and acting in a childlike manner. *Coping modes* involve attempts to protect oneself from pain by engagement in either avoidant, overcompensatory, or surrendering behaviours. *Parent modes* relate to self-directed criticism or demands that reflect internalised parent behaviour and emotional positions. *The healthy mode* refers to the expression of healthy, balanced self-reflection and associated feelings of pleasure and happiness (Young et al., 2003).

The overall aim of ST is to heal underlying child modes so that dysfunctional coping modes are no longer required.

Schema therapy with forensic patients

The effective use of individual ST has been widely evidenced within the literature (Arntz & Bogels, 2000; van Genderen & Arntz 2005; Young et al., 2003, 2005). ST has been evidenced to be an effective individual psychological treatment for individuals presenting with borderline personality disorder (BPD), both in terms of improvements in quality of life and cost-effectiveness for BPD (Giesen-Bloo et al., 2006; Nadort et al., 2009; van Asselt et al., 2008) and for other personality disorders (Bamelis et al., 2014, 2015; Gude & Hoffart, 2008; Gude, Monsen & Hoffart, 2001; Weertman & Arntz, 2007).

Giessen-Bloo et al. (2006) identified that 50% of their patients offered ST were deemed to have recovered from their BPD pathology whilst 70% evidenced a clinically significant improvement after three years of therapy and a one-year follow-up. It is hypothesised that these results are linked to the integrative nature of ST, which facilitates deeper-level and long-lasting personality change (Farrell, Shaw & Webber, 2009). Intervention with borderline and narcissistic patients led to the schema modes concept being developed and successfully utilised with individuals with these presenting personality types (Bamelis et al., 2012, 2014; Bernstein, Arntz & de Vos, 2007; Lobbestael, van Vreeswijk & Arntz, 2008).

Forensic patients, i.e. those whom have been convicted of a crime and are incarcerated for this crime either in a prison or secure forensic mental health hospital, often pose greater treatment needs in the areas of presenting aggression, impulsivity, and trust. Individuals presenting with antisocial, narcissistic, and borderline personality types are deemed to present a higher risk of recidivism (Jamieson & Taylor, 2004; Rosenfeld, 2003). This has often led many professionals to be sceptical as to whether offenders with a personality disorder can exact change and reduce their risk of reoffending.

Bernstein et al. (2007) introduced five forensic schema modes in order to encapsulate the motivations behind criminal behaviour. These modes were defined as *angry protector, bully and attack, paranoid overcontroller, conning and manipulative*, and *predator* modes. Table 4.3 below highlights the link between these modes, and their overall mode domains, as discussed above. Modes listed in italics are those that have been developed specifically for work with forensic patients.

Table 4.3 Mode domains and corresponding domains using ST in a forensic setting

Mode domains	Schema modes
Child modes	Vulnerable child Angry child Impulsive child Lonely child
Avoidant coping modes	Detached protector Detached self-soother Compliant surrenderer *Angry protector* Complaining protector
Parent modes	Punitive critic Demanding critic
Overcompensatory modes	Self-aggrandiser Bully and attack *Conning and manipulative* *Predator* Obsessive-compulsive overcontroller *Paranoid overcontroller*
Healthy modes	Healthy adult Playful child

Three main types of techniques are utilised within ST intervention: *behavioural*, *cognitive*, and *experiential*. Of these, *experiential* techniques are central to help individuals break through their emotional detachment. Experiential techniques such as role play and guided imagery are used to access and reprocess patients' emotions and have been found to be particularly effective in bypassing patients' detached modes in order to access more vulnerable emotions that need reprocessing (Holmes & Mathews, 2005). Typical experiential techniques are role play, (guided) imagery, and chair-work.

Role play involves the re-enactment of situations from the past or the present. During role play, rescripting is initiated (Kellogg, 2004; Landy, 2000), whereby the therapist seeks to intervene and change distressing elements in the scenes that are being relived in order for associated thoughts, feelings, and behaviours to be altered, and for change in these responses to be initiated (Rush et al., 2000; Smucker & Niederee, 1995). Chair-work involves the therapist coaching the patient to switch between chairs, each of which represents one of their modes. The therapist encourages the patient to initiate dialogue between these different modes (Kellogg, 2004). Imagery work refers to when the therapist asks the patient to visualise an upsetting or traumatic image or memory from their past, within which their emotions are explored and the therapist and/or the patient (through activation of their healthy adult mode and therapist guidance) intervenes in the scene with new, healthier responses (Rafaeli, Bernstein & Young, 2011; Smucker & Boos, 2005). This again serves the function of altering associated thoughts, feelings, and behaviours from these previous memories, and for new, non-abusive/traumatic responses to be processed within the image.

Traditional *cognitive* techniques are utilised to increase a patient's insight into their cognitions, feelings, and behaviours that serve to form the basis of each schema mode, with the aim of challenging and restructuring cognitive distortions. *Behavioural* techniques are utilised to target dysfunctional behavioural patterns and to replace these with more adaptive behavioural coping responses (Arntz & Jacob, 2013).

Patient background

At the time of engaging in therapy, Dave had been incarcerated for over 20 years after being found guilty of the murder of his wife through manual asphyxiation. This offence also included the raping of the victim after she had died. Dave received a life sentence for this offence with a 15-year minimum tariff. He was approximately six years over tariff at the time of the ST intervention commencing.

After serving the first half of his sentence in prison, Dave was transferred to a medium secure forensic mental health hospital after suffering from a psychotic illness, which was later diagnosed as being **schizoaffective disorder**. Dave was treated through the prescription of antipsychotic medication, nursing, and psychological support. His mental state had since been settled under his medication regime for a number of years. Dave was also diagnosed as suffering from a personality disorder, with elevated borderline and narcissistic traits.

Following his transfer to secure hospital care, Dave engaged in a number of different group and individual treatment programmes. Over the years, this work included CBT, **Cognitive Analytic Therapy (CAT;** Ryle, 1997), anger management groups, mental health group intervention, and completion of the **Sex Offender Treatment Programme (SOTP)** through community probation services.

Dave had progressed to the point where he was living in a low secure ward within a secure forensic mental health hospital, under Section 47/49 of the **Mental Health Act** (1983, as revised 2007). He had unescorted leave to the community on up to four occasions each week. He used this leave to go swimming, to the cinema, shopping, and for walks. Dave was in contact with his father, but not with any other relatives or friends.

During his most recent parole hearing, it was identified that Dave presented with a good insight into his index offence, including both the sexual and violent elements to this offence, his previous substance misuse, and mental health diagnoses. It was identified that Dave would benefit from gaining further insight into his own personality functioning and the role of this within previous relationships, including that with his wife and subsequent victim and ongoing current relationships with personal and professional support. This recommendation led to a referral for him to engage in ST to address this outstanding risk factor.

Prior to engagement in ST, it was important to consider Dave's background history. This is outlined below.

Childhood and education

Dave's biological mother left him on a street corner at six months old. He had no subsequent contact with her during his childhood, and no contact with his biological father until his late adolescence. Dave was fostered and eventually adopted.

Throughout his childhood, Dave received mixed messages as to why he had been fostered, resulting in the development of beliefs that he was worthless and unimportant and that people would reject him. Whilst his foster parents did provide for him physically, he always felt emotionally neglected by them. He described the other foster children as being treated with more love and affection than he received. He held a belief that his foster parents were only looking after him because of the money that they received for this. This belief was reinforced when he was asked to leave home at the age of 16, which coincided with his foster parents' funding being cut.

Dave's foster mother was emotionally neglectful and physically abusive to him. She would be critical and abrasive, giving him messages such as *"you'll never be any good / you're worthless / not good enough"*, which would arise seemingly without justification. Dave recalled generally being chastised rather than nurtured by her.

Dave was sexually abused by a scout leader at the age of eight. He recalled not knowing what was going to happen, where the abuse would lead, or when it would end. He described the subsequent fear and mistrust of the intentions of others in authority over him and felt unable to tell anybody about this abuse as a child for fear of further punishment.

Dave described his foster father as *"a doormat – and he wouldn't do anything with us"*. However, he recalled thinking that although they were emotionally neglectful, at least, in his opinion, they were not consistently abusive to him.

Dave sought to meet some of his own needs by seeking acceptance or nurturance from his friend's family. He also enjoyed regular trips to the seaside every month with his foster family from the age of six but preferred his own company during these trips.

Employment

Dave left school at the age of 16 after obtaining five GCSE qualifications. No specific problems are noted within his school life. He subsequently attended his local college to study carpentry. He worked on an ad hoc basis as a carpenter on a self-employed basis, leading up to his index offence.

Relationships and sexual history

Dave developed an intimate relationship at the age of 16 with a childhood friend. The couple then married at 19, and she was the subsequent victim of the index offence. Dave described spending more time riding his motorbike and watching television late at night rather than spending time with his wife. He also admitted to providing for her physically but not feeling able to connect with her emotionally (he later realised) – something which he was able to link to his own experiences within his relationship with his foster parents. At the time, he often assumed that he and his wife knew what the other was thinking without specifically discussing these thoughts.

Dave murdered his wife when he was aged 22, a number of months after they had separated and she had begun a new relationship. Shortly before the offence, his wife had informed him that she had ended the relationship through a solicitor and had also sold his possessions, including his dogs.

Following his incarceration, Dave contacted his biological mother, who stated that she did not want to have further contact with him because she had her own family to look after. Dave reignited contact with his father, which has continued to this day. There has been no contact between Dave and his foster parents since the index offence.

Substance misuse

Dave experimented with illicit substances prior to the index offence, smoking cannabis on an ad hoc basis each week. He drank beer regularly on weekends, but his intake appears to have increased in response to relationship difficulties. Looking forward, Dave planned to be abstinent from both drink and drug use for the remainder of his life.

Mental health

Prior to his transfer to secure forensic mental health hospital care, Dave had no formal diagnosis of mental disorder. However, he had experienced psychotic symptoms on an intermittent basis since the age of 12. These symptoms included auditory and visual hallucinations as well as delusional perception. Dave took an overdose of medication at the age of 16 following a disagreement with his foster parents. He also expressed suicidal ideation following the separation from his wife. He later attempted to suffocate himself in prison five years after his conviction and also attempted to hang himself during the initial stages of his detention in the mental health system.

Axis I Symptoms/Diagnoses

- Transient psychotic episodes.
- Schizoaffective disorder (suspected).

Axis II Symptoms/Diagnoses

- Personality disorder with elevated narcissistic and borderline traits.

Offending history

Dave was convicted of the murder of his wife at the age of 22. The victim was murdered through manual asphyxiation and was subsequently raped after she had died. He had no previous convictions.

Schema therapy with Dave

At the time of referral, Dave had recently been transferred back onto the low secure unit from a progressive step-down placement following disagreements with staff. Dave had an argument with one member of staff in particular regarding their role in his care and their trustworthiness. He also had difficulty accepting the boundaries between a professional's requirement to write reports and to provide daily care for him. Since his return to the low secure ward, Dave tended to isolate himself on the ward, spending the majority of time in his room rather than in communal areas with peers. Themes of avoidance, insecurity, and disinhibition were also noted within both Dave's historical and current relationships.

Dave had engaged well in previous therapeutic intervention (CBT, CAT, SOTP) and upon initial contact appeared motivated to explore his personality functioning and its root causes in more detail.

Schema therapy case conceptualisation formulation

The founder of ST, Jeffrey Young, identified the requirement to develop a case conceptualisation **formulation** with the individual at the beginning of therapy in order to identify the problems and symptoms of the individual, their interpersonal patterns, problematic emotions, and associated repeating life patterns (Young et al., 2003). In the case conceptualisation model for schemas, links between the past and current problems are mapped together with the individual, in order to develop a joint formulation. The process of case conceptualisation for Dave was developed from background information, clinical interviews, and completion of ST questionnaires.

Current major problems/life patterns

Problem 1

Hypervigilance and paranoia regarding others' intentions, and a sense that he refused to be outwitted and manipulated by others, *"...I'm not playing this game".*

Life pattern

Dave reported that when he sensed that others had gained control over him, he felt a loss of control and was overwhelmed by associated fears of abandonment, abuse, or humiliation. Historical experiences of abuse included him being sexually abused by his scout leader at the age of eight, being physically chastised by his foster mother on an ad hoc basis during his childhood, and being frequently subjected to emotional abuse and neglect.

At times, Dave had fought against this sense of losing control by fighting back against those whom he perceived to be mistreating or abusing him. Historically, this had included him committing the index offence against his ex-wife. More recently, and less severely, Dave had sought to verbally express his concerns regarding perceptions that members of staff had sought to abuse their power over him by misrepresenting his behaviour and interactions in their professional reports. This led him to raise his voice and threaten to complain about staff regarding these incidents.

Problem 2

Presenting as disconnected and detached because he did not expect his needs to be met.

Life pattern

Dave admitted to spending the majority of his life since the index offence (either in custody or secure mental health hospitals) detaching himself from others in a bid to retain a sense of control and calm over his life. This was a very strong coping mechanism for him, in that he had spent the majority of his time detaching himself from others and not trusting others with any information about himself or his life. As a result, he retained a superficial sense of control and calm but failed to get his core needs met consistently.

Dave recalled learning to cut himself off from others from a young age, largely because his foster parents never met his emotional needs, and he learnt to self-soothe. When he was involved in an intimate relationship with his ex-wife, he felt unable to engage emotionally with her, which eventually led her to end the relationship.

Problem 3

Surrendering to those in authority over him for fear of punishment, criticism, or loss of control.

Life pattern

At other times, Dave responded to situations whereby others were in authority and therefore (as he saw it) in control over him by presenting with an overly compliant, submissive stance. He had engaged in this pattern of behaviour during periods of his adult life for fear of being harshly punished should he seek to express his own needs, opinions, or beliefs.

Historically, Dave was often punished, criticised, and humiliated by his foster mother during his childhood when he sought to express his own needs, opinions, and beliefs. Indeed, such expression often led to negative consequences. Consequently, he had continued to engage in a mode of passively complying to the needs and requests of others at times, in a bid to avoid any further negative treatment.

After identifying these repeating life patterns, it was important to identify the origins of these life patterns, along with Dave's associated core memories and images from his early life.

Developmental origin (mother, father, siblings, peers, authority figures)

1   Mother abandoned him at the age of six months.
2   Father had no contact with him until early adulthood.
3   Foster father was a passive and avoidant character that rarely prioritised him or met his needs.
4   Foster mother was emotionally neglectful, providing little by way of nurturance or affection. She would also be a harsh critic, deriding his abilities and potential, and was physically abusive at times.
5   Siblings were not direct relations and received preferential treatment from Dave's foster parents. Dave did report a positive relationship with his younger foster brother at times.
6   Peers – described some positive friendships and spent time at one friend's house in particular in his early adolescence, seeing their family as being more supportive and nurturing than his own.

7   Authority figures – sexually abused by a scout leader at the age of eight.
8   Ex-wife – married at the age of 19, but struggled to emotionally connect with his wife, leading her to eventually have an affair and end the relationship. This sequence of events subsequently led to the index offence.

Summary of core childhood memories or images

1   Being sexually abused by a scout leader at the age of eight.
2   Foster father never having time for him / showing any interest in him, even when he received a good report at school aged ten.
3   Aged 11, he and his foster brother had both been out playing in the street too late. His foster brother received a hug to see if he was okay, whereas he was criticised and chastised for the same behaviour from their foster mother.
4   His foster mother telling him that he would never amount to anything or make a success of himself when he was doing his homework at the kitchen table aged 12.
5   His foster mother hitting him with a television cable at the age of 12, from which he felt shocked, but not angry, and asked her to stop before his father intervened.
6   Seeking a sense of warmth, nurturance, and acceptance from his friend's parents aged 13, recalling that they asked him to stay for dinner and enquired about his school work and home life.
7   Being asked to leave home at 16 for seemingly no specific reason or fault of his own.

Through the identification of these core early experiences, memories, and images, we could begin to identify Dave's core unmet needs from his early life.

Dave's core unmet needs

*   Secure attachments to others, including safety, stability, nurturance, and acceptance.
*   Freedom to express valid needs and emotions.
*   Spontaneity and play.

Dave's relevant schemas, developed from these early experiences and these core needs not being met, were then identified.

Dave's most relevant schemas, with origins

*   Emotional deprivation (Origin – foster mother more than foster father)
*   Mistrust/Abuse (Origin – birth mother, scout leader)
*   Abandonment/Instability (Origin – biological parents, foster parents)
*   Defectiveness/Shame (Origin – both foster parents, scout leader)

- Unrelenting standards (Origin – both foster parents)
- Punitiveness (Origin – foster mother more than foster father)
- Subjugation (Origin – from both foster parents, perhaps as a means of attempting to secure nurturance and affection from others)

Whilst it has been identified that Dave had been able to gain a significant degree of insight into his personality functioning since these early experiences, and during his current incarceration, through the collaborative formulation, it was identified that some of these schemas continued to be triggered.

Current schema triggers

1   Engaging with people in authority (Schema link: Defectiveness/Shame; Emotional Deprivation; Mistrust/Abuse; Punitiveness).
2   Building and maintaining secure friendships with others/socialising with peers (Schema link: Emotional deprivation; Abandonment/Instability; Defectiveness/Shame).
3   Maintaining relationship with father (Schema link: Emotional deprivation; Abandonment/Instability; Defectiveness/Shame).
4   Spending time on own (Schema link: Emotional deprivation; Defectiveness/Shame; Self-sacrifice).
5   Thinking about the future (Schema link: Emotional deprivation; Mistrust/Abuse; Punitiveness; Unrelenting standards).

Coping responses

In response to these schemas being triggered, Dave engaged in various deep-rooted coping mechanisms in an attempt to protect himself from the associated hurt and distress from these schemas being triggered.

Surrender behaviours

Dave often continued to give in to both real and perceived demands, threats, or expectations from others (especially when deemed to be in a position of power) in an anxious attempt to avoid pain, or in an attempt to get his needs met (*Schema link: Emotional deprivation; Mistrust/Abuse; Punitiveness*).

Avoidance behaviours

Dave continued to utilise emotional detachment to protect himself from the possibility of painful feelings, remaining physically and emotionally distant from others (*Schema link: Emotional deprivation; Abandonment/Instability; Defectiveness/Shame*).

Overcompensation behaviours

There was evidence of eliminating a threat, rival, or obstacle in a cold, ruthless, calculating manner in the index offence, and, to a far lesser extent more recently, in his recall from the step-down unit, following an argument with his keyworker. In short, under direct threat, Dave stood up for himself at times, but to a much lesser degree of severity now (*Schema link: Emotional deprivation; Abandonment/Instability; Mistrust/Abuse; Defectiveness/Shame*).

There was also ongoing evidence of Dave attempting to portray himself as perfect or beyond reproach in a bid to control everybody's perceptions of him and to avoid any level of criticism or punishment (*Schema link: Defectiveness/ Shame; Mistrust/Abuse; Unrelenting Standards*).

Due to the number of Dave's prominent schemas, and the promising evidence of utilising schema modes within interventions with forensic patients (Bernstein et al., 2012; Chakhssi, Bernstein & de Ruiter, 2014), the above information was utilised to create a collaborative schema mode model. This mode model is presented diagrammatically in Figure 4.1 below and is also discussed further.

Relevant schema modes

Vulnerable, lonely child mode (vulnerable, lonely little Dave)

Triggered when Dave felt unsafe, abandoned, not protected by others. Instead, he felt that others wanted to control and abuse him, leading him to feel unloved, abandoned, misunderstood, and confused. When in this mode, he often isolated himself from others and ruminated alone in his room within the hospital.

Punitive and demanding critic mode

The internalising of his foster mother's critical and punishing parental voice – particularly regarding not being good enough or equal in worth or ability to others. When in this mode, he presented as very hypersensitive and panicked, trying to please others and praise them to avoid any further criticism, chastisement, or rejection.

Detached protector mode

Removing himself from individuals and environments within which he sensed a threat or attempts to manipulate and control him. When in this mode, he presented with a strong belief that he needed to control his own immediate environment and behaviour and could meet all of his own needs. He believed that he must be free of any influence from others whatsoever in order to keep himself safe.

Vulnerable, Lonely Little Dave

This mode is triggered when I don't feel safe, and I don't feel protected by others.

I've felt like this previously when I was returned from the step-down unit, and when the Dr said he might transfer me back to prison.

I feel unsafe, that others don't care for me, or want to protect me, they want to control and abuse me.

I feel unloved, abandoned, confused, and misunderstood.

I can't cope with these feelings, something bad is going to happen, I can feel it.

Dave's SCHEMA MODE FORMULATION

Core Schemas:

Emotional Deprivation

Mistrust / abuse

Abandonment / instability

Defectiveness / shame

Unrelenting standards

Punitiveness

Subjugation

When triggered – How I Cope

Goals For 'Healthy Adult' Dave: To meet the needs of Vulnerable, Lonely Little Dave – I want to feel secure, loved, and cared for in relationships with others. If I do something wrong, people will still care for and look after me.

I want to work on expressing my emotions more, and feeling comfortable doing this with others. This can help me to have more meaningful friendships and familial relationships.

I also want to connect with others through the church.

I want to be comfortable living my life and exploring friendships and relationships, despite my past.

Fight

Violent Dave (fight) – This happens when my other coping mechanisms fail me, it is very rare. It was evident in my index offence, & in my move from the step-down unit.

When I'm in this mode, I feel out of control, unable to manage my emotions, very angry at my treatment from others – I feel abused, controlled and manipulated, leading me to react with violence, or anger. I don't like this mode, it is my hardest edge.

Overcompensator / Untrusting Dave (fight) – If I'm not perfect, and in control of everything, then others will take advantage of me, and harm me in some way.

I'm very aware of this, and must get all of the information before making a perfect decision, to keep me safe. I am very hypervigilant at these times.

Flight

Punitive and Demanding Critic (freeze) – I must be beyond reproach, because others will always try to criticise and chastise me. My mother used to tell me "...you'll never amount to anything...you're worthless...you're just like your dad".

If I do something wrong, or upset somebody, others will reject me, and I'm left feeling rejected and worthless.

Because I am hyper sensitive to other's reactions and rejection, I struggle to react calmly to people's emotions and projections, I can feel paralysed and panicked by their criticism & rejection.

Freeze

Surrender Dave (freeze) -I'd rather just give in to others, rather than be rejected by them if I don't do what they want, even if I think it's wrong / I don't agree. Their opinions are worth more than mine.

I need to meet their needs to stop anything bad from happening to me, it's easier that way, people will stay supporting me and I'll be left alone.

Detached Protector Dave (flight)

To keep myself safe, I must be on my own. I'm going to sit in my room and avoid others so that they can't try and manipulate, control, and influence me. Others are no good for me, they just bring me trouble and bad feelings.

If I control my own behaviour and environment, then nothing bad can happen to me. I'm happy on my own, I can meet my own needs.

Figure 4.1 Schema formulation.

Paranoid/Perfectionist overcontroller mode (overcompensator/ untrusting Dave)

This mode consisted of Dave believing that if he was not perfect and in control of everything, others would take advantage of him and harm him in some way. At such times, he was very hypervigilant and attempted to be beyond reproach and perfect within interactions with others in a bid to keep himself safe.

Predator/Bully-attack mode (violent Dave)

This mode was only triggered when all of his other coping modes failed him, which was very rare. When in this mode, he felt out of control and was unable to manage his emotions. He might attack others verbally and physically (bully/ attack) within this mode. It was noted that his index offence involved significant levels of planning, control, and explosive violence (predator mode). At times he was susceptible to feeling very angry at the treatment that he had received from others, which left him feeling abused, controlled, or manipulated. He described this as his "*hardest edge*" and the side of him that he liked the least.

Compliant surrenderer mode (surrenderer Dave)

This is the mode whereby he would just give in to others rather than be rejected by them. In doing so, he developed a belief that if he did not do as others wanted him to do, even if he thought it was wrong or did not agree, then he would be rejected, because of a belief that others' opinions were worth more than his. In this mode, he believed that he needed to meet others' needs to stop anything bad from happening to him, believing that it was easier that way, people would stay supporting him, and he would be left alone.

Possible temperamental/biological factors

Dave described himself as having a placid temperament. There was little documented evidence available to support or refute this.

Core cognitions and distortions

As a result of his early neglectful and abusive childhood experiences, Dave developed some significant negative core beliefs, including:

- People reject me when I am no longer of use to them.
- I am flawed compared to others.
- It is best if I keep myself to myself, others will reject or hurt me.
- I must be in control, otherwise bad things will happen to me.
- I must moderate my behaviour – others' needs are a priority over mine.
- My needs are unimportant compared to others'.

After completing the background history and subsequent collaborative schema mode formulation, it was important to identify a number of goals for subsequent ST sessions, how to meet Dave's core needs, and improve his insight into his personality functioning within both historical and current relationships.

Focus and plan for change

- Psycho-education of core schemas and modes, and childhood needs.
- Collaborative case formulation.
- Mode maps to increase self-awareness and as a reference point during sessions.
- Daily monitoring of schema modes.
- Pros and cons work regarding the importance of each maladaptive coping mode.
- Bypass the Detached Protector (DP) mode.
- Engagement in cognitive, experiential, and behavioural pattern breaking.
- Use of ongoing limited reparenting within therapy to meet the needs of the Vulnerable Child (VC) and bypass the DP mode.
- Use of consistent limited reparenting to provide a canvas for core needs to be met within the therapeutic relationship.
- Develop the happy child and happy adult modes through developing an awareness of and stronger focus on identifying and meeting his own needs.
- Reduce and limit the influence of the critical parent mode and attempt to banish it. Develop more empathy and compassion towards himself and provide him with the platform and confidence to begin to meet his needs more consistently.
- Use of experiential work to help explore the emotions of the vulnerable, lonely child mode.
- Longer-term goal – encouragement of the development of the healthy adult and happy child modes in order to actively meet his own needs in both the short term and long term, in areas such as building and maintaining healthy relationships with peers, father, and professionals, and looking to the future in terms of needs and life goals.

Therapeutic relationship

Dave was able to develop a trusting therapeutic relationship fairly quickly within therapy, and he was able to take the concepts of ST on board and apply them within his own formulation. Over time, he showed a growing awareness of the ST mode model and utilised schema language within the sessions. This proved to be a solid foundation for him to then build upon this knowledge and apply it within the subsequent strategy for change sessions (*experiential, cognitive, behavioural*). He was also able to open up and explore his vulnerabilities as the sessions developed.

Dave reacted well to the use of *limited reparenting* and *empathic confrontation* as the trust developed within this relationship. A reasonably strong, secure attachment was built within the therapeutic relationship, in which he was able to open up about his previous and current experiences.

Progress within ST

Dave engaged in over 50 ST sessions. Progress was measured through behavioural evidence regarding change within ward behaviour and response within treatment sessions.

By the end of therapy, Dave was able to reference his early experiences, within the VC mode and the role that his various coping mechanisms played in protecting himself from hurtful experiences but also in reinforcing that these coping behaviours served to perpetuate the underlying problems and did not serve to consistently meet his core needs. Dave was able to identify when he had engaged in a period of behaviour within a specific coping mode. These coping modes included 'Detached Protector Dave', whereby he detached from interactions with others in order to avoid potential fear, harm, or rejection from others. Dave was able to identify that he frequently engaged in this mode within his day-to-day living resulting in not meeting his own emotional needs and not feeling connected with others. Through engagement in experiential work (role play and guided imagery), and between-session behavioural work and diaries, Dave was able to challenge these behaviours and engage in more 'healthy adult' behaviours, whereby he began to socialise with peers more regularly and felt more connected and content within these interactions. Nursing staff fed back that Dave became increasingly more open in his interactions with peers and staff, further building the lines of trust and support within these professional relationships.

Significant time was also spent within the ST sessions exploring the links between Dave's coping modes and his index offence. Although this was not a specific requirement of ST, on account of Dave having already engaged in offence-focused treatment, it was invaluable in linking Dave's early experiences, subsequent schema mode formulation, and the role that his maladaptive coping modes played within the offence.

In short, a 'violent Dave' mode was developed, which was triggered only once all of his other coping modes had failed him. Through collaborative case formulation, it was deciphered that at the time of the index offence, Dave was incapable of expressing and managing his emotions. He lacked the skills to engage in meaningful communication within a relationship and engaged in a number of solo pursuits as opposed to emotionally connecting with his partner. These deficits ultimately led to his wife having an affair and leaving the relationship. Dave experienced an uncontrollable rage on the day of the offence and was incapable of managing the sense of rejection, hurt, and betrayal that he felt within this relationship dynamic.

Dave spent a considerable amount of time exploring his interactions with others, the needs that these fulfilled, why relationships were important, and his coping mechanism when experiencing strong feelings such as hurt, betrayal, or rejection. By the end of therapy, he was able to acknowledge that the strength of an emotion that he might experience for a current situation was likely to be influenced by his early experiences, and therefore, he was able to modify his response to a current situation accordingly. Engagement in experiential techniques such as chair-work and guided imagery was also invaluable in reprocessing previous abusive and neglectful experiences and the role that these early experiences played in the subsequent development of his schemas and various coping modes. Dave was also able to identify the different coping modes that he may engage in at different times and the requirement to continue to identify these modes and challenge himself to meet the needs of his 'healthy adult' mode.

In conclusion, after engaging in over 50 sessions of ST, Dave presented with a far greater understanding of the impact of his early experiences, particularly the impact that the punitive and critical voices from his foster mother had upon his subsequent personality development and coping modes. He was able to apply this understanding within the schema mode formulation to his index offence and his subsequent difficulties in meaningfully engaging with others. He was able to explore current difficulties and make sense of them within the ST model and his own ST formulation.

ST had therefore been effective in helping Dave to recognise and meet his core emotional needs. In doing so, the ST process had enabled the strength of these prominent EMS to reduce. His avoidant, overcompensatory, and surrendering coping modes had also reduced, as had the punitive and demanding critic mode, whilst he was able to meet the needs of his vulnerable child through his healthy adult mode developing and being able to recognise and meet his core emotional needs responsively. In activating these changes within ST, Dave's repeating life patterns had also been broken, including his hypervigilance and paranoia of others' intentions, disconnecting and detaching from others, and being avoidant and overly compliant within interactions with others.

By the end of therapy, Dave engaged in more meaningful trusting relationships with peers, his father, and professionals. He expressed hopes to develop and maintain further relationships in the future and expressed his happiness in meaningfully engaging with others to meet his core needs.

Conclusions

This case study has highlighted the use of ST with an adult male with a diagnosed personality disorder who had been incarcerated for the past 20 years after murdering and raping his wife. ST, and its adaption to forensic patients through the use of mode work, was found to be effective in helping Dave to gain a greater understanding of the impact of his early experiences upon his subsequent EMS, coping modes, and the impact of these upon his relationships with others, in line with existing research on ST's effectiveness (Bamelis et al., 2014, 2015; Bernstein et al., 2012; Chakhssi et al., 2014; Giesen-Bloo et al., 2006; Gude & Hoffart, 2008; Gude et al., 2001; Nadort et al., 2009; Weertman & Arntz, 2007; van Asselt et al., 2008). The core components of ST (therapeutic relationship, collaborative formulation, and behavioural, cognitive, and experiential techniques) enabled Dave to process previous neglect and trauma, break repeating life patterns, and develop more meaningful relationships with others in which he was able to meet his core emotional needs rather than continue to deprive himself of these.

ST continues to present with promising evidence as to its applicability within both the general and forensic populations in being able to enact positive therapeutic change in individuals with presenting personality difficulties/disorders. As with all therapeutic approaches, further validation and control studies are required to continue to drive the evidence base of ST, and its effectiveness within different populations, within both group and individual intervention.

References

Arntz, A., & Bogels, S. (2000). *Schemagerichte Cognitieve Therapie voor Perssonlijkheidsstoornissen.* Hooten: Bohn Stafleu van Loghum.

Arntz, A., & Jacob, G. (2013). *Schema therapy in practice – An introductory guide to the schema mode approach.* Chichester, UK: Wiley Blackwell.

Bamelis, L. L. M., Arntz, A., Wetzelaer, P., Verdoorn, R., & Evers, S. M. A. A. (2015). Economic evaluation of schema therapy and clarification-oriented psychotherapy for personality disorders: A multicenter, randomized controlled trial. *Journal of Clinical Psychiatry, 76,* 1432–1440.

Bamelis, L. L. M., Evers, S. M. A. A., & Arntz, A. (2012). Design of a multicentered randomized controlled trial on the clinical and cost effectiveness of schema therapy for personality disorders. *BMC Public Health, 12,* 75.

Bamelis, L. L. M., Evers, S. M. A. A., Spinhoven, P., & Arntz, A. (2014). Results of a multicenter randomized controlled trial of the clinical effectiveness of schema therapy for personality disorders. *American Journal of Psychiatry, 171,* 305–322.

Beck, A. T. (1976). *Cognitive therapy and the emotional disorders.* New York, NY: International Universities Press.

Beck, A. T., Freeman, A. M., & Davis, D. D. (Eds.) (2004). *Cognitive therapy for personality disorders* (2nd ed.). New York, NY: The Guilford Press.

Bernstein, D. P., Arntz, A., & de Vos, M. E. (2007). Schema-focused therapy in forensic settings: Theoretical model and recommendations for best clinical practice. *International Journal of Forensic Mental Health, 6*(2), 169–183.

Bernstein, D. P., Nijman, H., Karos, K., Keulen-de Vos, M. E., de Vogel, V., & Lucker, T. (2012). Schema therapy for forensic patients with personality disorders: Design and preliminary findings of a multicenter randomized clinical trial in the Netherlands. *International Journal of Forensic Mental Health, 11*(4), S312–S324.

Bowlby, J. (1969). *Attachment and loss.* New York, NY: Basic Books.

Chakhssi, F., Bernstein, D. P., & de Ruiter, C. (2014). Early maladaptive schemas in relation to facets of psychopathy and institutional violence in offenders with personality disorders. *Legal and Criminological Psychology, 19*(2), 356–372.

Cohen, P., Crawford, Th. N., Johnson, J. G., & Kasen, S. (2005). The children in the community study of developmental course of personality disorder. *Journal of Personality Disorders, 19*, 466–486.

Farrell, J. M., Shaw, I. A., & Webber, M. A. (2009). A schema-focused approach to group psychotherapy for outpatients with borderline personality disorder: A randomized clinical trial. *Journal of Behavior Therapy and Experimental Psychiatry, 40*, 317–328.

Giesen-Bloo, J., van Dyck, R., Spinhoven, P., van Tilburg, W., Dirksen, C., van Asselt, T., … Arntz, A. (2006). Outpatient psychotherapy for borderline personality disorder: A randomized clinical trial of schema focused therapy versus transference focused psychotherapy. *Archives of General Psychiatry, 63*, 649–658.

Gude, T., & Hoffart, A. (2008). Health and disability: Change in interpersonal problems after cognitive agoraphobia and schema-focused versus psychodynamic treatment as usual of inpatients with agoraphobia and Cluster C personality disorders. *Scandinavian Journal of Psychology, 49*, 195–199.

Gude, T., Monsen, J. T. & Hoffart, A. (2001). Schemas, affect consciousness, and cluster C personality pathology: A prospective one-year follow-up study of patients in a schema-focused short-term treatment program. *Psychotherapy Research, 11*, 85–98.

Holmes, E., & Mathews, A. (2005). Mental imagery and emotion: A special relationship? *Emotion, 5*, 489–497.

Jamieson, L., & Taylor, P. (2004). A re-conviction study of special (high security) hospital patients. *Journal of Criminology, 44*, 783–802.

Kellogg, S. (2004). Dialogical encounters: Contemporary perspectives on 'chair-work' in psychotherapy. *Psychotherapy: Theory, Research, Practice, Training, 41*(3), 310.

Kersten, T. (2015). Schema therapy in personality disorders and addiction. In M. V. Vreeswijk, J. Boerson, & M. Nadort (Eds.), *Schema therapy theory, research and practice* (pp. 415–424). Oxford, UK: Wiley Blackwell.

Landy, R. L. (2000). Role theory and the role method of drama therapy. In P. Lewis & D. Read Johnson (Eds.), *Current approaches in drama therapy* (pp. 50–69). Springfield, IL: Charles C. Thomas.

Lobbestael, J., van Vreeswijk, M. F., & Arntz, A. (2007). Shedding light on schema modes: A clarification of the mode concept and its current research status. *Netherlands Journal of Psychology, 63*, 75–85.

Lobbestael, J., van Vreeswijk, M. F., & Arntz, A. (2008). An empirical test of schema mode conceptualizations in personality disorders. *Behavior Research and Therapy, 46*, 854–860.

Maughan, A., & Cicchetti, D. (2002). Impact of child maltreatment and interadult violence on children's emotion regulation abilities and their socioemotional adjustment. *Child Development, 73*, 1525–1542.

Mental Health Act (2007). Department of Health.

Nadort, M., Arntz, A., Smit, J. H., Giesen-Bloo, J., Eikelenboom, M., Spinhoven, P., … van Dyck, R. (2009). Implementation of outpatient schema therapy for borderline personality disorder with versus without crisis support by the therapist outside office hours: A randomized trial. *Behavior Research and Therapy, 47*, 961–973.

Rafaeli, E., Bernstein, D. P., & Young, J. (2011). *Schema therapy: Distinctive features*. New York, NY: Routledge.

Rosenfeld, B. (2003). Recidivism in stalking and obsessional harassment. *Law and Human Behavior, 27*, 251–265.

Rush, M. D., Grunert, B. K., Mendelsohn, R. A., & Smucker, M. R. (2000). Imagery rescripting for recurrent, distressing images. *Cognitive and Behavioral Practice, 7,* 173–182.

Ryle, A. (1997). *Cognitive analytic therapy and borderline personality disorder: The model and the method.* Chichester, UK: Wiley.

Smucker, M. R., & Boos, A. (2005). Imagery rescripting and reprocessing therapy. In A. Freeman, M. Stone, & D. Martin (Eds.), *Comparative treatments for borderline personality disorder* (pp. 215–237). New York, NY: Springer Publishing.

Smucker, M. R., & Niederee, J. (1995). Treating incest-related PTSD and pathogenic schemas through imaginal exposure and rescripting. *Cognitive and Behavioral Practice, 2,* 63–93.

van Asselt, A. D., Dirksen, C. D., Arntz, A., Giesen-Bloo, J. H., van Dyck, R., Spinhoven, P., ... Severens, J. L. (2008). Outpatient psychotherapy for borderline personality disorder: Cost effectiveness of schema-focused therapy vs. transference-focused psychotherapy. *British Journal of Psychiatry, 192*(6), 450–457.

van Genderen, H., & Arntz, A. (2005). *Schemagerichte Cognitieve Therapie bij Bordeline Perssonlijkheidsstoornis.* Amsterdam: Utigeverij Nieuwezijds.

Weertman, A., & Arntz, A. (2007). Effectiveness of treatment of childhood memories in cognitive therapies for personality disorders: A controlled study contrasting methods focusing on the present and methods focusing on childhood memories. *Behaviour, Research and Therapy, 45,* 2133–2143.

Young, J. E. (1990). *Cognitive therapy for personality disorders: A schema-focussed approach.* Sarasota, FL: Professional Resource Press.

Young, J. E. (2005a). *Schema therapy rating scale.* New York, NY: Schema Therapy Institute.

Young, J. E. (2005b). *Young Schema Questionnaire: Long form, version 3.* New York, NY: Schema Therapy Institute.

Young, J. E., & Brown, G. (2003). *Young Schema Questionnaire: Short form, version 3.* New York, NY: Schema Therapy Institute.

Young, J. E., Klosko, J., & Weishaar, M. (2003). *Schema therapy: A practitioner's guide.* New York, NY: Guilford.

Young, J. E., Klosko, J., & Weishaar, M. (2005). *Schemagerichte Therapie. Handboek voor Therapeuten.* Houten: Bohn Stafleu Van Loghum.

Chapter 5

Neurodevelopmental disorder

Learning disability in secure forensic psychiatric services

Lyn Shelton

Introduction

Learning disability

In the UK, the Mental Health Act (MHA; 1983, as amended 2007) allows someone to be admitted, detained, and treated in hospital against their wishes, where suitable professionals deem this necessary to protect them or the public. This process is similar in many countries, and the law allows this type of detention where an individual is deemed to be suffering from a mental disorder which warrants their detention in a hospital for assessment or treatment. The decision to detain someone in hospital is taken after a comprehensive mental health assessment. In relation to people who have committed a crime, the process of mandatory detention can occur at various points in the criminal justice system, such as whilst they are waiting for trial or sentence in prison, or whilst they are serving a prison sentence. A Judge can also sentence a person to indefinite treatment in hospital, instead of a prison sentence, when recommended by healthcare professionals. Table 5.1 outlines the sections of the MHA that are used within forensic mental health settings. Transfers from prison to secure services aim to ensure that individuals with severe mental health problems have access to the right treatment and care.

Mental health difficulties in secure forensic settings include **psychosis, schizoaffective disorders, schizophrenia**, and **neurodevelopmental disorders**. Neurodevelopmental disorders are impairments of the growth and development of the brain (Reynolds & Goldstein, 1999). They cover a range of problems including interpersonal and intellectual skills (Kolb & Whishaw, 2015), some of which may influence a person's offending and general functioning.

Neurodevelopmental disorders, and conditions that can result in impaired cognitive functioning, include **Learning Disability (LD), Autism Spectrum Disorder (ASD)**, motor disorders, **Attention Deficit/Hyperactivity Disorder (ADHD),** and other neurodevelopmental disorders such as traumatic brain injury, genetic disorders, Down syndrome, schizophrenia, and schizotypal disorder.

Table 5.1 Sections of the Mental Health Act utilised within forensic mental health settings in the UK

MHA Section	Definition	Length of detention
37	The client can be sent to hospital for treatment; this could be before or after they have been convicted (Crown Court) or after conviction (Magistrate's Court). Two doctors need to provide evidence to the Court that the client has a mental disorder of a nature or degree that makes detention for medical treatment appropriate and that appropriate medical treatment is available for them.	Up to six months; can be renewed for a further six months, and then for one year at a time.
38	The Crown Court can remand an individual following conviction for offences leading to imprisonment (except for murder) under Section 38. This means that the client will be transferred to hospital for assessment and treatment. The client will then return to the Court for them to determine whether to sentence them to prison or under a hospital order.	Renewable to a maximum period of one year.
41	If the Crown Court has made a hospital order under Section 37, it can also impose a 'restriction order'. This means that the client can only be discharged, transferred, or given Section 17 leave with permission from the Ministry of Justice (MoJ). This is usually imposed in order to protect the public.	No fixed time limit.
47	The MoJ can order the individual to be transferred from prison to hospital for treatment of their mental health problems.	Up to six months, renewable for a second six months, and then one year at a time.
48	If a prisoner is on remand, two registered medical practitioners need to agree that the client is suffering from a mental health problem of a nature or degree which makes it appropriate for them to be urgently admitted to hospital for medical treatment.	N/A
49	If the MoJ has ordered an individual to be transferred from prison to hospital under Section 47, at the same time it can also impose a 'restriction direction' on them under Section 49. This means that they can only be discharged, transferred, and given leave from hospital with permission from the Secretary of State for Justice.	Until the end of the Section 47 or the date when they should be released from prison.

Although other terms are often used in the literature, the term LD will be used within this chapter to describe learning or intellectual disability. Patients with LD often have a co-morbid presentation, meaning that they have additional mental health difficulties (Glaser & Florio, 2004) as well as LD. Forensic inpatients with LD have some of the most complex needs (Lunsky et al., 2010). These individuals often overlap different systems including the criminal justice system and secure forensic hospitals. It can be difficult for an individual with LD to be appropriately placed within the criminal justice system, as it can be administratively difficult to transfer between prison and secure psychiatric environments because they are not synonymous with one another. This is a particular issue for those individuals who have not received a formal diagnosis and are placed on remand in prison without access to a comprehensive assessment of their mental health. Given that mental health problems (including LD) impact a person's day-to-day functioning and therefore on the person's ability to cope with prison life as well as the risk of offending (Hayes, 2007), this is an important issue both in the short-to-medium term in custody and the longer term in relation to risk.

LD can occur when brain development is affected before or during birth, or in early childhood (Fraser & Cooper, 2009). There are a number of elements that can impact the development of the brain, such as maternal illness during pregnancy, oxygen deprivation during birth, development of abnormal genes, inherited LD passed through maternal and/or paternal genes, and illness or injury during early childhood (for example, meningitis) (Sadler, 2010). However, it is important to highlight that there is no known cause of LD.

LD affects the way a person understands information and how they communicate. They can have difficulty understanding new or complex information, learning new skills, and coping independently. LD is an official diagnosis, where the individual must meet specific criteria in order to be diagnosed. The criteria include the following:

- The onset is prior to the age of 18,
- Intellectual functioning is assessed as an IQ below 70, and
- The individual has impaired adaptive functioning (BPS, 2015).

Adaptive functioning is a term used to describe how a person with LD may adapt to their difficulties in everyday life in order to function (BPS, 2015). The World Health Organisation's (WHO) International Classification of Functioning, Disability and Health (WHO, 2001, 2007) describes adaptive functioning as the distinction between the individual's ability and performance. As such, an individual with adaptive functioning difficulties may not have had the opportunity to acquire important skills. The Diagnostic and Statistical Manual of Mental Disorders, Fifth Edition (DSM-5; American Psychiatric Association, 2013) also lists criteria for the severity of LD: mild, moderate, severe, and profound.

The use of specifiers for these diagnoses enables a fuller description of the individual's case, how it impacts them, and what current symptoms they present with. In addition to specifiers such as the age of onset or severity ratings, neurodevelopmental disorders may also include the specifier 'associated with a medical (e.g., seizure disorder) or genetic condition (e.g., trisomy 21) or environmental factor (e.g., low birth weight)' (DSM-5, p. 33).

Learning disability and sexually motivated offending

Children are not born with the ability to regulate their emotions and/or understand their environment (Beech & Mitchell, 2005); those who are born with cognitive difficulties are likely to struggle to apply learning from relevant caregivers. In the absence of appropriate caregivers, the child is likely to develop maladaptive strategies to manage their emotions and behaviour and form insecure attachment styles (Smallbone & McCabe, 2003). This can often result in the delayed development of appropriate skills as the child matures, resulting in a childlike approach as an adult. This can lead to difficulties in forming appropriate adult intimate relationships (Beech & Mitchell, 2005), resulting in an emotional congruence with children and subsequent sexual offending against children. These clients tend to have poor self-identity, poor relationships with peers, and a lack of social knowledge (Hayes, 1991). Research has noted that there is an increased level of sexual offending within LD populations (Lindsay, 2002). It is therefore essential to consider the client's cognitive ability prior to treatment planning so that it can be tailored to meet their learning needs. Without these adaptations, it would be unlikely that the client would be able to engage in appropriate therapy and therefore have difficulty in progressing.

A forensic psychologist within a secure psychiatric facility is able to assess a patient in order to confirm (or not) a suspected diagnosis of LD. This is done by exploring the patient's cognitive and adaptive functioning utilising standardised tools, alongside clinical and observational information. A primary method for assessment of cognitive functioning is the Wechsler Adult Intelligence Scale-Fourth UK Edition (WAIS-IV; Wechsler, 2008). This is seen as the 'gold standard' in the cognitive assessment of intellectual ability (Hartman, 2009). If the individual has particularly poor concentration or the assessor has limited time available, the Wechsler Abbreviated Scale of Intelligence-Second Edition (WASI-II; Wechsler, 2011) can be used; however, the information provided is limited due to its screening nature. For individuals who have limited verbal ability and/or cultural differences including English not being their first language, an alternative consideration is the Leiter International Performance Scale, Third Edition (Leiter-3, Roid et al., 2013). However, this measure is not validated within the UK and should therefore be used with caution. Adaptive functioning assessments aim to measure the social, practical, and conceptual ability of the individual. Adaptive functioning can be more difficult to measure due to less clear definitions (Avery & Sullivan, 2013). There are a number of measures available; this case study utilised the Adaptive Behaviour Assessment System, Third Edition (ABAS- 3; Harrison & Oakland, 2015); this assessed the majority of the areas of potential adaptive functioning that would be considered when diagnosing LD; of particular importance is that an adult who knows the client well should also complete the assessment so that it is not reliant on patient self-report. An alternative measure is the Functional Living Scale (UK version; Cullum, Sine & Weiner, 2012); this focuses on instrumental activities of daily living. However, this measure does not focus on conceptual skills. The Vineland Adaptive Behavior Scales, Third Edition (Vineland-3; Sparrow, Cicchetti & Saulnier, 2016) is a further alternative; however, the Vineland has some psychometric deficiencies when utilised with an LD population (Loeb, 1996). Additionally, the norms are based on an American sample and reflect slightly different means and standard deviations in the UK comparison (Wechsler, 2000).

Patient history

Referral

One of the difficulties when working with patients in a secure forensic psychiatric setting is the lack of diagnosis, which then impacts their treatment pathway. Patrick resided in a ward specifically for males with LD within a medium secure hospital. Whilst Patrick had previously been considered to have an LD, it had been noted by his clinical team that he was having difficulties in making any treatment gain and presented with uncorroborated and improbable stories about his past. Patrick was therefore referred for an assessment of his LD with the consideration of potential cognitive decline.

In order to assess Patrick, a battery of tests described below was used, including the WAIS-IV for cognitive functioning, the ABAS-3 for adaptive functioning, the Behavioural Assessment of **Dysexecutive Syndrome** (BADS; Wilson et al., 1996) for executive functioning. In this case, following neuropsychological assessments, risk was reviewed using a structured professional judgement approach in order to develop a **formulation** that took into account the assessment findings. This allowed Patrick's most appropriate short- and medium-term treatment pathway to be considered.

Background

Childhood

Patrick is a 57-year-old male who was born following an uneventful pregnancy and no recorded history of developmental delay. Patrick's parents divorced when he was young. His father was a violent man who drank heavily. He died when Patrick was in his early 20s. Patrick's mother has LD, and as a result, Patrick spent a lot of time with his maternal grandparents when he was a child. Their death when he was in his early 20s led to his mother becoming unable to cope alone. Aged 11 years, Patrick was subjected to physical and sexual abuse by his mother's boyfriend; he also involved Patrick in the grooming of other male children to sexually abuse. Patrick reported telling his family about the abuse but he was not believed. The abuse ended when the family caught his abuser in bed with Patrick and they told his abuser to leave.

Education and employment

Patrick truanted from school and was suspended because he struggled with his peers and displayed many behavioural problems. He attended mainstream school until the age of ten and he was then transferred to a school for children with additional needs.

Patrick has had a number of unskilled jobs. He stated that his longest period of legitimate employment was six to seven weeks as a car mechanic. He stated that this ended because he started to talk to a child in a car seat and tried to touch the child's genitalia whilst the child's father was not in the car. He stopped when the boy's father saw and shouted at him.

Relationships and sexual development

Patrick said that he recognised he had a sexual preference for males at the age of 11. He was unsure if this was as a result of being sexually abused by a male. He described a formative incident when a school friend had come to visit him. Patrick stated that he *"did something bad"*. He described telling his friend that he loved him and tried to hug him. He was rebuffed and his friend said that he *"didn't do that with boys"*.

Patrick said that when aged 16 years, he abused a younger boy in the toilets of his school. He said he had always spent time around younger males. He stated that he took the boy into the bathroom and hugged, held, and kissed him, who later told a teacher and *"got him in trouble"*.

Patrick said that, in his 30s, he had a single sexual contact with an adult male who was a child sexual offender. He said that he engaged in receptive and penetrative anal intercourse, and that this occurred on one occasion, and it made him feel embarrassed. He has denied ever having any sexual contact with adult or child females.

Patrick had previously said that he loved young boys and was sexually attracted to them. However, he retracted this statement and said he had never been attracted to children.

Mental health and cognitive functioning

Patrick had previously been assessed as having a mild LD. He experienced some anxieties and frustrations that resulted in difficulty establishing prosocial relationships with others. Historically, he used maladaptive strategies to discharge his feelings, such as being intimidating, making harassing phone calls to members of the public, and making persistent complaints about others, which caused interpersonal frictions. Patrick reported that he did not consider himself to have any mental illness or LD.

Offending history

Index offence

During his late 20s, Patrick was convicted of child abduction and false imprisonment. He enticed an eight-year-old boy to his bedroom where he lived independently. The victim lived nearby and knew Patrick. He reported that the victim wore clothes that *"turned people on"*. Patrick stated that he offered the victim £20 to *"sleep with him"* (i.e. have sexual relations with him), and that the victim refused. He subsequently kept the victim imprisoned in his bedroom for 48-hours. He wrote a letter pretending to be the victim, stating that he was staying at a friend's house so his parents would not get suspicious. Patrick said he threatened the victim that he would never see his parents again if he did not do what he told him. He reported kissing the boy and admitted to lying on top of him and rubbing the boy's genitals. He locked the victim in a cupboard without food or drink for two days.

Previous convictions

There were a number of discrepancies across historical reports regarding details and dates of Patrick's past offending, which can lead to difficulties when applying static risk tools such as the Risk Matrix 2000 (Thornton, 2010). Collation of information indicated that Patrick had a total of four convictions comprising four non-sexual and non-violent offences. These included the theft of a motor vehicle and forgery.

Although he did not receive a conviction, records indicated that Patrick once lured a male child, aged 11, back to his house by stating that he had a computer which the boy could use. He was reported to have attempted to kiss and cuddle the boy, and Patrick tried to put his hand in the child's trousers. In relation to an additional un-convicted incident, Patrick reported that he touched a male child's genitalia and incited the victim to touch Patrick's genitalia. He also stated that he threatened, whilst holding a toy gun, to kill the victim and his family if the victim told anyone about the abuse.

Cognitive and neurological assessment

There are many psychometric assessments available to psychologists, and psychologists use their clinical judgment based on client presentation and the research literature in order to select appropriate tests. Some types of tests are based heavily on client self-report of their thoughts, feelings, and behaviour, and others are based on an 'informant' reporting on these issues. These sorts of tests have the limitations of subjectivity and the assessment being influenced by factors such as client presentation on that particular day, or perceived situational demands. Other types of tests, such as cognitive functioning assessment, involve asking the client to perform various tasks and assessing their performance, accuracy, and speed in doing so. This type of test can be influenced by a number of clinical factors such as client fatigue, client effort, and malingering.

Despite the limitations of psychometric testing, some of which are detailed above, psychologists can administer supplementary tests in order to examine the nature and degree of some of the factors influencing assessment. Clinical observations are also useful; spotting patterns or unusual findings within cognitive assessment provides useful evidence. The current assessment involved administering a clinical interview and supplementary psychometric testing in order to consider the validity of the functioning assessment findings.

When an assessment is taking place in a hospital context, it is important to consider the possibility that situational demands may impact client performance, in that it may serve the purpose of the client to perform well, or to perform poorly, within an assessment. With that in mind, and based on Patrick's previous presentation, a supplementary test of effort specific to memory malingering was administered. In line with the British Psychological Society's recommendation (BPS, 2009), the specifics of this measure will not be detailed in this case study, so as not to share information that might invalidate its continued use with those at risk of malingering.

Examination of the supplementary test results did not highlight concern regarding the amount of effort Patrick put into the testing procedure. My clinical observations of Patrick's performance throughout the assessment were that he understood instructions, asked questions where appropriate, and appeared to try hard. Conclusions about examinee effort should be based on several sources of converging evidence (Iverson, 2010). Therefore, the full and critical analysis of the psychometric (WAIS-IV) findings was considered in relation to consistency with my clinical observations and the psychological assessment. Based on this, it was my opinion that Patrick tried his best to comply and engage fully with the assessment, and therefore it is my view that the overall assessment and outcome is valid.

Wechsler Adult Intelligence Scale-Fourth Edition

The WAIS-IV (Wechsler, 2008) is an individually administered assessment of a person's cognitive and intellectual functioning. It examines non-verbal reasoning skills, spatial processing skills, visual-motor integration, attention to detail, and acquired knowledge such as verbal reasoning and comprehension. The WAIS-IV comprises up to 15 subtests measuring both verbal and non-verbal abilities, from which index scores and composite scores are derived. The Full-Scale Intelligence

Table 5.2 Summary table using the WAIS index scores

Scale	Composite score	Percentile rank	Confidence intervals	Descriptive classification
Full-scale IQ	65	1	62–70	Lower extreme / Normative weakness
Verbal Comprehension Index	68	2	64–75	Lower extreme / Normative weakness
Perceptual Reasoning Index	71	3	66–79	Below average / Normative weakness
Working Memory Index	69	2	64–78	Lower extreme / Normative weakness
Processing Speed Index	74	4	68–85	Below average / Normative weakness

Quotient (FSIQ) consists of many composite parts and provides an overall estimate of a person's intellectual ability. This test yields five composite scores: Verbal Comprehension Index (VCI), Perceptual Reasoning Index (PRI), Working Memory Index (WMI), Processing Speed Index (PSI), and the FSIQ. All 15 subtests were administered. IQ scores are based around an average of 100. Any scores within 20 points on either side are considered to fall within the average range of ability. This is further subdivided into low average, average, and high average categories. Approximately 80% of the population would fall into one of these three categories according to the WAIS-IV normative sample (Wechsler, 2008). Table 5.2 summarises the results for Patrick.

Full-scale intellectual quotient

When considering overall IQ, it is important to consider any differences between the indexes making up the overall IQ score. This is so that it can be decided as to whether the FSIQ provides an accurate summary of functioning. In Patrick's case, the difference between his highest scoring index (PSI = 74, 4th percentile) and his lowest scoring index (VCI = 68, 2nd percentile) was 6 points. This indicated that the spread was within acceptable limits; therefore, Patrick's general FSIQ was interpretable. His FSIQ was assessed as 65 (1st percentile) and fell into the lower extreme, indicating that 99% of the general population would perform better than him. There was a 95% certainty that Patrick's results on the WAIS-IV would fall within the *lower extreme* range when considering the confidence interval levels. Scores obtained on a measure of cognitive ability are based on observational data and represent only *estimates* of an examinee's *true* scores. They reflect an examinee's true ability combined with some degree of measurement error. An examinee's score is more accurately represented by establishing a confidence interval: a specified range of scores in which the true score is likely to lie. Confidence interval estimates therefore provide a means of expressing score precision and serve as a reminder that measurement error is inherent in all test scores.

Verbal comprehension index

Patrick's verbal reasoning abilities were in the *below average* range, being above 2% of his age-related peers (VCI = 68). This index is intended to measure verbal abilities including reasoning, conceptualisation, and knowledge acquisition and can be impacted by educational achievement, interests, and outside reading. Patrick's performance indicated that he had learnt to recall verbal interaction and repeat this back, but that he may not understand what had been said to him. It was therefore considered that it would be helpful to Patrick to be given simple instructions and that he should be encouraged to repeat back and share his understanding of the meaning of those instructions.

Perceptual reasoning index

Patrick's non-verbal reasoning abilities were in the *below average* range (PRI = 71). This index is intended to measure visual processing, perceptual organisation, visual-motor integration, and non-verbal fluid reasoning. It can be impacted by cerebral damage. Patrick's abilities in this area were a relative weakness for him compared to other subscales assessed using the WAIS-IV. This may impact his ability to manipulate information in his mind and then make sense of it. This can also impact his ability to make sense of visual material, particularly if it relates to an abstract concept, which may negatively influence Patrick's ability to engage fully with tasks and he may struggle to move quickly between tasks that are new to him.

Working memory index

Patrick's WMI was considered to be a normative weakness and fell in the *lower extreme* range (WMI = 69). Patrick can struggle to recall information, as reflected in his performance on the digit span subtest, where the participant is required to recite a string of digits; Patrick struggled to recall more than four digits. This difficulty is likely to impact his ability to engage in group discussions. He is also more likely to lose track of what has been said and may therefore struggle to relate the information to himself. He is therefore more likely to respond better to information provided at a slower pace and/or on a one-to-one basis.

Processing speed index

The PSI relates to the participant's ability to quickly process information. Compared to the other indexes, Patrick's processing speed was a strength in his cognitive profile. However, it was still considered a normative weakness. Patrick's index score was in the *below average* range (PSI = 74). When compared to his age-related peers, Patrick's abilities were higher than only 4% of the sample population. This means that he may take longer to complete work such as note-taking or assignments, suggesting that the time Patrick requires to complete tasks and comprehend information will be longer than some of his peers. However, the level of processing speed assessed indicated that he should be able to process information, for instance, within a psychological intervention, as long as the speed of material delivery is responsive to his needs.

Adaptive Behaviour Assessment System, Third Edition

The ABAS-3 (Harrison & Oakland, 2015) provides a comprehensive assessment of adaptive skills for individuals from birth to 89 years of age. The tool may be used to assess an individual's adaptive skills for diagnosis and classification of disabilities and disorders and can be used for highlighting the individual's strengths and weaknesses. The measure assesses nine main (and one optional) areas of adaptive functioning, including *communication, community use, functional academics, home living, health and safety, leisure, self-care, self-direction, social*, and *work*.

The ABAS-3 assessment uses information from staff to assess skills. This was completed by a member of nursing staff who was familiar with Patrick. The interpretation of the assessment found that Patrick's General Adaptive Composite (GAC) fell into the *low* range (GAC = 71) and indicated that 97% of people were likely to have better overall adaptive functioning than Patrick. The results showed that communication and home living were personal strengths for Patrick, and fell into the *average* range. Social and health and safety skills fell within the *extremely low* range and were marked difficulties for Patrick. He also had a weakness in self-direction, which could negatively influence his motivation to do well at other tasks and/or utilise his abilities.

The composite score profile showed a lower social and conceptual profile (both within the *extremely low* range) in comparison to Patrick's practical skills, which fell in the *low* range. It is likely that the environment he grew up in significantly affected his adaptive skills, which resulted in a *below average* adaptive functioning.

Behavioural Assessment of the Dysexecutive Syndrome

The BADS (Wilson et al., 1996) is designed to predict everyday problems which arise from Dysexecutive Syndrome (DES; Baddeley & Wilson, 1988; Godefroy et al., 2010), including difficulties in attention, focusing, and learning new tasks. This can lead to individuals being distracted, acting impulsively, displaying inappropriate behaviour in social situations, and finding it difficult to utilise feedback. There are six subtests within the BADS: *rule shift cards test, action programme test, key search test, temporal judgment test, zoo map test,* and *modified six elements test.*

Before commencing each subtask, the rules for each task were reviewed with Patrick several times. However, Patrick was not always able to apply the rules to the task, indicating difficulty in higher-order cognitive tasks such as translating rules into action.

Patrick's total profile score fell within the low average range as compared to a control group of a similar age. Patrick was unable to shift between two sets of 'rules' or instructions. His performance indicated that his executive functioning is likely to impact his day-to-day functioning in terms of how he may respond to changes in ward rules or variation in the implementation of existing rules. Despite being able to repeat new rules, Patrick struggled to apply this knowledge into action. This means that those working with Patrick would need to ensure that he fully understands what is being asked of him.

The assessment revealed that Patrick had strengths in applying logic; however, this did not always extend to the completion of a task. This is particularly relevant if Patrick believes he has come to the end of a task but he has not actually completed it. The results of the assessment indicated that Patrick had impaired reasoning and indicated the presence of DES. This could have caused many problems with everyday life decisions and may have affected Patrick's ability to realistically assess and manage the problems of everyday living. New problems and situations may be especially poorly handled because of the inability to transfer previous knowledge to the new event.

Individuals with DES are likely to have a poor working memory and short-term memory (Baddeley & Wilson, 1988); this is also reflected in Patrick's WMI score on the WAIS-IV assessment. This can increase the likelihood of the individual suffering **confabulation**, which is the spontaneous reporting of events that never happened (Thornton, 2008). It is thought that individuals may not be able to assess the accuracy of memory retrieval, and may therefore elaborate on implausible memories. Additionally, individuals with DES often struggle with social skills because their judgements and insights into what others may be thinking are impaired. They may have trouble knowing how to behave in group situations and may not know how to follow social norms. This was in line with Patrick's presentation.

Overall assessment results

The above assessments revealed an overall level of intellectual functioning as extremely low and that Patrick also had adaptive skills across a range of domains. This is consistent with the DSM-5 description of mild LD. Patrick was also assessed as having impaired executive functioning, consistent with a diagnosis of DES. These important results were then considered in the context of his offending in order to inform treatment and risk management planning.

Formulation of sexual offending

Based on the neuropsychological assessments and guided by the assessment of Patrick's risk using the *Risk for Sexual Violence Protocol* (RSVP) instrument (Hart et al., 2003), a narrative formulation of Patrick's sexual offending was developed to aid the understanding of his case in order to best advise how to work with him. A case formulation provides hypotheses about a person's problems so that the problem can be understood.

In Patrick's case, the area being considered as the 'problem' or 'presenting issue' was his index offences, which were considered as being sexually motivated offences. Patrick was exposed to violence at an early age, which is likely to have made this approach to problem-solving a more normalised approach. As Patrick's mother had learning disabilities, it is unlikely that she was able to establish boundaries, resulting in Patrick struggling to establish social norms/rules in his formative years; this was likely to have been exacerbated by his cognitive difficulties. It appears that Patrick learnt as a child that persistent complaining to his mother would get his needs met, which in turn led to an entitlement **schema** whereby Patrick continued to struggle as an adult if he perceived that his needs were not met quickly enough. As an adult, this has manifested in Patrick making an increased number of complaints when he was anxious or worried about an issue that felt important to him. Persevering in this manner is likely to be linked to Patrick's DES, whereby he struggles to change a cycle of behaviour once he feels immersed in it.

Patrick experienced sexual abuse at the hands of an adult male whilst he was an adolescent. Despite discrepancies in the details, it was clear that Patrick believed that he experienced some level of trauma that he stated continued to affect him. Those early sexual experiences were likely to have had an impact on Patrick's developing sexual identity, as well as possibly contributing to a distorted sense of appropriate relationships with children, likely compounded by his level of intellectual functioning. Patrick acknowledged that he went on to tell a male friend that he had sexual feelings for him; he believed that this was a direct result of being sexually abused. It is likely that due to his friend not reciprocating, Patrick felt rejected. Given his later difficulties establishing social norms and developing friendships, it can be hypothesised that Patrick feared the rejection of others and so developed an emotional congruence with children whom he considered as less likely to reject him, and with whom he felt that he had more in common, as a result of his cognitive capacity.

Patrick has acknowledged that he had struggled with his sexual identity. It is likely that he had also struggled with his general identity, and as a result of this, he had compensated for his perceived inadequacies by developing an image representative of confidence. It is suggested that this presentation acted as a 'mask' for Patrick, who underneath lacked confidence in his social competence. He was likely to have developed an **Avoidant-Fearful Attachment Style** in response to perceived rejection by males as an adolescent, as well as rejection from family as he grew up (both his brother and mother at times) and the violence experienced in the home. Patrick has a tendency to confabulate; this is directly linked to his DES and has likely become a way to help him feel more adequate around others. He often overcompensated for his attachment style by utilising his entitlement schema; this can often be perceived by those working with him as a **Dismissive Attachment Style** whereby Patrick attempts to present himself as confident and independent. However, based on an examination of his case in detail, it is hypothesised that his default attachment style is to view both himself and others negatively and that he overcompensates for this.

Discussion

The results of the assessments above were critical in informing risk-reduction treatment planning for Patrick. Within secure psychiatric hospital settings, patient numbers are on a smaller scale when compared to the number of people residing on a prison wing. This means that patients within hospital settings can often be offered more bespoke treatment packages rather than the generic treatment groups usually offered within a prison setting. This is an especially relevant consideration for Patrick, who was assessed as having a number of difficulties including mild LD and DES, and so it was considered that mainstream group-based psychological treatment would be unlikely to meet his individual needs in relation to responsivity and risk and that a tailored responsivity plan would need to be in place if he were to engage with group-based interventions.

Based on risk assessment and Patrick's identified LD, as well as his deficient abilities related to social skills and emotional recognition and management, he was offered a place on the 'I Can Feel Good' (ICFG) programme (Ingamells & Morrissey, 2014). This programme is based on **Dialectical Behavioural Therapy** (DBT; Linehan, 1993) and is adapted to meet the responsivity and treatment needs of individuals with LD. The modules of the programme cover **mindfulness** skills, managing feelings, coping in crisis, and people skills, all of which were identified as problems for Patrick within the case formulation. This includes group and individual sessions. Early preliminary research (Ashworth & Brotherton, 2018) indicates a positive effect for a male sample in managing feelings, coping in crisis, and people skills. There has also been evidence of positive effect on the client's adaptive coping strategies (Ashworth, Mooney & Tully, 2017). Patrick took part in this programme for approximately one year. He was supported in his engagement through a responsivity plan, and as a result, he participated well in group discussions and enjoyed doing group activities; he particularly enjoyed aspects of the programme that involved role play and mindfulness. Despite significant effort by therapists to adapt material and communication to meet Patrick's learning needs, he struggled to understand some of the material, particularly if it was new or of a complex nature. This sometimes led to superficial treatment engagement, which could be linked to his cognitive difficulties or his DES (Alderman, Fry & Youngson, 1995), and/or his motivation to engage (Medalia & Richardson, 2005).

Conversely, it could have been that Patrick was at a stage of ambivalence, which is a normal stage on the route to change (Prochaska & Norcross, 2013). Patrick was advised to continue to engage with the ICFG programme in order to enhance retention of information through repetition, which was considered in line with his learning needs, and staff continued to support him to manage any difficulties he experienced as a result of DES.

Patrick was also offered weekly psychology sessions, which he attended for approximately one year. The sessions focused on rapport-building initially, and then focused on his offence utilising a sex offender treatment model approach (Craig, Lindsay & Browne, 2010). During this treatment, Patrick was initially open about his sexual interest in children, and he shared the concerns he was having about his sexual thoughts. A treatment approach exploring strategies to challenge these thoughts was used, as well as helping Patrick to generate ways of managing thoughts and feelings with techniques such as distraction. However, part way through therapy, Patrick's level of openness about his sexual thinking changed, with him stating that he did not have a sexual interest in children and that he had fabricated any previous admission of sexual interest in children. Patrick continued to focus on learning gained from the ICFG programme, which was considered as evidence of good progress; however, he maintained his stance regarding his sexual interests, and therefore it was difficult to work directly on his sexual offending risk.

Various recommendations were made to those working with Patrick, taking into account his cognitive and adaptive functioning abilities. Patrick's personal strength was his processing speed. However, it was still in the below average range. It was therefore considered essential that he be given time to formulate responses to enable him to apply the knowledge processed. Using a variety of ways to present information was advised as being likely to benefit Patrick in order to support him with processing and retaining information. Patrick's weakness was his verbal comprehension. Subsequently, it was advised that Patrick would be likely to benefit from being given simple instructions and that he should be encouraged to repeat back and share his understanding of the meaning of those instructions.

With regard to his adaptive functioning, Patrick's weakness in self-direction was considered as being likely to impact his motivation to do well at other tasks and/or utilise his abilities. It was recommended that any further interventions should take into account his cognitive and adaptive profile and that any in-depth work should be completed on a one-to-one basis in order to be responsive to his needs.

DES can be difficult to work with, particularly when present alongside other co-morbid presentations such as LD (Burgess et al., 1998). Literature suggests the use of response cost (Alderman & Ward, 1991) as a successful approach in behaviour management, but its focus on the punishment cycle means that the emphasis is on the negative aspects of the client rather than reinforcing desired behaviours. Therefore, there is a reluctance for its use in current practice

(Alderman et al., 1995). A more favourable approach is cognitive rehabilitation through restructuring and over-learning (McDonald, Flashman & Saykin, 2002); this approach was recommended as an approach that was also likely to meet Patrick's cognitive needs.

Given that Patrick's engagement with office-focused psychological intervention had been superficial, and his stance had changed to deny a sexual interest in children, it was considered that alternative approaches should be tried to enhance **protective factors** for Patrick. It was recommended to engage in a positive behavioural support (PBS) model such as Reinforce Appropriate Implode Disruptive (RAID; Davies, 2013). RAID (2017) is described as a positive approach to working with extreme and challenging behaviour. The aim is for the patient to focus on 'green' (positive) behaviours in order to eliminate opportunities for 'red' (challenging or less positive) behaviours through developing a therapeutic milieu (RAID, 2017). Research has shown the RAID model significantly reduced the number of incidents of challenging behaviour on a medium secure LD ward. Results also indicated that there was an increase in the number of periods of escorted leave recorded, thus indicating an increase in quality-of-life experiences (Summers, unpublished). Staff were advised to utilise this approach with Patrick in order to engage him in a more fulfilling life including gradual access to community leave. It was also recommended that this should be complemented with recovery activities through **occupational therapy**, which would help develop Patrick's skills in activities of daily living, in line with the functioning defects identified using the ABAS.

Those working with Patrick in the future were also advised to take a trauma-focused approach to treatment in order to support him to explore the abuse he suffered as a child, although any intervention would need adaptation to meet his learning needs. A variety of treatment models were recommended to be explored in order to find the most suitable approach for Patrick. These included **Cognitive Behavioural Therapy**, Eye Movement Desensitisation and Reprocessing (**EMDR**; Shapiro, 2005), and psychodynamic-based treatments (Mevissen & De Jongh, 2010). EMDR has been reported to be an applicable psychological trauma treatment for individuals with limited cognitive and/or verbal abilities (Barol & Seubert, 2010) and so this was advised as a potential future treatment to help target difficulties that were identified in the case formulation as being relevant to his offending risk.

Conclusions

Research has found that there is a higher prevalence of sexual offending within the LD population; this has been found to be particularly relevant to those who have also been victims of abuse. Traits among sexual offenders with LD include poor self-identity, difficulty developing appropriate adult intimate relationships, lack of sexual knowledge, behavioural and emotional management problems, and psychiatric illnesses. This client group has been found to be more likely to offend against young children and male children (Blanchard et al., 1999). With this in mind, it was essential to assess Patrick's cognitive, adaptive, and executive functioning in order to aid formulation and identify an appropriate treatment pathway. The formulation led to a multimode approach to treatment including group therapy, individual trauma-focused therapy, and support using the PBS system RAID. There is limited available research on treating clients with this co-morbid presentation, particularly with the element of DES. Future research should therefore focus on evaluating the effectiveness of ICFG in relation to risk-related treatment needs, RAID in relation to environmental and supportive factors to aid progress, and EMDR with forensic LD patients.

References

Alderman, N., Fry, R. K., & Youngson, H. A. (1995). Improvement of self-monitoring skills, reduction of behaviour disturbance and the dysexecutive syndrome: Comparison of response cost and a new programme of self-monitoring training. *Neuropsychological Rehabilitation, 5*(3), 193–221.

Alderman, N., & Ward, A. (1991). Behavioural treatment of the dysexecutive syndrome: Reduction of repetitive speech using response cost and cognitive overlearning. *Neuropsychological Rehabilitation, 1*(1), 65–80.

American Psychiatric Association (2013). *Diagnostic and statistical manual of mental disorders (DSM-5®)*. Arlington, VA: American Psychiatric Publication.

Ashworth, S., & Brotherton, N. (2018). "We can feel good": Evaluation of an adapted DBT informed skills programme in medium security. *Advances in Mental Health and Intellectual Disabilities, 12*(5/6), 184–194.

Ashworth, S., Mooney, P., & Tully, R. J. (2017). A case study demonstrating the effectiveness of an adapted-DBT program upon increasing adaptive emotion management skills, with an individual diagnosed with mild learning disability and emotionally unstable personality disorder. *Journal of Forensic Psychology Research and Practice, 17*(1), 38–60. doi:10.1080/15228932.2017.1251098

Avery, G., & Sullivan, F. (2013). Use of the Vineland Adaptive Behaviour Scales (2nd ed.) in the assessment of adults with intellectual disabilities: Clinical observations. *Clinical Psychology Forum, 246*, 13–17.

Baddeley, A., & Wilson, B. (1988). Frontal amnesia and the dysexecutive syndrome. *Brain and Cognition, 7*(2), 212–230.

Barol, B. I., & Seubert, A. (2010). Stepping stones: EMDR treatment of individuals with intellectual and developmental disabilities and challenging behavior. *Journal of EMDR Practice and Research, 4*(4), 156–169.

Beech, A. R., & Mitchell, I. J. (2005). A neurobiological perspective on attachment problems in sexual offenders and the role of selective serotonin re-uptake inhibitors in the treatment of such problems. *Clinical Psychology Review, 25*, 153–182.

British Psychological Society (BPS) (2009). *Assessment of effort in clinical testing of cognitive functioning for adults*. Retrieved from www.bps.org.uk

British Psychological Society (BPS) (2015). *Guidance on the assessment and diagnosis of intellectual disabilities in adulthood*. Retrieved from www.bps.org.uk

Craig, L. A., Lindsay, W. R., & Browne, K. D. (Eds.) (2010). *Assessment and treatment of sexual offenders with intellectual disabilities: A handbook.* Chichester, UK: John Wiley & Sons.

Cullum, C. M., Saine, K. C., & Weiner, M. F. (2012). *The Functional Living Scale, UK Version.* London, UK: Pearson Clinical.

Davies, W. (2013). *The RAID course* (10th ed.). Leicester, UK: The ATP Press.

Fraser, D. M., & Cooper, M. A. (2009). *Myles textbook for midwives: The world's favourite midwifery textbook!* London, UK: Churchill Livingstone.

Glaser, W., & Florio, D. (2004). Beyond specialist programmes: A study of the needs of offenders with intellectual disability requiring psychiatric attention. *Journal of Intellectual Disability Research, 48,* 591–602.

Godefroy, O., Azouvi, P., Robert, P., Roussel, M., LeGall, D., Meulemans, T., & Behalf of the Groupe de Réflexion sur l'Evaluation des Fonctions Exécutives Study Group (2010). Dysexecutive syndrome: Diagnostic criteria and validation study. *Annals of Neurology, 68*(6), 855–864.

Harrison, P., & Oakland, T. (2015). *Adaptive Behaviour Assessment System - Third Edition.* San Antonio, TX: Pearson Clinical.

Hart, S. D., Kropp, P. R., Laws, D. R., Klaver, J., Logan, C., & Watt, K. A. (2003). *The Risk for Sexual Violence Protocol (RSVP).* Burnaby, BC: The Mental Health, Law, and Policy Institute of Simon Fraser University.

Hartman, D. E. (2009). Wechsler Adult Intelligence Scale IV (WAIS-IV): Return of the gold standard. *Applied Neuropsychology, 16*(1), 85–87.

Hayes, S. (1991). Sex offenders. *Australia and New Zealand Journal of Developmental Disabilities, 17,* 221–227.

Hayes, S. (2007). Missing out: Offenders with learning disabilities and the criminal justice system. *British Journal of Learning Disabilities, 35*(3), 146–153.

Ingamells, B., & Morrissey, C. (2014). *I can feel good: Skills training for people with intellectual disabilities and problems managing emotions.* London, UK: Pavilion Publishing and Media.

Iverson, G. L. (2010). Detecting exaggeration, poor effort and malingering in neuropsychology. In A. Horton & L. C. Hartlage (Eds.), *Handbook of forensic neuropsychology* (2nd ed., pp. 91–135). New York, NY: Springer.

Kolb, B., & Whishaw, I. Q. (2015). *Fundamentals of human neuropsychology* (7th ed.). New York, NY: Macmillan.

Lindsay, W. R. (2002). Research and literature on sex offenders with intellectual and developmental disabilities. *Journal of Intellectual Disability Research, 46*(s1), 74–85.

Linehan, M. M. (1993). *Cognitive behavioral treatment of borderline personality disorder.* New York, NY: Guilford Press.

Loeb, P. (1996). *Independent living scales: Manual.* San Antonio, TX: Psychology Corp.

Lunsky, Y., Gracey, C., Koegl, C., Bradley, E., Durbin, J., & Raina, P. (2010). The clinical profile and service needs of psychiatric inpatients with intellectual disabilities and forensic involvement. *Psychology, Crime & Law, 17*(1), 9–23.

McDonald, B. C., Flashman, L. A., & Saykin, A. J. (2002). Executive dysfunction following traumatic brain injury: Neural substrates and treatment strategies. *NeuroRehabilitation, 17*(4), 333–344.

Medalia, A., & Richardson, R. (2005). What predicts a good response to cognitive remediation interventions? *Schizophrenia Bulletin, 31*(4), 942–953.

Mental Health Act (2007). Ch. 43. Retrieved from http://www.opsi.gov.uk/acts/acts2007/ukpga_20070012_en_1

Mevissen, L., & De Jongh, A. (2010). PTSD and its treatment in people with intellectual disabilities: A review of the literature. *Clinical Psychology Review, 30*(3), 308–316.

RAID (2017). Retrieved from www.apt.ac

Reynolds, C. R., & Goldstein, S. (1999). *Handbook of neurodevelopmental and genetic disorders in children* (pp. 3–8). New York: The Guilford Press. ISBN 1-57230-448-0.

Roid, G. H., Miller, L. J., & Koch, C. (2013). *Leiter international performance scale.* Wood Dale, IL: Stoelting.

Sadler, T. W. (2010). *Urogenital system in Langman's medical embryology.* Philadelphia, PA: Walters Kluwer.

Shapiro, F. (2005). *Eye movement desensitization and reprocessing (EMDR) training manual.* Watsonville, CA: EMDR Institute.

Smallbone, S. W., & McCabe, B. (2003). Childhood attachment, childhood sexual abuse, and onset of masturbation among adult sexual offenders. *Sexual Abuse: A Journal of Research and Treatment, 15*, 1–9.

Sparrow, S. S., Cicchetti, D. V., & Saulnier, C. A. (2016). *Vineland Adaptive Behavior Scales, Third Edition (Vineland-3).* Bloomington, MN: Pearson Clinical.

Summers, K. (unpublished). Reviewing RAID implementation across learning disability services. Unpublished manuscript.

Thornton, T. (2008). *Ed. Dysexecutive syndrome: Dealing with day-to-day decision-making.* Aged Services, Royal Hobart Hospital, Tasmanian Department of Health and Human Services, Australia. Retrieved March 11, 2011.

Thornton, D. (2010). Scoring guide for the Risk Matrix 2000. National Offender Manager Service.

Wechsler, D. (2000). *Wechsler Adult Intelligence Scale-Third Edition: Administration and scoring manual.* London, UK: Psychology Corp.

Wechsler, D. (2008). *Wechsler Adult Intelligence Scale-Fourth Edition.* San Antonio, TX: Pearson Clinical.

Wechsler, D. (2011). *Abbreviated Scale of Intelligence Second Edition.* San Antonio, TX: Pearson Clinical.

Wilson, B. A., Emslie, H., Evans, J. J., Alderman, N., & Burgess, P. W. (1996). *Behavioural assessment of the dysexecutive syndrome (BADS).* London, UK: Pearson Clinical.

World Health Organization (2001). *International classification of functioning, disability, and health.* Geneva. Author.

World Health Organization (2007). *International classification of functioning, disability, and health: Children and youth version.* Geneva. Author.

Chapter 6

Autism spectrum disorder

Females in secure forensic psychiatric services

Sarah Ashworth

Introduction

Autism Spectrum Disorder (ASD) is a neurodevelopmental disorder defined within the **Diagnostic and Statistical Manual, Fifth Edition** (DSM-5; American Psychological Association, APA, 2013) by persistent deficits in social communication, interaction, and imagination, associated with restricted, repetitive patterns of behaviour, interests, and activities and potential sensory difficulties. Lyall et al. (2017) found only one rigorous study of ASD prevalence rates to date, which estimates a prevalence of 1% in the general population (Brugha et al., 2011), with males significantly over-represented (Whiteley et al., 2010) leading some to question the accuracy of these gender-biased figures (Zwaigenbaum et al., 2012). However, the 1% prevalence rate has been replicated within the literature (e.g. Simonoff, 2012), though exact figures are not known (Fernell et al., 2012), especially within forensic contexts (Ashworth, 2016).

The increased identification of individuals with ASD in the community in addition to forensic services has raised the profile of the relationship between ASD and offending within the public domain (Melvin, Langdon & Murphy, 2017). There are some who suggest that individuals with ASD are more likely to offend (Barry-Walsh & Mullen, 2003; Howlin, 2004; Katz & Zemishlany, 2006), whereas others promote the generally law-abiding nature of such individuals (Cederlund et al., 2008). Chown (2010) highlights the multifaceted nature of the relationship between ASD and involvement with the criminal justice system. He presents ASD as a risk factor for certain offending typologies as influential regarding interactions with the criminal justice system (Debbaudt, 2002), and as a factor which increases an individual's vulnerability during investigation procedures (Allen et al., 2008). Certain features associated with ASD have been suggested to increase an individual's vulnerability to becoming involved with the criminal justice system (Sappok, Heinrich & Underwood, 2015). These may include social and communication difficulties, rigid thinking styles and behavioural patterns, difficulty understanding social rules, and obsessions or special interests (Attwood, 2007; Baron-Cohen, 1989; Tantam, 2011). Specifically, difficulty with social understanding and empathy have been linked with arson, violence, and sexual offending (Baron-Cohen, 1988; Griffin-Shelley, 2010).

It is important to note that although having a diagnosis of ASD may not necessarily increase an individual's risk of offending, it is essential to consider the potential role associated features play within offending behaviour in order to fully understand, manage, and treat such individuals. It is acknowledged that the clinical features of ASD may act as possible barriers to assessment and therapy, which may impact negatively upon treatment (Melvin et al., 2017). These may include individual characteristics such as cognitive rigidity and difficulties with empathy and social perspective-taking (Griffin-Shelley, 2010; Murphy, 2010a, 2010b) in addition to practical issues such as difficulties within group contexts and associated issues within capacity and consent (e.g. Milton et al., 2002). There is increasing evidence that early identification of individuals with ASD increases the effectiveness of intervention (Anderson, Liang & Lord, 2014; Dawson et al., 2010; Makrygianni & Reed, 2010; Orinstein et al., 2014). This issue appears exacerbated within forensic contexts due to a range of factors including insufficient staff awareness training, lack of resources, and a lack of awareness of available specialist services (Ashworth, 2016). Despite the apparent over-representation of ASD in forensic settings (Brugha, McManus & Bankart, 2011), many with associated difficulties remain masked, missed, or overlooked (Ashworth & Tully, 2016). Despite the advantages of early identification, those with ASD often remain undetected and subsequently unsupported (Sappok et al., 2013; Saemundsen et al., 2010).

In addition to the potential benefits that accurate assessment and diagnosis attract within the community, such as acting as a prerequisite for financial support and access to specialised intervention programmes (Sappok et al., 2015), the lack of an accurate understanding of an individuals' traits within forensic contexts may affect additional factors. This includes effective risk assessment, offence analysis, risk management, and subsequent pathway progression. It may inhibit awareness of increased vulnerability to bullying or exploitation, heightened risk of psychiatric **co-morbidity**, and the potential need to manage challenging behaviour resulting from deficits in social and communication skills (Ashworth, 2016).

ASD is often co-morbid with low cognitive functioning and specifically **Learning Disabilities** (LD; Sappok et al., 2010), mental health issues (anxiety disorders; White et al., 2009; affective disorders; Matson & Williams, 2014), and severe challenging behaviours (Sappok et al., 2014). ASD is frequently recorded as a cause for psychiatric hospital admission, specifically for individuals with co-morbid LD, and may lead to additional mental or behavioural disorders (Bhaumik et al., 2008; Sappok et al., 2014; Underwood et al., 2010). Diagnostic clarification of potential ASD is essential in providing appropriate treatment options for the associated co-morbidities (Sappok et al., 2015).

As stated, there are concerns regarding the identification of ASD within female populations (Zwaigenbaum, et al., 2012). Additionally, it is recognised that female offenders differ significantly from men in relation to offending, psychiatric diagnosis, and mental health needs (Coid et al., 2000). It has been reported that 51% of female inmates in prison have severe and enduring mental health problems (The Cabinet Office Social Exclusion Task Force, 2009), and despite representing 5% of the prison population, females make up 25% of the forensic health population (Woods & Collins, 2003). Despite this, Hellenbach et al. (2015) highlight the paucity of research and subsequent evidence base regarding specific service provision for female offenders with LD and additional mental health needs.

Taking all of these factors into consideration, it appears important that individuals, and more specifically females, diagnosed with LD in forensic contexts should be appropriately screened and assessed for other co-morbid disorders. This is to inform understanding, the development of management strategies, and treatment with the ultimate aim of increasing quality of life and reducing future risk of reoffending. Therefore, this case study explores the potential influence of ASD traits upon forensic inpatient presentation and risk, outlining the assessment and **formulation** process within a medium secure psychiatric hospital for an adult female diagnosed with ASD within the LD pathway. It serves to highlight the need to comprehensively assess, formulate, and intervene with those within forensic contexts, considering ASD profiles and idiosyncrasies.

Patient history

This clinical case study summarises psychological assessment and **psycho-education** intervention completed with a 21-year-old female psychiatric inpatient who was detained under Section 37 of the **Mental Health Act** (1983, 2007) within a medium secure LD setting. There are three levels of psychiatric hospital setting in England; high secure, medium secure, and low secure. Each differs in relation to physical security and staffing. Throughout the case study, the client will be referred to as Jane in order to maintain anonymity. Informed consent was obtained from Jane utilising a structured consent sheet, in line with guidance from the British Psychological Society (BPS), (2006, 2008) Division of Forensic Psychology (DFP, 2002), and Health and Care Professionals Council (HCPC, 2015).

Childhood and education

Very little information is available regarding Jane's early life. She was born prematurely but achieved all developmental milestones. Jane's mother has learning difficulties (although the details of these are unclear) alongside **depression**, alcoholism, and agoraphobia with some possible **obsessive-compulsive** traits. Jane's father does not have any known physical or mental health problems. She has several siblings.

Jane attended primary and secondary school but she did not attempt any exams. It is reported that Jane started to present with 'odd' behaviours when she was 15, including taking off her clothes, wetting herself, and attempting to strangle herself at school. At times of distress, she threatened herself, her mother, and other children in the street with a knife on different occasions. She also took a knife into school secreted in her underwear leading to her exclusion from school. She went to college, training in hairdressing, although she was excluded after stabbing a male member of staff in the hand with scissors.

There is a history of vulnerability to sexual abuse in Jane's past, with several reports against her father, an unknown male, and reported indecent assault by a group of young males whilst on a bus. Collateral history indicates that Jane was placed in the care of the local authority after she disclosed an allegation of sexual abuse by her father when she was 15. When she was 16, Jane was placed under a Child Protection Plan under the category of Sexual Abuse and Neglect.

Prior to her offence, Jane lived with her parents with occasional contact with her siblings. She spent most of her time in her room watching TV and went out shopping alone sometimes. Jane lived a solitary life, rarely going out.

Psychiatric history

Jane has a diagnosis of **foetal alcohol syndrome** and mild-moderate learning difficulties. The psychological report when she was 16 reports a full-scale IQ of 52 on the Wechsler Adult Intelligence Scale-Fourth Edition (WAIS-IV; Wechsler, 2008) with particular difficulties in Perceptual Reasoning Index (0.3%), Working Memory Index (0.1%), and Processing Speed Index (0.3%). This supports a diagnosis of mild-moderate learning disability. Jane has a diagnosis of pervasive developmental disorder unspecified, and a formal assessment for ASD was recommended based on her history.

Jane's first suspected episode of **psychosis** was when she was 15, when she was admitted to hospital for a period of three weeks. She had previously been treated with antipsychotic medication to good effect and had input from the early intervention service. Her most recent episode prior to detention was when she was aged 18. At the time she was commenced on medication to good effect, with improvement in her sleep and a reduction in both auditory and visual hallucinations.

Jane has a history of self-harm via superficial cuts and scratches to her arms and wrists, tying ligatures, and she made attempts to get out of a moving car when she was 15.

Forensic history

Jane was convicted of the harassment of a former teaching assistant and the teaching assistant's daughter by making contact via social media and setting up fake accounts in the victim's name, causing significant distress including the loss of her job and ongoing trauma. After being convicted when she was 18, and released on probation, Jane breached probation by continuing to harass her victim using social media, contacting the victim on over 100 occasions, and when the Police took her into custody, several different devices were found in her bed-room, which she had been using to offend. She was remanded in prison. Jane has no other known offences, although it was reported that she had stabbed a teacher in the hand with scissors in the past. Whilst in prison, Jane continued to threaten that if released, she intended to attempt to contact the victim and cause her harm by stabbing her.

Referral

Whilst in prison, Jane was considered to have a mental disorder and considerable risks which warranted admission to psychiatric hospital under the Mental Health Act for further assessment and management. The assessing team ini-tially considered whether Jane could be safely managed in a low secure hospital; however, in view of the level of risk posed, a period of assessment in a medium secure hospital was recommended. Since admission to hospital, Jane continued to show risk behaviours in the ward, such as attacking staff (including attempts at strangulation), weapon use (stabbing with pens), extensive property dam-age (including ripping flooring and chairs), and self-harm (including superficial scratching and ligating). She was also at risk of self-neglect, as she required prompts regarding self-care. She was a highly vulnerable individual and there-fore potentially at risk from other patients.

The role of a psychologist in a forensic psychiatric hospital is varied and can involve training, consultancy, supervision, assessment, and treatment. Jane was referred for assessment by her clinical team, and I was asked to consider specifically whether she may meet the criteria for ASD.

Assessment(s)

Initial assessment(s)

Jane attended and participated in just under half of the 14 initial assessment sessions offered to her across three months. She engaged relatively well with the initial assessment process. When she attended sessions, at times she strug-gled to identify potential treatment needs and showed limited insight into her current risk and difficulties. However, she was able to identify some potential sensory issues related to increases in agitation, and these were explored with her. She engaged well with more structured assessments.

It has been reported that individuals diagnosed with LD are more susceptible to emotional and psychological problems than the general population (Beail, 2016). However, the majority of existing assessment instruments are not appropriate for application with this population (Hogue et al., 2007). Therefore, the use of self-report measures within LD populations can cause problems (Finlay & Lyons, 2001). The need to develop staff-report measures in addition to self-report measures has been suggested (Nadarajah et al., 1995; Prosser & Bromley, 1998).

Therefore, regarding the current case, a combination of staff- and self-report measures was utilised to develop a comprehensive case conceptualisation of Jane's presenting difficulties.

This included assessment of her risk of violence utilising a structured professional judgement tool providing a set of professional guidelines for violence risk assessment and management (Historical Clinical Risk-20 Version 3, HCR-20^{V3}; Douglas et al., 2014). The HCR-20^{V3} acts as a significant predictor of violent and general reconviction in offenders with LD (Gray et al., 2007) and is used widely within forensic services (Douglas et al., 2014). Additional assessment of her emotional, psychological, and behavioural problems was undertaken (Emotional Problems Scale-Behaviour Report Scale; Prout & Strohmer, 1991). This tool was considered appropriate for measuring global treatment outcomes (Hogue et al., 2007). Observational assessment of her interpersonal styles was undertaken by staff (Chart of Interpersonal Reactions in Closed Living Environments; Blackburn & Renwick, 1996) and self-report measures of her psychological distress as a result of her well-being, symptoms, functioning, and risk, utilised two outcome measures: the Clinical Outcomes in Routine Evaluation – Outcome Measure (Evans et al., 2002) and the Clinical Outcomes in Routine Evaluation – Learning Disability (Brooks, Davies & Twigg, 2013).

Screening assessment

The referral was for a comprehensive diagnostic assessment regarding the potential for a diagnosis of ASD. Jane was offered weekly sessions to complete these assessments. She attended over half of the additional 14 screening and diagnostic sessions offered and generally engaged well, asking relevant questions about the assessment process and outcomes. In my opinion, there was sufficient interview and assessment time to comprehensively assess Jane's needs. The screening assessment package comprised the following measures.

The Adult Autism Spectrum Quotient-10

The Adult Autism Spectrum Quotient-10 (AQ-10; Allison, Auyeung & Baron-Cohen, 2012) is a short screening tool developed from the Adult Autism Spectrum Quotient (AQ) containing ten binary items. This test is recommended in 'Autism: recognition, referral, diagnosis and management of adults on the autism spectrum' (National Institute of Health and Care Excellence, NICE, clinical guideline CG142). It should be noted that it is recommended for individuals who do not have LD; however, it was considered appropriate as, with support, Jane appeared able to understand the items. Scores of 6 or higher indicate the need for further exploration. Jane scored 8 on this assessment, indicating that further assessment was warranted.

The Adult Autism Spectrum Quotient

The AQ (Baron-Cohen et al., 2001) is a questionnaire that identifies the degree to which any individual adult may have features of ASD. It comprises 50 questions, made up of 10 questions assessing five different areas: social skills, attention switching, attention to detail, communication, and imagination. In short, 80% of adults with Asperger Syndrome (AS) or high-functioning ASD (HFA) scored a critical minimum of 32 in the development sample. Jane completed this assessment and engaged very well. She scored 35/50, which is indicative of ASD, as 32 or higher indicates a strong likelihood of ASD. Notable deficits were reported in her ability to switch tasks (9/10), social skills (8/10), in regard to her imagination (7/10), high attention to detail (6/10), and some deficits in her communication skills (5/10).

Empathy Quotient

The Empathy Quotient (EQ; Baron-Cohen & Wheelright, 2004) is designed for use with adults of normal intelligence. It contains 40 empathy items and 20 filler/control items. Support has been given by Baron-Cohen et al. (2004) for the EQ to be used as a screening instrument within clinical settings. Their study showed that 80% of adults who had a diagnosis of AS or HFA scored below 30 on the EQ. Jane scored 19/60 demonstrating deficits in empathic functioning. It must be taken into consideration that this assessment is designed for individuals with average intelligence whereas Jane is diagnosed with mild LD, although with support she was considered to have understood the items.

Reading the mind through the eyes (Eyes Test)

The Eyes Test (Baron-Cohen et al., 2001) involves the recognition of a wide variety of facial expressions, including basic emotions (e.g., happiness, anger) and social emotions (e.g., guilt, admiration, flirtatiousness). This tool is widely accepted as a screening tool within clinical settings and is inversely correlated with the AQ. Lower scores are indicative of ASD, and 80% of adults who had a diagnosis of ASD or HFA scored below 16. Jane scored 13/36 on this assessment, indicating deficits in emotion recognition.

Screening assessment summary

In summary, the screening assessments completed with Jane suggest that she may be likely to have traits of ASD, including difficulty switching tasks, poor social skills, difficulty with imagination, deficits in empathy, and deficits in emotion recognition. Following the completion and outcomes of the ASD screening assessments, a full diagnostic assessment took place, as described below and using assessment tools which meet the NICE (2016) guideline recommendations regarding ASD diagnosis.

Diagnostic assessment

Autism Diagnostic Interview-Revised

The Autism Diagnostic Interview-Revised (ADI-R; Le Couteur, Lord & Rutter, 2003) is a standardised, semi-structured clinical interview for caregivers of children and adults. The ADI-R provides a diagnostic algorithm for ASD as described in both the International Statistical Classification of Diseases and Related Health Problems 10th Revision (ICD-10) and DSM-IV. The interview contains 93 items and focuses on behaviours in three content areas or domains: qualities of reciprocal social interaction; communication and language; and restricted and repetitive, stereotyped interests and behaviours.

Following gaining consent from Jane, contact was made with her parents, with the main line of communication being with her father. He reported being willing to engage with the ADI-R assessment but was able to provide little information, and so, a thorough developmental history was not obtained. He did report that he perceived Jane to be *"a normal little girl"* until she was removed from the family home following reports of sexual abuse, which he denies. He attributed this change in presentation to this removal and involvement of social services.

Autism Diagnostic Observation Schedule, Second Edition, Module 4

The Autism Diagnostic Observation Schedule, Second Edition (ADOS-2; Lord et al., 2012) is a semi-structured, standardised assessment of communication, social interaction, and play for individuals who have been referred because of possible ASD or other pervasive developmental disorders. Administration consists of a series of planned social occasions or 'presses' in which a behaviour of a particular type is likely to occur. Across the session, the examiner presents numerous opportunities for the individual being assessed to exhibit behaviours of interest in the diagnostic process. A module chosen to be appropriate to a particular language level dictates the protocol. At the end of the administration, ratings are completed based on the observation period. The obtained scores are compared with the ADOS-2 cut-off scores to assist in diagnosis. Scores at or above the cut-off indicate a higher likelihood of an ASD.

For this assessment, all of the required items from Module 4 were administered. Module 4 is appropriate for an adolescent or an adult who has fluent speech. The descriptions provided below involve only those behaviours and clinical impressions that are needed to ascertain the presence of autistic traits (Table 6.1).

Language and communication

Jane's scores were at the cut-off for autism spectrum in the language and communication domain. This suggested that language and communication may be an area of relative strength for her. She demonstrated a well-developed range

Table 6.1 Jane's ADOS-2 scores

Area	Score	ADOS-2 cut-off	
		Autism spectrum	Autism
Language and communication	2	2	3
Reciprocal social interaction	8	4	6
Communication and social interaction total	10	7	10
Stereotyped behaviours/Restricted interests	2	No cut-offs determined	
Imagination/Creativity	1	No cut-offs determined	

of verbal language skills and an ability to maintain social communication with others. However, her speech appeared unusual at times with occasional echolalia and odd intonation; this was often in times of perceived anxiety or excitement.

Reciprocal social interaction

Jane scored above the cut-off for autism regarding the reciprocal interaction domain. This suggested that this may be an area in which she experiences relative difficulty. There was a definite unusual quality to her social inter-action and she appeared to be content in her own company the majority of the time, with some attempts at engaging others in conversation either following a social press or to get her needs met. She demonstrated little understanding of typical social relationships and did not appear to consider social relationships as a priority for her. Although she was able to describe her own emotional experiences, she did so to a limited degree, and there was a marked absence of identification or understanding of emotional states in others.

Stereotyped behaviours / Restricted interests

There is no cut-off determined for the stereotyped behaviours and restricted interests domain. Jane demonstrated definite evidence of sensory interests both in her actions and reported behaviours and interests. This is an area which war-ranted further exploration.

Imagination/Creativity

There is no cut-off determined for the imagination/creativity domain. Jane demonstrated an ability to be creative, although this appeared not to be an automatic tendency for her.

Other abnormal behaviours

There is no cut-off determined for the other abnormal behaviours domain. However, her marked underactivity, stiff posture, and unusually restricted gait may be suggestive of sensory modulation issues relating to difficulties with proprioception and balance. This may warrant further exploration of sensory modulation issues.

Conclusions and recommendations

The information obtained from the ADOS-2 suggested that Jane presented in a manner suggestive of ASD. Specifically, she demonstrated persistent deficits in her reciprocal social interaction and sensory issues. However, due to the lack of developmental history obtained through the ADI-R or collateral information, it was impossible to ascertain the aetiology of the current presentation. It is acknowledged that individuals with foetal alcohol syndrome often present with 'autism like' features (APA, 2013) and there is no reliable way of pulling apart her behaviours and attributing these to one condition or the other.

The severity of ASD symptoms tends not to be a good prognosis indicator. Good prognostic factors include functional language, adaptive functioning, and mental health. Jane demonstrated limited stereotyped behaviours and/or restricted interests, and despite deficits regarding social interactions, her language and communication skills are relatively well-developed. This will likely benefit her in the future, not only increasing her functional ability but also when developing social relationships, a potential **protective factor** against mental health difficulties.

Once accurately assessed and identified, the importance of psycho-education for individuals with LD (Beail, 2016) and ASD (Melvin et al., 2017) has been highlighted. Therefore, for Jane, it was recommended that subsequent psychological intervention should initially involve giving her feedback of the assessment outcomes and the subsequent collaborative development of materials designed to increase her understanding of ASD, and how this relates to her personally. It was suggested that psychological intervention regarding social skills and relationships would be beneficial, specifically concerning appropriate behaviours, relationship types, and boundaries (Melvin et al., 2017). Additionally, education regarding the use and misuse of information communication technology and social media was considered valuable in reducing her specific risk and potential vulnerabilities.

In order to comprehensively understand Jane's sensory profile and potential processing difficulties, it was also recommended that a full sensory integration assessment be completed by a suitably qualified **Occupational Therapist** (e.g. Sensory Integration and Praxis Tests, SIPT; Ayres, 1989). This may inform ward-based sensory interventions and sensory management strategies regarding her problem behaviours, such as providing her with alternative adaptive sensory stimuli to reduce the maladaptive problem behaviours she displays (e.g. ripping flooring). Such intervention is designed to increase her effective sensory integration and modulation abilities (Ayres & Robbins, 2005). Finally, it was recommended that the issues identified within the formulation presented below be consideration in any future treatment and management plans designed to reduce the risk of reoffending relapse.

Formulation

A formulation is a revisable hypothesis developed to explain why an individual presents as they do (Eells & Lombart, 2011). Its development serves multiple purposes, including information structuring, therapy blueprint development, and facilitating the development of the therapist-client relationship (Eells, 2007). Its development reflects a scientist-practitioner approach (Kennedy & Llewelyn, 2001).

The formulation developed and presented here provides a narrative about the possible causes, triggers, and perpetuating factors in an attempt to explain Jane's current presentation, which included a range of difficulties. It utilises a structured approach taking into account central factors; the presenting problem(s), predisposing, perpetuating, and protective factors (Johnstone & Dallos, 2006). Specifically regarding risk treatment and management, based on the assessment outcomes, the formulation includes areas identified as likely contributory factors to her offending behaviours. This formulation approach was used to communicate the psychological knowledge derived from the assessment process to Jane and to her clinical team in a concise and understandable manner.

Presenting problems

Harm to others

Jane's conviction of harassment was considered her presenting issue, alongside her physical violence risk to others. Jane continued to make threats to kill the victim of her harassment by stabbing her, and at the time of assessment she offered no alternative; she believed there was a high probability she would engage in this behaviour in the community. Based on the repetitive nature of this behaviour and her continued threats, it was considered highly likely that Jane would attempt to use a knife to harm herself or others in the future, and the level of risk was deemed to potentially cause serious harm or even death.

Harm to self

Jane continued to pose a risk to herself from self-harming. Due to the impulsivity of her behaviour, there remained a risk of accidental death, especially if she were to use a ligature and not be found in time. Jane was also at risk of self-neglect, and she continued to engage in risk behaviours in the ward, including attacking staff, weapon use, property damage (which is potentially associated with sensory seeking behaviours), and self-harm (including ligating).

Contributory factors

Diagnoses

Jane's diagnoses include possible ASD, mild LD and foetal alcohol syndrome, which could contribute to difficulties when attempting to solve problems. Her ability to learn and apply new behavioural responses to external or internal triggers may be limited, which may inhibit her ability to develop new ways of coping.

Lack of understanding regarding typical social situation and relationships

Jane demonstrated little understanding of appropriate social relationships. This may therefore cause her to cross certain social boundaries without realising how these may be interpreted by others, potentially leading to the interpersonal nature of her primary offence.

Difficulties with social communication

Jane's unusual presentation when anxious or excited, involving fixed eye contact and loud speech, could be interpreted as threatening or unpredictable.

Difficulty identifying or processing emotional experience in others

Jane demonstrated little empathy or remorse following her violent and antisocial actions, which may be attributable to an empathy deficit linked to ASD traits and not simply poor victim empathy.

Childhood trauma

There are reports of childhood trauma including sexual abuse and difficulties with **attachment**, which may also have contributed to her current difficulties regarding attachment and social interaction.

Physical presence

Jane presented as relatively young and non-threatening in her physical appearance. Her quiet demeanour could be perceived as shy and vulnerable, which may lead others to underestimate her risk, perhaps putting themselves in situations of increased risk (e.g. spending time alone with Jane). Whilst not directly contributing to her risk, this may provide Jane opportunities she may not otherwise have had, increasing the opportunity to display risk behaviours such as increasing the potential for Jane to target and victimise individuals.

Sensory issues

Due to the existence of patterns of behaviour associated with certain sensory sensations (such as stabbing and ripping) across several contexts, it was considered whether these were contributory factors involved in her offending behaviour.

Maintaining factors

Difficulties with social interaction

Jane's ASD symptoms may contribute to the maintenance of difficulties when attempting to engage therapeutically, which would subsequently limit the opportunity to engage in therapy to be able to learn new skills and new patterns of behaviour. Problems with social skills and deficits in problem-solving may contribute to her risk. In the past, a perceived lack of consequences and not enough external risk management may have helped to maintain her problem behaviours.

Cognitive rigidity

Jane's rigid, 'black or white' thinking could serve to perpetuate her difficulties relating to her over-reliance upon specific thought and behavioural processes. This may contribute to fixation on particular people, resulting in harassment.

Limited sense of responsibility for her actions

Jane demonstrated a limited sense of responsibility for, or consideration of, the consequences of her actions. Due to this, there is limited opportunity for interventions which utilise behavioural reinforcement. Some of her actions appear to be impulsive in nature.

Protective factors

Insight

Jane demonstrated limited insight into her current risk and difficulties but often responded with *"I don't know"* when questioned about her thoughts, feelings, and behaviours. She was able to identify some potential sensory issues related to increases in agitation, and she showed a willingness to explore these in more detail.

Engagement and motivation

Jane expressed an interest in learning new ways of coping with her emotions by attending a skill- building group. She also expressed a willingness to engage in psychological intervention. However, her attendance and engagement with sessions offered were known to fluctuate. She reported a wish to change her current behaviour (likely in part due to external factors, such as having to pay for items she had damaged), which was considered a promising starting point for engaging her with psychological intervention.

Discussion

The literature highlights the difficulties faced when attempting to assess, formulate, treat, and manage females with LD and additional mental health needs within forensic services (Hellenbach et al., 2015). de Vogel et al. (2015) argue for the need to gain insight into this increasing population to be able to effectively intervene by developing gender-responsive assessment tools and treatment programmes.

Regarding the assessment phase of this process, the majority of risk assessment tools utilised within forensic services are developed and validated with male samples (e.g. HCR-20^{V3}; Douglas et al., 2014). The recognition of this issue has led to the development of female-specific assessment tools (e.g. Female Additional Manual; de Vogel et al., 2012). However, such gender-specific tools are still uncommon within forensic practice; therefore, the ability to apply such tools to the increasing forensic female population is limited. Furthermore, the majority of existing forensic psychometric tools are validated with non-LD samples (e.g. CORE-OM; Evans et al., 2002). The common practice of obtaining self-report measures in psychological assessment has been highlighted as problematic within LD settings (Finlay & Lyons, 2001). Therefore, again, the ability for conclusions to be generalised to the potentially more diverse and complex populations, such as those placed within LD settings (Beail, 2016), may be questionable (Hogue et al., 2007).

Additional difficulties arise when we consider co-morbid diagnoses of ASD (Melvin et al., 2017), as again, the majority of assessment instruments are not validated with ASD samples and furthermore do not take into consideration how the manifestation of the disorder within female populations may impact accurate identification (Dworzynsky et al., 2012). Additionally, diagnostic criteria and concepts of ASD have historically been biased towards the typical male presentation (Dworzynsky et al., 2012). This impacts professionals' ability to accurately assess and identify ASD within female populations due to symptom masking (camouflage hypothesis; Dworzynsky et al., 2012) or atypical presentations, missed by standard screening tools

(Andersson et al., 2013). Therefore, the combination of the pre-existing gender bias regarding forensic LD research, with the gender-skewed nature of ASD diagnostic criteria and assessment approaches, create an unstable landscape in which to attempt to comprehensively assess, formulate, and intervene with this complex population.

This case study highlights the valuable role forensic psychology plays within this process. The ability to combine clinical knowledge with forensic awareness in order to develop a meaningful psychological formulation, which can subsequently inform treatment and management plans, lies within the remit of a forensic psychologist. Despite the need to screen and appropriately assess individuals, specifically females with LD within forensic settings, forensic psychologists are faced with additional logistical and practical difficulties within such contexts. In Jane's case, the issue of obtaining full, reliable developmental histories as part of the ADI-R assessment process was encountered despite contact with her parents to complete the ADI-R. This limited the ability to draw conclusions about the potential aetiology of her current presentation. Although attempts were made to obtain historical professional reports to provide developmental information where possible, this was limited in terms of the wealth of information acquired. This is a common issue within this and other forensic contexts, such as prisons, with a significant number of individuals with LDs coming from backgrounds with histories of abuse or neglect (Stinson & Robbins, 2014), involvement with social services and time spent in care, and institutionalisation from a young age (Hackett et al., 2013), all of which may result in inconsistent caregiving. Assessors therefore face problems when trying to identify a reliable source of information. Additionally, issues such as parental substance misuse, mental health issues, and lifestyle choices, may also limit the assessors' ability to obtain or rely on information gained from parents or caregivers. Further to this, there are practical difficulties faced in forensic environments when attempting to complete the ADOS-2 assessment. Individual **risk factors** can limit the safe use of the materials used in the assessment. The ADOS-2 kit often includes items restricted within secure environments (e.g. shoelaces, pens, metal clips) which need to be controlled and accounted for throughout the assessment where necessary.

This case study serves to highlight not only the practicalities but also the importance of comprehensively assessing, formulating, and intervening with females with LD within forensic contexts, considering ASD profiles. This case study has also highlighted the valuable role forensic psychology plays within this process in a secure setting with the aim of informing understanding, developing management strategies, and adapting interventions with the goal of increasing quality of life and reducing future risk of reoffending.

References

Allen, D., Evans, C., Hider, A., Hawkins, S., Peckett, H., & Morgan, H. (2008). Offending behaviour in adults with Asperger syndrome. *Journal of Autism and Developmental Disorders, 38*(4), 748–758.

Allison, C., Auyeung, B., & Baron-Cohen, S. (2012), Toward brief 'red flags' for autism screening: The short autism spectrum quotient and the short quantitative checklist for autism in toddlers in 1,000 cases and 3,000 controls corrected, *Journal of the American Academy of Child and Adolescent Psychiatry, 51*(2), 202–212.

American Psychiatric Association (2013). *Diagnostic and statistical manual of mental disorders (DSM-5)*. Washington, DC: American Psychiatric Association.

Anderson, D. K., Liang, J. W., & Lord, C. (2014). Predicting young adult outcome among more and less cognitively able individuals with autism spectrum disorders. *Journal of Child Psychology and Psychiatry, 55*(5), 485–494.

Ashworth, S. (2016). Autism is underdiagnosed in prisoners. *British Medical Journal, 353,* i3028.

Ashworth, S., & Tully, R. J. (2016). Adult autism – Hidden in forensic settings. *The Psychologist, 29*(9), 660–661.

Attwood, T. (2007). *The complete guide to Asperger's syndrome*. London, UK: Jessica Kingsley.

Ayres, A. J. (1989). *Sensory integration and Praxis test (SIPT)*. San Antonio, TX: Pearson Clinical.

Ayres, A. J., & Robbins, J. (2005). *Sensory integration and the child: Understanding hidden sensory challenges*. Los Angeles, CA: Western Psychological Services.

Baron-Cohen, S. (1988). An assessment of violence in a young man with Asperger's syndrome. *Journal of Child Psychology and Psychiatry, 29*(3), 351–360.

Baron-Cohen, S. (1989). Autism spectrum disorder: A survey of adults in the United Kingdom. *Journal of Autism Developmental Disorder, 44,* 3033–3044.

Baron-Cohen, S., & Wheelwright, S. (2004). The empathy quotient: An investigation of adults with Asperger syndrome or high functioning autism, and normal sex differences. *Journal of Autism and Developmental Disorders, 34*(2), 163–175.

Baron-Cohen, S., Wheelwright, S., Skinner, R., Martin, J., & Clubley, E. (2001). The autism-spectrum quotient (AQ): Evidence from Asperger syndrome/high-functioning autism, males and females, scientists and mathematicians. *Journal of Autism and Developmental Disorders, 31*(1), 5–17.

Barry-Walsh, J., & Mullen, P. E. (2003). Forensic aspects of Asperger's syndrome. *Journal of Forensic Psychiatry & Psychology, 15*(1), 96–107.

Beail, N. (2016). *Psychological therapies and people who have intellectual disabilities*. Leicester, UK: The British Psychological Society.

Bhaumik, S., Tyrer, F. C., McGrother, C., & Ganghadaran, S. K. (2008). Psychiatric service use and psychiatric disorders in adults with intellectual disability. *Journal of Intellectual Disability Research, 52*(11), 986–995.

Blackburn, R., & Renwick, S. J. (1996). Rating scales for measuring the interpersonal circle in forensic psychiatric patients. *Psychological Assessment, 8,* 76–84.

Brooks, M., Davies, S., & Twigg, E. (2013). A measure for feelings – Using inclusive research to develop a tool for evaluating psychological therapy (Clinical Outcomes in Routine Evaluation–Learning Disability). *British Journal of Learning Disabilities, 41*(4), 320–329.

Brugha, T., McManus, S., Bankart, J., Scott, F., Purdon, S., Smith, J., ... Meltzer, H. (2011), Epidemiology of autism spectrum disorders in adults in the community in England, *Archives of General Psychiatry, 68*(5), 459–466.

Cabinet Office Social Exclusion Task Force (2009). *Short study on women offenders.* London, UK: Home Office.

Cederlund, M., Hagberg, B., Billstedt, E., Gillberg, I. C., & Gillberg, C. (2008). Asperger syndrome and autism: A comparative longitudinal follow-up study more than 5 years after original diagnosis. *Journal of Autism and Developmental Disorders, 38*(1), 72–85.

Chown, N. (2010). 'Do you have any difficulties that I may not be aware of?' A study of autism awareness and understanding in the UK police service. *International Journal of Police Science & Management, 12*(2), 256–273.

Coid, J., Kahtan, N., Gault, S., & Jarman, B. (2000). Women admitted to secure forensic psychiatry services: I. Comparison of women and men. *The Journal of Forensic Psychiatry 11*, 275–295.

Dawson, G., Rogers, S., Munson, J., Smith, M., Winter, J., Greenson, J., ... Varley, J. (2010). Randomized, controlled trial of an intervention for toddlers with autism: The early start Denver model. *Pediatrics, 125*(1), e17–e23.

de Vogel, V., de Vries Robbé, M., van Kalmthout, W., & Place, C. (2012). *Female Additional Manual (FAM). Additional guidelines to the HCR-20 for assessing risk for violence in women* (English version). Utrecht, The Netherlands: Van der Hoeven Kliniek.

de Vogel, V., Stam, J., Bouman, Y. H. A., Ter Horst, P., & Lancel, M. (2015). Violent women: A multicentre study into gender differences in forensic psychiatric patients. *The Journal of Forensic Psychiatry & Psychology, 27*(2), 145–168.

Debbaudt, D. (2002), *Autism, advocates, and law enforcement professionals. Recognising and reducing risk situations for people with autism spectrum disorders.* London, UK: Jessica Kingsley.

Douglas, K. S., Hart, S. D., Webster, C. D., Belfrage, H., Guy, L. S., & Wilson, C. M. (2014). Historical-Clinical-Risk Management-20, Version 3 (HCR-20V3): Development and overview. *International Journal of Forensic Mental Health, 13*, 2.

Dworzynsky, K., Ronald, A., Bolton, P., & Happe, F. (2012). How different are girls and boys above and below the diagnostic threshold for autism spectrum disorders? *Journal of the American Academy of Child and Adolescent Psychiatry, 51*(8), 788–797.

Eells, T. (2007). *Handbook of psychotherapy case formulation.* New York, NY: Guildford Press.

Eells, T. D., & Lombart, K. G. (2011). Theoretical and evidence based approaches to case formulation. In P. Sturmey & M. McMurran (Eds.), *Forensic case formulation* (pp. 3–32). Cambridge, UK: John Wiley and Sons.

Evans, C., Connell, J., Barkham, M., Margison, F., McGrath, G., Mellor-Clark, J., & Audin, K. (2002). Towards a standardised brief outcome measure: Psychometric properties and utility of the CORE-OM. *British Journal of Psychiatry, 180*(1), 51–60.

Finlay, W. M. L., & Lyons, E. (2001). Methodological issues in interviewing and using self-report questionnaires with people with mental retardation. *Psychological Assessment, 13*, 319–335.

Gray, N. S., Fitzgerald, S., Taylor, J., MacCulloch, M. J., & Snowden, R. J. (2007). Predicting future reconviction in offenders with intellectual disabilities: The predictive efficacy of VRAG, PCL–SV, and the HCR–20. *Psychological Assessment, 19*(4), 474–479.

Griffin-Shelley, E. (2010). An Asperger's adolescent sex addict, sex offender: A case study. *Sexual Addiction & Compulsivity, 17*(1), 46–64.

Hackett, S, Phillips, J., Masson, H., & Balfe, M. (2013). Individual, family and abuse characteristics of 700 British child and adolescent sexual abusers. *Child Abuse Review, 22*, 232–245.

Hellenbach, M., Brown, M., Karatzias, T., & Robinson, R. (2015). Psychological interventions for women with intellectual disabilities and forensic care needs: A systematic review of the literature. *Journal of Intellectual Disability Research, 59*, 319–331.

Hogue, T. E., Mooney, P., Morrissey, C., Steptoe, L., Johnston, S., Lindsay, W. R., & Taylor, J. (2007). Emotional and behavioural problems in offenders with intellectual disability: Comparative data from three forensic services. *Journal of Intellectual Disability Research, 51*(10), 778–785.

Howlin, P. (2004). Legal issues. In P. Howlin (Ed.), *Legal issues, in autism and Asperger syndrome: Preparing for adulthood* (pp. 300–312). London, UK: Routledge.

Johnstone, L., & Dallos, R. (2006). *Formulation in psychology and psychotherapy: Making sense of people's problems.* Oxton, UK: Routledge.

Katz, N., & Zemishlany, Z. (2006). Criminal responsibility in Asperger's syndrome. *Israel Journal of Psychiatry and Related Sciences, 43*(3), 166–173.

Kennedy, P., & Llewelyn, S. (2001). Does the future belong to the scientist practitioner? *The Psychologist, 142*, 74–78.

Le Couteur, A., Lord, C., & Rutter, M. (2003). *Autism Diagnostic Interview-Revised.* Torrance, CA: Western Psychological Services.

Lord, C., Rutter, R., Dilavore, P. C., Risi, S., Gotham, K., & Bishop, S. L. (2012). *ADOS-2: Autism Diagnostic Observation Schedule. Second Edition Part 1: Modules 1–4.* Torrance, CA: Western Psychological Services.

Lyall, K., Croen, L., Daniels, J., Fallin, M. D., Ladd-Acosta, C., Lee, B. K., … Newschaffer, C. (2017). The changing epidemiology of autism spectrum disorders. *Annual Review of Public Health, 38*, 81–102.

Makrygianni, M. K., & Reed, P. (2010). A meta-analytic review of the effectiveness of behavioural early intervention programs for children with autistic spectrum disorders. *Research in Autism Spectrum Disorders, 4*(4), 577–593.

Matson, J. L., & Williams, L. W. (2014). Depression and mood disorders among persons with autism spectrum disorders. *Research in Developmental Disabilities, 35*(9), 2003–2007.

Melvin, C., Langdon, P. E., & Murphy, G. (2017). Treatment effectiveness for offenders with autism spectrum conditions: A systematic review. *Psychology Crime and Law, 23*(8), 748–776.

Milton, J., Duggan, C., Latham, A., Egan, V., & Tantam, D. (2002). Case history of co-morbid Asperger's syndrome and paraphilic behaviour. *Medicine, Science and the Law, 42*(3), 237–244. https://doi.org/10.1177/002580240204200308

Murphy, D. (2010a). Extreme violence in a man with an autistic spectrum disorder: Assessment and treatment within high-security psychiatric care. *Journal of Forensic Psychiatry & Psychology, 21*(3), 462–477.

Murphy, D. (2010b). Understanding offenders with autism-spectrum disorders: What can forensic services do? Commentary on … Asperger syndrome and criminal behaviour *Advances in Psychiatric Treatment, 16*(1), 44–46.

Nadarajah, J., Roy, A., Harris, T. O., & Corbett, J. A. (1995). Methodological aspects of life events research in people with learning disabilities: A review and initial findings. *Journal of Intellectual Disability Research, 39*(1), 47–56.

National Institute for Health and Care Excellence (NICE, 2016). *Autism spectrum disorder in adults: Diagnosis and management. Clinical guideline {CG142}.* London, UK: Author.

Orinstein, A. J., Helt, M., Troyb, E., Tyson, K. E., Barton, M. L., Eigsti, I. M., ... Fein, D. A. (2014). Intervention for optimal outcome in children and adolescents with a history of autism. *Journal of Developmental and Behavioral Pediatrics, 35*(4), 247–256.

Prosser, H., & Bromley, J. (1998). *Interviewing people with intellectual disabilities.* In E. Emerson, C. Hatton, J. Bromley, & A. Caine (Eds.), *The Wiley series in clinical psychology. Clinical psychology and people with intellectual disabilities* (pp. 99–113). New York, NY: John Wiley & Sons Ltd.

Prout, H. T., & Strohmer, D. C. (1991). *Emotional Problems Scales. Professional manual for the Behaviour Rating Scales and the self-report inventory.* Lutz, FL: Psychological Assessment Resources Inc.

Saemundsen, E., Juliusson, H., Hjaltested, S., Gunnarsdottir, T., Halldorsdottir, T., Hreidarsson, S., & Magnusson, P. (2010). Prevalence of autism in an urban population of adults with severe intellectual disabilities–a preliminary study. *Journal of Intellectual Disability Research, 54*(8), 727–735.

Sappok, T., Bergmann, T., Kaiser, H., & Diefenbacher, A. (2010). Autism in adults with intellectual disabilities. *Der Nervenarzt, 81*(11), 1333–1345.

Sappok, T., Budczies, J., Dziobek, I., Bölte, S., Dosen, A., & Diefenbacher, A. (2014). The missing link: Delayed emotional development predicts challenging behavior in adults with intellectual disability. *Journal of Autism and Developmental Disorders, 44*(4), 786–800.

Sappok, T., Diefenbacher, A., Budczies, J., Schade, C., Grubich, C., Bergmann, T. ... Dziobek, I. (2013). Diagnosing autism in a clinical sample of adults with intellectual disabilities: How useful are the ADOS and the ADI-R? *Research in Developmental Disabilities, 34*(5), 1642–1655.

Sappok, T., Heinrich, M., & Underwood, L. (2015). Screening tools for autism spectrum disorders, *Advances in Autism, 1*(1), 12–29.

Simonoff, E. (2012), Autism spectrum disorder: Prevalence and cause may be bound together, *British Journal of Psychiatry, 201*, 88–89.

Stinson, J. D., & Robbins, S. B. (2014). Characteristics of people with intellectual disabilities in a secure U.S. Forensic Hospital. *Journal of Mental Health Research in Intellectual Disabilities, 7*, 337–358.

Sturmey, P., & McMurran, M. (Eds.) (2011). *Forensic case formulation.* Chichester, UK: John Wiley & Sons.

Tantam, D. (2011). *Autism spectrum disorders through the life span.* London, UK: Jessica Kingsley Publishers.

Underwood, L., McCarthy, J., & Tsakanikos, E. (2010). Mental health of adults with autism spectrum disorders and intellectual disability. *Current Opinion in Psychiatry, 23*(5), 421–426.

Wechsler, D. (2008). *Wechsler Adult Intelligence Scale-Fourth Edition.* San Antonio, TX: Pearson.

White, S. W., Oswald, D., Ollendick, T., & Scahill, L. (2009). Anxiety in children and adolescents with autism spectrum disorders, *Clinical Psychology Review, 29*(3), 216–219.

Whiteley, P., Todd, L., Carr, K., & Shattock, P. (2010). Gender ratios in autism, Asperger syndrome and autism spectrum disorder. *Autism Insights, 2,* 17–24.

Woods P., & Collins M. (2003). Exploring relationships between inside communication and social skills in mentally disordered offenders. *Journal of Psychiatric and Mental Health Nursing,* 10, 518–525.

Zwaigenbaum, L., Bryson, S., Szatmari, P., Brian, J., Smith, I., Roberts, W., ... Roncadin, C. (2012). Sex differences in children with autism spectrum disorder identified in a high-risk infant cohort. *Journal of Autism and Developmental Disorders, 42*(12), 2585–2596.

Chapter 7

Female sexual sadism

Psychological assessment for prison parole review

Jennifer Bamford

Introduction

Her Majesty's Prison and Probation Service, herein referred to as HMPPS, is the largest employer of forensic psychologists in England and Wales. Whilst some prisons have their own local psychology teams, often comprising one or more Chartered and Registered Psychologists as well as trainees and assistant psychologists, there are also regionally based teams who operate across a number of prisons within that local area. Due to resourcing difficulties, there are times when independent psychologists are commissioned to complete reports on prisoners. On other occasions, independent psychologists may be instructed to complete a report on a prisoner by the prisoner's solicitor, sometimes as a means of getting a 'second opinion'. Regardless of the source of the referral, the role of the independent psychologist is to meet the agreed instructions or directions supplied as part of the assessment referral in a fair, ethical manner, irrespective of the referral source. In fact, declaring that the psychologist's duty is to the Court or Panel is an important part of the psychologist's statement of duty contained within the report; for a psychologist's opinion to be swayed depending on who commissioned the report would be unethical and dangerous.

The vast majority of offenders are male; estimations from 2015 concluded that around 16% of all individuals arrested are female, the average sentence length for women was 9.5 months (compared to 16.9 months for men), 18% of women reoffend (compared to 26% of men), and that the UK prison population in 2015 was comprised of just 4.5% of women. Only 15.5% of the probation-supervised caseload are females (Ministry of Justice, 2015). Female offenders are therefore in a significant minority across criminal justice services. The female prison estate, although comparatively smaller, offers a breadth of interventions deemed appropriate and unique to this client group, catering for both juvenile and adult female offenders. As the prevalence of **personality disorder** is higher amongst the female prison population than the general community (Singleton et al., 1998), the treatment services offered to female prisoners are largely focused on managing problematic personality traits. Of the women thought to meet the criteria for personality disorder, 31% meet the criteria for **Antisocial Personality Disorder** (ASPD), 20% for **Borderline Personality Disorder** (BPD), otherwise referred to as **Emotionally Unstable Personality Disorder** (EUPD), and 16% for **Paranoid Personality Disorder** (Department of Health, 2011). HMPPS have a specialist treatment pathway for those diagnosed with a personality disorder. This is referred to as the Offender Personality Disorder (OPD) pathway. The female OPD includes community services, e.g. **Psychologically Informed Planned Environments** (PIPE) hostels in the community, **Community Mental Health Teams** (CMHT) and women's projects, specialist prison-based units/programmes (e.g. **Therapeutic Communities**, PIPEs and other specialist units), and secure psychiatric hospital units (high–low secure units for women). Women with personality disorder, particularly Cluster B personality disorders, are more likely to offend than those without a diagnosis of personality disorder (Esbec & Echeburua, 2010), and women with **Psychopathic Personality Disorder** demonstrate a higher recidivism rate than women without this disorder (Salekin et al., 1998).

As psychologists, we now know much more about women and personality disorder, and how this may functionally link to their offending (e.g. Howard et al., 2008). However, we know a lot less about personality disordered women who engage in sexual sadism (Pflugradt & Allen, 2012), most likely because female sexual offenders are estimated to make up just 1% of all known sex offenders (Vandier & Walker, 2002). One of the common misconceptions regarding female offenders is the assumption that the literature and knowledge about male sexual offenders can be applied to female sexual offenders (Blanchette & Brown, 2006). Even less clear is how female sexual offenders with sadistic interests differ from male offenders. The concept of sexual sadism, like many forensic definitions in psychology, has been widely debated. Marshall and Hucker (2006) offer a useful behavioural scale to identify male sexual sadists which include the following:

- The offender is sexually aroused by sadistic acts.
- The offender exercises power/control/domination over a victim.
- The offender humiliates or degrades the victim.
- The offender tortures the victim or engages in acts of cruelty on the victim.
- The offender mutilates sexual parts of the victim's body.
- The offender has a history of choking consensual partners during sex.
- The offender engaged in gratuitous violence towards the victim.
- The offender has a history of cruelty to other people or animals.
- The offender gratuitously wounds the victim.
- The offender attempts to, or succeeds in, strangling, choking, or otherwise asphyxiating the victim.
- The offender keeps trophies of the victim.
- The offender keeps records of the offence.
- The offender carefully pre-plans the offence.
- The offender mutilates non-sexual parts of the victim's body.

- The offender engages in bondage with consensual partners during sex.
- The victim is abducted or confined.
- There is evidence of ritualism in the offence.

The concepts listed above were derived from knowledge of male offenders, and literature on female paraphilias is limited, although there is empirical evidence suggesting that deviant sexual arousal may be a contributory factor in the committing of sexually assaultive behaviour in women (Logan, 2008). More recently, Pflugradt and Allen (2012) used grounded analysis on a small sample of five female sexual sadists to reveal the following common behaviour patterns:

- The process of breaking the victim down emotionally/psychologically seemed just as arousing as the physical torture.
- Female perpetrators often used manipulation to direct others to torture whilst she observed and/or participated passively.
- Physical torture was severe and escalated over time.
- Physical torture occurred within a social context involving several people – each having a vaguely defined role in a loosely defined family structure.
- The infliction of pain and/or torture was at times vicarious (i.e. forcing the victim or co-offender to watch or participate in abusing another person/victim).
- Physical/psychological control was further obtained or enhanced by nurturing the victim.
- The torture progressed from psychological to physical due to some precipitating event with concomitant emotional responses such as anger, jealousy, fear, and revenge.
- Control was a central theme which involved not only controlling the victim but also the co-offenders.
- Some of the sexual arousal appeared vicarious.
- Victims were chosen for their psychological vulnerability rather than physical weakness.
- Perpetrators created emotional dependence in their victims.
- A primary cognitive distortion was that the victims deserved to be tortured.
- Control was more sexually arousing to the subjects than inflicting pain.

Notably, there are some differences between the set of factors derived from male samples by Marshall and Hucker (2006) and those derived for female offenders as listed above. In particular, there is a strong element of psychological control or abuse with female offenders which is not prominent in male offenders. Additionally, the use of co-offenders appears more common in female offenders, and this dynamic leaves open the opportunity for vicarious pleasure through watching others commit abusive acts. There are also a number of overlapping themes, in regard to the enjoyment of pain and humiliation, as well as likely keeping the victim for some time, e.g. the offence occurring within a kidnapping or false imprisonment scenario where the intention is not to kill the victim straight away but to spend time causing harm or humiliation. From a diagnostic perspective, the **Diagnostic and Statistical Manual of Mental Disorders** (**DSM-5;** American Psychiatric Association, 2013) specifies two distinct criteria for diagnosing an individual with **Sexual Sadism** (302.84).

1   Over a period of at least six months, recurrent and intense sexual arousal from the physical or psychological suffering of another person, as manifested by fantasies, urges or behaviors.
2   The individual has acted on these sexual urges with a nonconsenting person, or the sexual urges or fantasies cause clinically significant distress or impairment in social, occupational, or other important areas of functioning. (p. 695)

Having a good understanding of the diagnostic criteria balanced against psychological research regarding common behaviours in sexual sadism is important to understanding this very distinct group of individuals.

The case study referred to within this chapter details an adult female in her 30s who had been found guilty of attempted murder. The patient, who will be referred to as Amy to protect her confidentiality, had been in prison for around 12 years at the time when she was referred for an independent psychological assessment through her solicitor. She had completed a course of long-term therapy in prison. The solicitor requested an assessment of risk and progress, as well as a personality disorder assessment, and recommendations for further treatment and/or progression.

Patient history

Childhood and education

Amy had a largely straightforward upbringing, having been raised by both of her biological parents as an only child. Although she had a half-brother, Amy never lived with him and they did not have a close relationship. Amy noted feeling closer to her mother than her father and described her father as controlling. She had previously been violent towards her father and described thoughts of wanting to kill him when she was younger. As a child, Amy was often looked after by her maternal grandmother when her parents were working, and she described a close relationship with her grandmother, who died when Amy was seven years old.

Amy reported during interview that she did not like school, and she recalled an incident in which a teacher had humiliated her in front of the class, which appears to have been a formative memory for Amy. The experience left her feeling fearful and embarrassed. She reported that she bullied other children at school, which she found entertaining, and she was violent to other children at school. Amy was never suspended or expelled from school, despite her violent behaviour which, she reported, largely went unnoticed, and she continued into the college/post-16 provision. Amy did not pass her college exams, as by this point, she had become involved in drug and alcohol abuse.

Employment

Amy reported that she had various jobs in the community in the past, although she was sacked from some of these due to her behaviour. Amy's longest job was for six years, although there were problems within this role, and Amy had left work a few weeks before the index offence occurred. In prison, Amy had been employed and her job at the time of meeting her was as a cleaner within the prison gym; a job which she reported finding a lot of pleasure in, although she noticed emerging signs that she was becoming preoccupied with her own physical fitness.

Relationships and sexual history

Amy identified as heterosexual, and she reported that she had less than ten male sexual partners in the community. Amy first had full sexual intercourse at the age of around 20, although she described this as abusive and reported it as rape. She did not have sex for many years after this. Amy reported that she was dominant in many of her relationships and felt that she could easily manipulate her partners. At the time of meeting Amy, she was in a relationship with James. She had been with James for a few months before the index offence occurred, and this relationship had continued during her time in prison. Amy felt that James was more independent and did not accept her attempts at manipulating him. Amy was open about her sexual interests during interview, stating that she began to feel sexual pleasure through violence as a teenager and that she continues to have fantasies of violence within which she feels sexually aroused. Amy had also used knives during consensual sex with her partner James, during which she held a knife to his throat.

When speaking about friends, Amy identified having close friends throughout her life, but these appeared seemingly fleeting. Amy had been violent towards her friends in the past, and the year before the index offence, she attacked her friend Jane with a knife, apparently for no particular reason. Amy told me during interview that she felt she does not need other people, although she also recognised that she is sensitive to people not liking her and becomes anxious if she thinks a friend of hers no longer likes her. Amy described herself as 'picky' when it came to her friends, and she reported a particularly low tolerance for certain types of people whom she has had violent fantasies about, including people she deems to be stupid, weak, overweight, vulnerable, homeless, or of a different ethnicity than her own.

Drugs

Amy began taking drugs when she was 12 years old. She used many different types of drugs in the community, including crack cocaine, ecstasy, and heroin, which she used intravenously. Amy reported that even when she managed to abstain from drugs, she would be under the influence of alcohol and described an enduring compulsion towards daily substance misuse. She reported that in the year before the index offence, she relapsed into heroin use but was being managed on a methadone (heroin substitute) prescription at the time of the offence. She was also prescribed anti-anxiety medication at the time of the offence, although she stated that she did not take her medication on the morning of the offence. Amy continued to use drugs in prison, and at the time that I met her, she disclosed that she was still using drugs in prison. Amy stated that the weekend before I met her, she had become desperate and had drunk air freshener liquid in an attempt to feel the effects of the alcohol contained within it.

Personality

Amy was referred to as being 'psychopathic' at the time of her sentencing, although to my knowledge, she had never formally been assessed for psychopathic personality disorder. Later in her sentence, Amy was diagnosed with ASPD, with traits of BPD and **Narcissistic Personality Disorder** (NPD). It was suggested that Amy's personality traits overlap with those constituting psychopathic personality disorder. Amy told me during interview that she agreed with these diagnoses.

Violent thoughts/behaviour

A few months before the index offence occurred, Amy went to see a psychologist due to her reporting violent fantasies. During her interview with this psychologist, Amy said that she had violent fantasies which made her feel excited and sexually aroused. She said that these fantasies started at an early age and were impacted by violent films that she was allowed to watch from the age of around four. Amy reported that she felt aroused not just by death, but also by harm or torture caused to others. She described fantasies using knives, during which she would stab her victims in the eyes and then pull their intestines out. Amy previously told a psychologist that she would feel so aroused by these fantasies that she would orgasm without having to masturbate physically. She told me that in the lead up to the offence, she felt a physical drive to kill someone and that it made her body ache to have to restrain herself. She had previously reported that this urge was especially difficult to manage at night and that on occasion it became so overwhelming that she would cut herself and consume her own blood as an alternative.

Amy reported that at the age of seven, she began to behave violently towards animals. She described tying her cat's paws together and kicking and punching it, spitting in its eyes, and putting it in a bag. She was also violent to cats she found in the street and once set a dog on a chicken to watch it kill it. Amy said that she was violent to animals until the age of 13, when she started to have violent thoughts about people instead.

Mental health

There was a pattern of depression and anxiety throughout Amy's life, contributing to episodes of suicidality, for which she had been medicated. She described times when she wanted to end her life, but also times when she had self-harmed in order to evoke guilt in others, calling her friends to tell them that she had attempted suicide because of their maltreatment. At the time of meeting Amy, she was prescribed antidepressant medication and reported finding it very helpful, stating that her last suicide attempt had been more than five years ago. Amy was hospitalised for mental health problems twice in the past in the community, and she had a brief period of around one-and-a-half years where she was detained in a high secure forensic psychiatric hospital during her sentence. Amy also disclosed having some obsessional traits consistent with **Obsessive-Compulsive Disorder (OCD)**, which began in the community and continued throughout her prison sentence. She reported that these traits manifested in her aligning things and cleaning meticulously.

Offending history

Index offence

Amy was convicted of attempted murder committed against an adult male unknown to her. Amy tried to kill the individual by stabbing him with a knife. She attacked him from behind stabbing him in his side, in the direction of his lungs. The victim fell to the ground and Amy pursued him, trying to stab him again, but members of the public intervened and she escaped from the scene, although she was eventually apprehended. Amy reported during interview that she had woken up that day knowing she was going to kill someone. She took a knife and went to the home of a drug dealer whom she knew, who had once sold her what she considered to be overpriced drugs, with the intention of killing him. He was not home and Amy then decided she would kill the next person she saw, which was the adult male victim. Amy had not been drinking or taking drugs on the day of the offence. It was reported that during the subsequent Court proceedings and sentencing, Amy was seen laughing and smiling.

When asked about the index offence Amy said that after she committed the offence, she felt calm and serene and that it had felt great. She said that when she was at the Police Station, she overheard a Police Officer refer to the victim's injuries as 'non-life changing' and that she felt disappointed by this, but that she also felt a sense of relief and satisfaction at having committed the offence, which lasted a few days afterwards. For Amy, the offence was a buildup of events over time. The precipitating factors she identified as starting the year before the index offence.

Previous convictions

Amy had no convictions prior to the index offence. She had been cautioned twice for battery and harassment, although no formal reprimands were exercised. Amy described a feeling of invincibility, believing that she would be able to get away with things. She reported that she had committed thefts over many years, stealing items from shops whenever she wanted something but also for the thrill of it. Amy also said that she was violent before the index offence, running after some children with a knife after they had vandalised her car, and attacking a man in an incident of road rage. She also reported going out in the evenings, attempting to antagonise men whom she wanted to fight her. Shortly after Amy came into prison, she was found with a knife and told staff that she had planned on murdering another inmate. She was reported to have made threats to other prisoners during her sentence and had attempted to attack another prisoner around four years ago.

Psychometric assessment

Psychometric assessment was conducted with Amy in order to aid the assessment of treatment need/change and response style.

Several psychometric tests were utilised with Amy during clinical interview. The response style assessment using the Paulhus Deception Scale (PDS; Paulhus, 1998) did not indicate distorted responding, for instance through impression management. The Beck Anxiety Inventory (BAI; Beck & Steer, 1990) indicated minimal symptoms of anxiety, and the Beck Depression Inventory (BDI-II; Beck, Steer & Brown, 1990) suggested that she was suffering from a moderate level of depressive symptoms. These measures of mental health difficulties were consistent with Amy's presentation and self-report, and importantly, they were not of a level that appeared to impact her ability to engage with the assessment.

Self-esteem was measured using the Rosenberg self-esteem measure (Rosenberg, 1965) and indicated below average self-esteem, which Amy herself noted as a current difficulty. Impulsivity was assessed using the Barratt Impulsivity Scale (BIS-11; Patton, Stanford & Barratt, 1995), and Amy's results were compared with a sample of violent prisoners (Smith et al., 2006). Her results indicated continued difficulties across all three sub-scales of the BIS-11 (attentional, motor, and non-planning), and her coping style, as assessed through the Coping Style Questionnaire (Roger, Jarvis & Najarian, 1993) was primarily of an emotional nature, indicating that during times of stress, Amy was most likely to respond with anger or anxiety, these being prominent themes in her affective history. The results of these various psychometric measures were taken into consideration as part of the overall risk assessment.

Personality disorder assessment

Amy's solicitor instructed that she be reassessed for the presence of personality disorder using the International Personality Disorder Examination (IPDE) (Loranger, 1999). Unbeknown to her solicitor, Amy had recently been assessed by a psychologist working on behalf of HMPPS the month before her independent assessment. Upon meeting Amy and her seeing the length of the IPDE assessment interview, she indicated that she would not be willing to repeat the full IPDE interview. She said that she had found the assessment lengthy and tiresome and that despite this, she largely agreed with the outcome of the assessment which, she reported, was consistent with previous comments regarding her personality. Given that I also did not dispute the findings of the HMPPS-authored IPDE, I instead used a non-diagnostic measure of personality and clinical syndromes with Amy in order to gain an understanding of her personality on a dimensional, rather than categorical, level.

The assessment chosen was the Millon Clinical Multiaxial Inventory-IV (MCMI-IV; Grossman, Millon & Millon, 2015), the recently updated version of the MCMI-III (Millon et al., 2009). It is a measure of adult psychopathology, which amongst other things identifies deeper and pervasive personality characteristics that may underlie a patient's symptoms or behaviour. It can be used as a tool to aid the **formulation** of a patient's difficulties and presentation, as it identifies personality patterns and clinical syndromes. The tool is used with adults aged 18 and over who have come to the attention of services including psychiatric, counselling, and correctional services, and it can be used to aid the planning of an individual's treatment pathway. It is a 195-item self-report measure, and Amy engaged with assessment using the MCMI-IV during the interview sessions held with her. The interpretation of Amy's assessment is informed by the work of Groth-Marnat (2016) as well as Millon's theories. The MCMI-III was updated to form the current version in order to take into account advances in research and the publication of the DSM-5 (American Psychiatric Association, 2013), and although a full correctional/offender sample is not yet available, the clinical sample remains a valid comparator for Amy, this being comprised of those whose personality and/or distress were such that their personality was considered in need of assessment, using the MCMI-IV to form the comparator base rates. The main areas assessed by the MCMI-IV are *clinical personality patterns*, *severe personality pathology*, *clinical syndromes*, and *severe clinical syndromes*. The MCMI-IV personality scale scores are in order of increasing severity, from being considered 'not elevated', elevated to the level of personality 'style', to the level of a personality 'type', or to the level of being considered a personality 'disorder'.

It is important to note that the MCMI-IV does not diagnose personality disorder; the terminology 'disorder' used is designed to describe the level of pathology, but not to diagnose. The results of Amy's MCMI-IV revealed *antisocial personality* (to the level of disorder), *sadistic personality* (to the level of a type), *narcissistic personality* (to the level of a type), and *borderline personality* (to the level of a style). Within the assessment report, each of these elevations was described and related back to Amy's self-report and presentation to aid those working with her in future. The constellation of traits identified by the MCMI-IV in Amy's case was considered an accurate summation of her behaviour, beliefs, and presentation.

When considering the clinical syndrome scales of the MCMI-IV, Amy's results suggested that she was suffering from an adjustment disorder with anxiety, as well as substance use and alcohol use disorders. It is important to note that Amy had a tendency to respond in a self-disparaging way using the MCMI-IV, and whilst this was adjusted for within the assessment, it was also clinically reflective of her general disposition during the assessment insofar as Amy appeared open and honest during the assessment and reported that she spoke about things during the assessment which she has not done for many years. Amy said that the independent nature of the assessment (i.e. the fact that I was not employed by HMPPS) gave her more confidence to speak freely, which could have contributed to an elevated score for what the MCMI-IV terms *debasement*.

Dynamic risk assessment and case formulation

Historical-Clinical-Risk management 20 – Version 3

The Historical-Clinical-Risk management – Version 3 (HCR-20v3; Webster et al., 2013) is a structured professional judgement violence risk assessment tool. It is an updated version of the older HCR-20 violence risk assessment tool (Webster et al., 1997), which was modified to take into account developments in research, theory, and practice over the years. The HCR-20v3 is a clinical checklist of risk factors for the assessment and management of the risk of violence, with violence being considered to be *the actual, attempted, or threatened physical harm to a person or persons*. This definition may include threats of harm where they are clear and unambiguous or behaviours likely to induce fear, such as stalking. The **risk factors** included in the tool were determined from an extensive review of the literature on violence. The HCR-20v3 is not intended to be used as a *predictor* of violence, rather, it is a method to structure clinical judgement in helping to *identify relevant risk factors, develop a formulation for an individual's violent behaviour,* and *establish effective risk management plans to prevent future violence from occurring*. The tool is designed to facilitate scenario planning that aids risk management.

In administering the HCR-20v3, clinicians are required to evaluate and document the presence of each risk factor and its relevance to violence.

The HCR-20v3 includes the generation of risk scenarios to aid the planning of those supervising Amy's case. There are no 'cut-off' scores to determine the nature or degree of risk posed; the presence of a single risk factor may suggest a high risk for future violence. Each risk factor is defined, and users are encouraged to consider risk factors alone and as part of the 'bigger picture' in order to evaluate and formulate risk. Additionally, in order to also consider gender-specific risk factors that may be present for Amy, in line with good practice, I also applied the female-specific factors outlined by de Vogel et al. (2014) in the Female Additional Manual (FAM). The FAM is designed to be applied alongside structured professional guidelines like the HCR-20v3 so that the assessment additionally considers gender-specific risk factors that differ from those of men, thus aiding clinical case formulation. Relevant literature suggests that men and women have differing criminal profiles (e.g. de Vogel & de Vries Robbe, 2013). It is therefore relevant to consider whether the risk tools applied to women are valid and appropriate to use. The use of the HCR-20v3 has been supported with females both in the UK (e.g. Coid et al., 2009; O'Shea et al., 2014) and internationally (e.g. Singh, Grann & Fazel, 2011).

HCR-20v3 assessment

The HCR-20v3 first considers ten historical items, with the option to add in 'other' items as needed. Historical items are coded across a lifetime, and their presence and relevance to future risk are both considered by assessors. Table 7.1 summarises the findings in this historical domain.

The HCR-20v3 considers clinical items which assess the person as they have been recently. The authors of the tool recommend an optimal time frame of six months for the clinical items, but this can be adjusted depending on the nature

Table 7.1 Summary of historical items (e.g. past means 'ever' across the lifespan, even if the problems have recently lessened)

H Items: Past problems with...	Rating
H1: Serious violence	Present
H2: Non-violent antisocial behaviour	Present
H3: Relationship instability	Present
H4: Employment	Present
H5: Substance misuse	Present
H6: Major mental illness	Present
H7: Personality disorder	Present
H8: Traumatic experiences	Present
H9: Violent attitudes	Present
H10: Treatment or supervision response	Present
H11: Prostitution	Not present
H12: Parenting difficulties	Not present
H13: Pregnancy at young age	Not present
H14: Suicidality/Self-harming	Present

Table 7.2 Summary of clinical items (present over the last 12 months)

C Items: Recent problems with...	Rating
C1: Insight	Partially present
C2: Violent ideation or intent	Present
C3: Symptoms of major mental illness	Partially present
C4: Instability	Present
C5: Treatment or supervision response	Present
C6: Covert/Manipulative behaviour	Partially present
C7: Low self-esteem	Present

Table 7.3 Summary of risk management items (e.g. in the next 12 months)

R Items: Future* problems with...	Closed conditions	Open conditions (community)
R1: Professional services and plans	Not present	Not present (not present)
R2: Living situation	Partially present	Partially present (present)
R3: Personal support	Partially present	Partially present (partially present)
R4: Treatment or supervision response	Partially present	Present (present)
R5: Stress and coping	Present	Present (present)
R6: Problematic childcare responsibilities	Not present	Not present (not present)
R7: Problematic intimate relationships	Partially present	Partially present (partially present)

of the case. In Amy's case, the last one year was considered as 'recent' given that her risk was seemingly chronic. Table 7.2 summarises the assessment of these HCR-20V3 and FAM items.

The HCR-20v3 considers future problems across five factors. These are known as the risk management items. There is conceptual overlap between the risk management items and the clinical items discussed above, and it is important to remember that the risk management items consider the likelihood of *future* problems in the five areas, for instance in the next 12 months, whereas the clinical items consider *recent* problems, in the last 12 months. These are summarised in regard to Amy's case in Table 7.3.

Formulation of violent offending

A *formulation* of Amy's violent offending was devised in order to aid the understanding of her case and risk. There are various approaches to psychological formulation, although in Amy's case, the template known as the 5Ps was used. The 5P structure adopts a template approach for filling in lists of factors deemed relevant to the formulation as is advocated in psychology (e.g. Weerasekera, 1996) and in psychiatry (Royal College of Psychiatrists, 2010). This approach to case formulation identifies:

- *The Problem*: This is the problem being formulated. Often in forensic psychological assessments and violence risk assessments, this is the offending behaviour, although other problems may also be those that contribute to offending but are not illegal, such as alcohol misuse.
- *Predisposing factors*: These are factors which might have made the person vulnerable to the 'problem'. They are often factors that occur in the patients' early life: in childhood or adolescence. Predisposing factors common in forensic psychology include parental neglect or early victimisation (Rivera & Widom, 1990).
- *Precipitating factors*: These are events, thoughts, and feelings which happened in the lead up to the 'problem', in this case the index offence. Sometimes this is referred to as an 'offence chain' and the time frame from precipitating events can be long, e.g. 12 months, or very short, e.g. 24 hours before. The client will often be a useful source of information regarding the onset of precipitating factors.
- *Perpetuating factors*: These are factors that could contribute, or did contribute to the problem being repeated. These are often issues that can keep a person in a cycle of offending if the issues are not changed or managed. Perpetuating factors in forensic psychology often include beliefs that patients hold about themselves or others, sometimes referred to as cognitive distortions (Maruna & Mann, 2006).
- *Protective factors*: In relation to violence, these are factors that will aid the person in desistance from future violence. Protective factors are often assessed using a structure such as the Structured Assessment of Protective Factors (SAPROF) (de Vogel et al., 2012), which includes considering of internal, motivational, and external protective factors.

Each of the five 'P's will be described below in regard to Amy's case. The issue being considered the 'problem' is her index offence of attempted murder, and the case formulation attempts to make sense of this from Amy's life circumstances and her unique perspective on life (Table 7.4).

Scenario planning

Much like other dynamic risk assessment tools, the HCR-20v3 is structured to allow for scenario planning in regard to how a future offence may look, what warning signs there might be, who the likely victim might be, and what the triggering factors might be.

Table 7.4 5Ps formulation

Presenting problem	• Index offence of attempted murder
Precipitating factors	• Little emotional connection to her parents growing up > difficulties sharing things with her parents > secrecy within their relationship and a distant relationship with them modelling lack of close affection within relationships
	• Felt her parents weren't interested in her due to working all of the time > impacting her attachment style > spending a lot of time alone and learning to only rely on herself > when left with childminders would rebel against this through violence and antisocial behaviour
	• Grandmother gave her attention and formed a good relationship with her but she then died > not being able to process this loss and viewing herself as more alone
	• Father controlling > learning that to achieve in life you have to control other people
	• Exposed to violent films from early age > violence of an extreme nature normalised > viewing this as exciting and as real life > not understanding the distinction between real life and fantasy > blurring lines leading to disinhibition and later violence
	• Only child and difficulties forming friends in school > limited chance to emotionally connect with others > failure to understand others > perspective-taking poor
	• Teacher humiliating her > internalised anger and fear but unable to do anything about it > frustration and mounting vengefulness which she expressed through violence at school, possibly controlling others so as to not be left vulnerable to humiliation again
	• Found enjoyment in bullying others > I like hurting other people, gives me a sense of power > wanting more of this
	• Developing antisocial behaviour and stealing for thrill-seeking > not getting caught and the benefits outweighing the risk
	• Being violent to peers and enjoying this > signs of interest in harming others > fantasising over violence and finding arousal to this
	• Difficulties understanding others > poor empathy > antisocial traits
	• Parents had difficulties related to her father's affair and money problems > feeling anxious and uncertain over family circumstances with low self-esteem > I can't rely on others, can only rely on myself > I don't need other people
	• Learning how to manipulate others > exploiting people and viewing them as instrumental to meeting her needs but failing to form emotional connections to them
	• Financially indulged by parents > parasitic approach to life, not experiencing financial responsibility, learning others will help her get the things she needs depending on her approach to them
	• Lack of consequences to her violence encouraging more violence > I can get away with it
	• First sexual experience was abusive > avoiding and not having sex and not achieving sexual gratification in a healthy way
	• Lack of convictions despite persistent acquisitive offending > I won't get caught > increasing the desire to be violent due to lack of perceived negatives to breaking rules

- Enjoying thrill of crime and beliefs that she is untouchable
- Developing sexual interest to violence during puberty when she becomes sexually aware > relating sex and arousal to violence
- Increasing and reinforcing sexual arousal through seeking out of violent material and having orgasms to violent fantasies
- Being preoccupied with violent thoughts > spending much of her time thinking about or watching violence > using this as an escape from the mundaneness of life and as a way in which she can feel power and control, as well as arousal
- Fluctuating mood > depressive periods, self-harming and suicidal intent > using violent fantasies to make herself feel better, reinforcing these fantasies as helpful in her life
- Using drugs to mask low mood and mute violent thoughts > dependency developing upon avoidant coping > drugs escalating risk through disinhibition and aggression
- Using suicide or self-injury to inflict guilt on others whom she perceives to have wronged her > development of BPD traits and extension of her ability to manipulate others
- Not accepting rejection or disrespect by others > this impacting her self-esteem > not tolerating negative emotions well > I need to teach them a lesson > learning that revenge is satisfying
- Possible childhood sexual abuse that remained unprocessed

P-ecipitating factors	

- A preoccupation with violence controlling her life and dominating her thoughts
- Physical and sexual arousal to violence, which drives her desire to continue evoking fantasies
- Watching violent films and increasing desire to commit violence
- Feeling easily antagonised and disrespected by others; e.g. feeling that local children were mocking her by damaging her car
- Being "laughed at" by people when she had a car accident > violent, vengeful thoughts and "hatred" > unable to process these feelings appropriately
- Decision to keep a knife in her car in case she finds a victim
- Substance misuse contributing to a chaotic lifestyle
- Mental health poor > leaving work due to stress > increased time without structure leading to more opportunity to plan violence and fantasise about it
- Not feeling as though fantasies of violence were satisfying enough anymore
- Seeking help but this not being enough > other people don't understand, there is nothing they can do
- Deciding to commit offence and seeking out known drug dealer to kill > disappointment at him not being home and feeling compelled physically and cognitively to inflict harm upon someone
- Choosing victim and acting out violent fantasies using a knife

(Continued)

Perpetuating factors

- Ongoing violent fantasies and emotional and sexual arousal to violence
- Feeling powerful and in control through violence
- Achieving sexual arousal through violence
- Desire for thrill-seeking
- Antisocial attitudes towards rules and authority
- Believing that she will not get caught
- Not caring about the consequences
- Limited empathic ability
- Drug and alcohol abuse and ongoing sensation seeking
- Antisocial associates condoning behaviour
- Not engaging with treatment efforts or sharing her violent thoughts with professionals
- Avoidant and emotional coping styles
- Lack of formal supervision / risk management strategies
- Continued carrying of a weapon

Protective factors

- Internal: Intelligence: At least average intelligence
- Internal: Secure attachment in childhood: Positive attachment with mother noted, some possible attachment difficulties with father due to controlling and possible abusive behaviour
- Internal: Empathy: Some ability to consider the perspective of others, although limited empathic concern
- Internal: Coping: Some coping skills present and improved coping evidenced over time, e.g. no recent violence, no recent self-harm
- Internal: Self-control: Some self-control present, may need additional support in times of acute distress, in particular to avoid alcohol or drug use upon release
- Motivational: Work: Completed vocational skills training and has plans for areas of employment in the future
- Motivational: Leisure activities: Enjoys arts and crafts and plans on working in this trade in the future
- Motivational: Financial management: Able to better manage and support self through work or benefits
- Motivational: Motivated for treatment: Completed long-term individual psychotherapy and speaks positively regarding this
- Motivational: Attitudes towards authority: Willing to work with Offender Manager (OM) in the community and reports a good relationship with prison staff
- Motivational: Life goals: Plans are realistic and prosocial
- Motivational: Medication: From her self-report, she is medication compliant and views her medication as helpful
- External: Social network: Some social support evident through friends in the community and her parents, although would benefit from forming further prosocial friendships once released
- External: Intimate relationship: Has partner who is considered by her to be supportive and protective (although was her partner at the time of the index offence)
- External: Professional care: Due to long licence will have OM and mental health input as needed
- External: Living circumstances: Planned due to sentence type, e.g. a probation-approved hostel (or similar) eventually
- External: External control: Long-term licence conditions due to sentence type

In Amy's case, a repeat scenario was considered the most likely, which could be a repeat of a significantly violent offence using a weapon against an unknown adult. A repeat offence is likely to occur within the context of deteriorating mental health (primarily depression or anxiety), significant stress, a preoccupation with violent fantasies and desires, alcohol and/or drug misuse, feeling disrespected, and feeling vengeful. A future victim is most likely to be an adult, although the nature of their relationship with her may well be known or unknown; Amy offended against a stranger, although she has also described a desire to inflict harm upon those known to her who have wronged her in some way, and indeed, she had initially intended on killing a drug dealer known to her on the day of the index offence. She has also reported previous violent thoughts about a child but did not act on this. If known to her, a potential victim is likely to be someone whom Amy feels has threatened or 'wronged' her in some way. A stranger offence is likely to be committed with the motivation of arousal to violence rather than revenge, although it may be a way of indirect revenge by offending against a specific person to 'get back' at people or the world in general. An alternative scenario could involve less severe violence through, for example, engaging in a physical fight with another without the use of a weapon. Similar triggers are likely to be relevant in this type of scenario, in that Amy may seek to engage in violence with another person as a cathartic, thrill-seeking exercise. Alternatively, she may use violence when she feels threatened, disrespected, or antagonised by another person and may use it in an instrumental way to restore a sense of power over the other person through physical intimidation or harm.

The imminence of risk in Amy's case was considered moderate when considering closed prison, and if in open conditions or the community, it was considered high. Warning signs of increased risk may include lifestyle instability, substance misuse, violent fantasies and indulging in these, Amy spending time watching violence, discussing violence with others, feeling violent compulsions, carrying weapons (predominantly knives), feeling vengeful, ruminating on the wrongs done to her, avoidant coping, antisocial associations, poor emotion management generally over and above what is considered 'normal' for her, decline in mental health and possible failure to use prescribed medication, disengagement from supervision and her prosocial support network (e.g. withholding information from professionals or from her parents), and not accepting support.

Monitoring and supervision to manage risk (in prison or the community) was recommended to include regular searches of accommodation as per usual practices in prison (linked to general propensity for violence and use of weapons), residence at probation-approved premises in the community, careful support and therapeutic monitoring of her relationships (family and intimate), exclusion zones as appropriate in relation to past victims (if needed), monitoring of engagement, curfew, drug and alcohol testing, monitoring of medication compliance, and engagement with therapeutic services.

Overall risk and manageability

The HCR-20v3 structured professional judgement assessment, including the additional female items, carefully examined 28 factors linked to violent offending and aided a case formulation alongside scenario planning in Amy's case. Although Amy had completed a relatively long-term psychological intervention in prison, when balancing the clinical items of the HCR-20v3 with the risk management items and protective factors, it was my opinion that she posed a moderate-to-high level of risk of future violent offending, meaning that specific risk management strategies would be required in order to keep the public safe. I did not recommend that Amy progress to a low-security open prison or the community at the time of the assessment. Instead, I made several recommendations for her future risk management and treatment.

Recommendations for The Parole Board to consider

Psychological intervention for sexual interests

Amy had engaged in a number of years of individualised therapy, albeit somewhat inconsistently due to changes in therapist. She reported having worked on her anger, her violent thoughts, her anxiety, and her personality. Reasonable insight in several areas suggested that some progress had been made, notwithstanding the fact that Amy has the ability to manipulate other people. Amy appeared to be honest with me in saying that she had not ever discussed the sexual element to her violent thoughts and felt uncomfortable speaking about this with most people, stating that up until the current assessment, she had not mentioned it since meeting a psychologist prior to her index offence. The records verified that this indeed was the case. In my opinion, this was an important area for therapeutic focus, as Amy reported that she continued to experience sexual arousal to violence, and it was my view that she would benefit from exploring this as well as masturbatory redirection strategies to encourage healthier sexual fantasies and to avoid ongoing reinforcement of these sexual thoughts. I noted within the assessment that Amy's ability to engage in this intervention would largely be down to the strength of the therapeutic relationship and her ability to speak openly and freely about this subject, which she found difficult to discuss. I noted that Amy would also need to be able to manage any sexual and/or emotional arousal which may occur through the discussion of her violent fantasies.

Psychological intervention for self-esteem and coping

In addition to exploration of her sexual arousal to violence, I recommended that Amy use individualised intervention to continue to explore her self-efficacy and self-esteem, what motivates her and makes her happy, and to set herself realistic and prosocial goals for her immediate and long-term future. She appeared during clinical interview to struggle with recognising progress, which has led to thoughts of sabotaging her progress through succumbing to her hedonistic desires, which could include violence in particular circumstances. I viewed it especially important that a future therapist help Amy to build her resilience and tolerance to negative mood states, given the close relationship this has to her substance misuse, which from her self-report remained an active problem at the time of the assessment. It was recommended that a **Dialectical Behavioural Therapy (DBT)**-based approach be taken to this, to include modules on emotion regulation and distress tolerance with Amy, which have been found to have a positive impact on those with BPD (Choi-Kain et al., 2017). It was my view that this work should continue to be delivered on an individual basis due to Amy's anxiety in groups but also because of the bespoke nature of some of her treatment needs. At the time of meeting Amy, she felt positive about her ability to trust her new therapist, and I noted that she may be able to achieve these treatment goals within this forum. It was recommended that this be viewed as a long-term intervention, and it should be anticipated that the patient-therapist rapport-building process would take time and patience.

Personality disorder and management

Amy had been diagnosed with ASPD with traits of BPD and narcissism. There were also strong indications of psychopathic traits which overlap with these diagnoses, although her presentation was well-understood in the context of personality. In my view, progression through the personality disorder pathway was relevant in Amy's case, and of several available prison-based personality disorder treatment units, she had identified a particular unit as her preferred choice because of the location and proximity to her support network. I recommended within my report that if Amy were to transfer to this unit, she should be offered individualised intervention rather than group work due to her high levels of anxiety, her personality make-up, and the possibility that she would not be able to participate sufficiently in the group to benefit. I also noted within my report that there may be a real risk that her behaviour in a group could negatively impact the treatment progress of other group members. I recommended that personality disorder support services would be important at each stage of the prison progression route and also when she is eventually released into the community.

Mental health

Amy had suffered with symptoms of anxiety and obsessional traits for many years, but she felt at the time of meeting her that these were reasonably managed through medication and her ability to control her environment at that time. Amy told me during interview that her primary concern about transferring to a new prison was her fear about the cleanliness of the cell, related to her obsessional thoughts. I recommended that staff planning for a prison transfer formulate a care plan alongside her mental health worker and/or therapist to manage these anxieties. I also recommended that Amy continue with regular reviews of her medication with the prison mental health team.

Drugs

Amy had a long history of substance misuse and had also completed a number of interventions for substance misuse in prison. Despite these interventions, she disclosed that she was using drugs at the time of meeting her. It appeared, from Amy's description, that this was a psychological rather than physical/addictive dependency, and that her substance misuse would not stop until she wanted it to. I reported that I felt further **psycho-educational** intervention would have limited impact because of this; that it was not Amy's knowledge that contributed to her continued use of drugs, but rather her stage of change. In this sense, I considered that it was Amy's resilience and coping abilities that needed further development, and I therefore recommended that this form part of her individualised therapy in prison alongside drug testing.

Relationships

Amy had been violent in the past towards her friends, her father, and a previous partner, and she had acknowledged engaging in vengeful acts towards those close to her, within which she put herself at risk. Amy also talked about having violent thoughts about others when they do not do as she asks or when they say no to her. I therefore suggested that Amy continues to pose a risk to those people she is close to, including intimate relationships, friendships, and family members, and therefore, her close relationships should be carefully monitored by those supervising her.

Risk to others

When I met Amy, she told me that she was still having thoughts of being violent to others and that these fantasies aroused her physically and sexually. Amy had not been violent in prison since 2014, although I was of the view that her substance misuse could potentially destabilise some of her self-control. Amy also told me that if her parents were to pass away, she would have little motivation to exercise control over her violent thoughts. I therefore recommended within my report that Amy's risk to others be taken seriously in prison and openly explored with her as part of the recommended individualised intervention. Losing her parents was a situation which I identified as high-risk, whether this occurred in prison or in the community.

Conclusions

The case study described in this chapter was completed in the context of Amy's forthcoming parole review. She was applying for progression to Category D conditions (minimum-security prison) at her upcoming review, and my assessment was that this was not a safe management option and that Amy required further psychological treatment in closed prison conditions. The report was disclosed to her by her solicitor, and my clinical view of Amy was that she was bright, reflective, and interested in herself, and therefore I was of the opinion that Amy would have found some benefit in reading the report, particularly in relation to her personality assessment. Whether she engages in the recommendations will depend on her motivation and the availability of treatment in the prison setting (Grella & Rodriquez, 2011).

Amy represented a seemingly rare population; a female offender with a sexual interest in violence. In Amy's case, the aggravating factor for her violence was that it was not just about emotional dyscontrol, but there was a planned, volitional element to her offending in order to satisfy her enduring arousal to violence. In Amy's case, she wanted to offend not just because of anger and vengefulness at others, but also because she found violence physically and sexually arousing. Amy's outstanding psychological treatment needs are related to emotional control and coping strategies as well as her arousal to violence and helping her to meet her arousal needs through healthier fantasies and behaviours which do not involve harm to others. Her sexual interest is likely to remain an ongoing issue, although it is possible that she could develop strategies to not act on this interest and to be able to enjoy sex without violence in the future.

If we consider Amy's case in the context of the research presented earlier in this chapter, she, interestingly, meets many of the common behavioural patterns of both male and female sexual sadists. Amy experienced sexual arousal to violence, torture, and death, she engaged in consensual choking in her own intimate relationship, she had a history of cruelty towards animals, and she had pre-planned the offence. These are all qualities of male sexual sadists according to Marshall and Hucker (2006). Furthermore, if we look at the setting of the offence, this is also uncommon in female offenders, with Amy having committed the offence alone and against a stranger. Female offenders are statistically more likely to be violent towards those known to them, either as a family member or a spouse (Wallace, 1986), as a degree of emotional connection often precipitates the offence, i.e. feeling betrayed by the victim and this contributing to high levels of anger and vengeance (Wallace, 1986). However, research has indicated that those who commit sexually motivated offences, categorised as 'sexualised murder' by Higgs et al. (2017) are less likely to know their victims (Beauregard & Proulx, 2002; Beech, Fisher & Ward, 2005), and therefore, Amy's characteristics seem more similar to what is known about sexually driven murderers rather than female sexual sadists. Additionally, due to the context of the offence, Amy did not engage in any of the psychological abuse or manipulation that we might be more likely to see in female sexual sadists (as identified by Pflugradt & Allen, 2012), and in contrast to female offenders, she was more aroused to the idea of inflicting pain than simply having control over the victim; Amy recognised a very specific arousal to torture and to death.

When considering why Amy may be somewhat different from other female sexual sadists, one might also consider personality as a relevant factor. Amy was suggested to have psychopathic personality disorder and, although there was no evidence of formal assessment, her past behaviour did support this clinical view. I also considered it unlikely that she would consent to engage in interview for formal assessment using the Hare Psychopathy Checklist-Revised (PCL-R; Hare, 2003) for the same reasons she was reluctant to engage again with the IPDE personality disorder assessment. A number of studies have demonstrated that the offences of psychopathic sexual offenders are likely to be more violent and demonstrate more sadistic acts than those of other sexual offenders (e.g. Barbaree et al., 1994), and that psychopathic sexual offenders are more likely to recidivate than non-psychopaths (e.g. Quinsey, Rice & Harris, 1995).

In summary, Amy represents a very small sample of the population; she is a female offender, with an interest in sexual sadism, who demonstrates more of the behavioural patterns associated with male sexual sadists and with sexual murderers than with female sexual sadists. This case study demonstrates that whilst it is important to be aware of research-derived commonalities between offenders, there are cases where adopting a nomothetic approach to an individual does not significantly inform, or may even mislead, our understanding and analysis of the case in front of us. For this reason, individualised assessment and case formulation is essential in understanding the risks posed by people who commit serious offences.

References

American Psychiatric Association (2013). *Diagnostic and statistical manual of mental disorders* (5th ed.). Arlington, VA: American Psychiatric Publishing.
Barbaree, H., Seto, M., Serin, R., Amos, N., & Preston, D. (1994). Comparisons between sexual and nonsexual rapist subtypes. *Criminal Justice and Behavior, 21*, 95–114.
Beauregard, E., & Proulx, J. (2002). Profiles in the offending process of nonserial sexual murderers. *International Journal of Offender Therapy and Comparative Criminology, 46*(4), 386–399.
Beck, A. T., & Steer, R. A. (1990). *Beck Anxiety Inventory manual*. San Antonio, TX: The Psychological Corporation.
Beck, A. T., Steer, R. A., & Brown, G. K. (1990). *Beck Depression Inventory-II manual*. San Antonio, TX: The Psychological Corporation.
Beech, A. R., Fisher, D., & Ward, T. (2005). Sexual murderers' implicit theories. *Journal of Interpersonal Violence, 20*(11), 1366–1389.
Blanchette, K., & Brown, S. L. (2006). *The assessment of treatment of women offenders: An integrated perspective*. Chichester, UK: John Wiley & Sons.

Choi-Kain, L. W., Finch, E. F., Masland, S. R., Jenkins, J. A., & Unruh, B. T. (2017). What works in the treatment of borderline personality disorder, *Current Behavioural Neuroscience Reports*, 4(1), 21–30.

Coid, J., Yang, M., Ullrich, S., Zhang, T., Sizmur, S., Roberts, C., & Rogers, R. D. (2009). Gender differences in structured risk assessment: Comparing the accuracy of five instruments. *Journal of Consulting and Clinical Psychology*, 77(2), 337–348. doi:10.1037/a0015155

Department of Health (2011). *Offender personality disorder strategy for women: Executive summary*. http://www.womensbreakout.org.uk/wp-content/uploads/downloads/2012/07/Offender-Personality-Disorder-Strategy-Summary.pdf

de Vogel, V., de Ruiter, C., Bouman, Y., & de Vries Robbé, M. (2012). *SAPROF: Structured Assessment of PROtective Factors*. Utrecht, The Netherlands: Van Der Hoeven Stichting.

de Vogel, V., & de Vries Robbé, M. (2013). Working with women. Towards a more gender-sensitive violence risk assessment. In L. Johnstone & C. Logan (Eds.), *Managing clinical risk: A guide to effective practice* (pp. 224–241). London, UK: Routledge.

de Vogel, V., de Vries Robbé, M., van Kalmthout, W., & Place, C. (2014). *Female Additional Manual*. Utrecht, The Netherlands: Van Der Hoeven Kliniek.

Esbec, E., & Echeburua, E. (2010). Violence and personality disorder: Clinical and forensic implications. *Actas Esp Psiquitar*, 38(5), 249–261.

Grella, C. E., & Rodriguez, L. (2011). Motivation for treatment among women offenders in prison-based treatment and longitudinal outcomes among those who participate in community aftercare. *Journal of Psychoactive Drugs*, 7, 58–67.

Grossman, S., Millon, C., & Millon, T. (2015). *Millon Clinical Multiaxial Inventory – IV*. Bloomington, MN: Pearson.

Groth-Marnat, G. (2009). *Handbook of psychological assessment*. London, UK: John Wiley and Sons.

Hare, R. D. (2003). *Hare Psychopathy Checklist-Revised (PCL-R). Technical Manual* (2nd ed.). Toronto, ON: Multi Health Systems Inc.

Higgs, T., Carter, A. J., Tully, R. T., & Browne, K. D. (2017). Sexual murder typologies: A systematic review. *Aggression and Violent Behavior*, 35, 1–12.

Howard, R. C., Huband, N., Duggan, C., & Mannion, A. (2008). Exploring the link between personality disorder and criminality in a community sample. *Journal of Personality Disorder*, 22(6), 589–603.

Logan, C. (2008). Sexual deviance in females: Psychopathology and theory. In D. R. Laws & W. T. O'Donohue (Eds.), *Sexual deviance: Theory, assessment, and treatment* (2nd ed., pp. 486–507). New York, NY: Guilford Press.

Loranger, A. (1999). *International Personality Disorder Examination manual: DSM-IV module*. Washington, DC: American Psychiatric Press.

Maruna, S., & Mann, R. E. (2006). A fundamental attribution error? Rethinking cognitive distortions. *Legal and Criminological Psychology*, 11, 155–177.

Millon, T., Millon, C., Davis, R., & Grossman, S. (2009). *Millon Clinical Multiaxial Inventory-III manual* (4th ed.). Minneapolis, MN: Pearson.

Ministry of Justice (2015). *Statistics on women and the criminal justice system 2015*. https://www.gov.uk/government/statistics/women-and-the-criminal-justice-system-statistics-2015

O'Shea, L. E., Piccioni, M. M., Mason, F. L. Sugarman, P. A., & Dickens. G. L. (2014). Differential predictive validity of the Historical Clinical and Risk Management Scales (HCR-20) for inpatient aggression. *Psychiatry Research*, 220(1–2), 669–678.

Patton, J. H., Stanford, M. S., & Barratt, E. S. (1995). Factor structure of the Barratt Impulsiveness Scale. *Journal of Clinical Psychology, 6*, 768–774.

Paulhus, D. L. (1998). *Paulhus Deception Scales (PDS): The balanced inventory of desirable responding-7.* North Tonawanda, NY: Multi-Health Systems Inc.

Pflugradt, D., & Allen, B. (2012). A grounded theory analysis of sexual sadism in females. *Journal of Sexual Aggression, 18*(3), 325–337.

Quinsey, V. L., Rice, M. E., & Harris, G. T. (1995). Actuarial prediction of sexual recidivism. *Journal of Interpersonal Violence, 10*, 85–105.

Rivera, B., & Widom, C. S. (1990). Childhood victimization and violent offending. *Violence and Victims, 5*(1), 19–35.

Roger, D., Jarvis, G., & Najarian, B. (1993). Detachment and coping: The construction and validation of a new scale for measuring coping strategies. *Personality and Individual Differences, 15*(6), 619–626.

Rosenberg, M. (1965). *Society and the adolescent self-image.* Princeton, NJ: Princeton University Press.

Royal College of Psychiatrists (2010). *A competency-based curriculum for specialist core training in psychiatry.* London, UK: Author.

Salekin, R. T., Rogers, R., Ustad, K. L., & Sewell, K. W. (1998). Psychopathy and recidivism among female inmates. *Law and Human Behavior, 22*(1), 109–128.

Singh, J. P., Grann, M., & Fazel, S. (2011). A comparative study of violence risk assessment tools: A systematic review and metaregression analysis of 68 studies involving 25,980 participants. *Clinical Psychology Review, 31*(3), 499–513.

Singleton, N., Meltzer, H., Gatward, R., Coid, J., & Deasy, D. (1998). *Psychiatric morbidity among prisoners in England and Wales: A survey carried out in 1997 by the social survey dimension of ONS on behalf of the Department of Health.* London, UK: HMSO.

Smith, P., Waterman, M., & Ward, N. (2006). Driving aggression in forensic and non-forensic populations: Relationships and self-reported levels of aggression, anger and impulsivity. *British Journal of Psychology, 97*, 387–403.

Vandiver, D. M., & Walker, J. T. (2002). Female sex offenders: An overview and analysis of 40 cases. *Criminal Justice Review, 27*, 284–300.

Wallace, A. (1986). *Homicide: The social reality.* Sydney: New South Wales Bureau of Crime Statistics and Research.

Webster, C. D., Douglas, K. S., Eaves, D., & Hart, S. D. (1997). *HCR-20: Assessing risk for violence (version 2).* Burnaby, BC: Mental Health, Law & Policy Institute.

Webster, C. D., Douglas, K. S., Eaves, D., & Hart, S. D. (2013). *HCR-20: Assessing risk for violence (version 3).* Burnaby, BC: Mental Health, Law and Policy Institute, Simon Fraser University.

Weerasekera, P. (1996). *Multiperspective case formulation: A step towards treatment integration.* Malabar, FL: Krieger.

Chapter 8

Mental health and violence

Forensic risk assessment and formulation

Ruth J. Tully

Introduction

Forensic psychology and mental health

Forensic psychology is a discipline of psychology with many applications. Just a few settings in which forensic psychology is practised include mental health settings, prisons, community, and Court settings (family, criminal, mental health, and immigration law). Forensic psychologists work with people throughout the justice system, including offenders and victims. The overlap of these settings and client groups can be considerable. For example, people in prison can present with mental health problems (offence-related or otherwise), and offenders can have a significant history of past victimisation themselves, as adults or as children. Forensic psychology therefore as a discipline has a wide range of applications, and the case study discussed in this chapter relates to an adult male who was in prison and aged 19 when I worked with him. Sam (not his real name) had an existing diagnosis of Post-Traumatic Stress Disorder (PTSD) as his primary mental health problem. PTSD is an anxiety disorder caused by very stressful, frightening, or distressing events. Causes can vary and PTSD can develop immediately or even years after the event occurs. Symptoms include nightmares, flashbacks, feelings of isolation, irritability, and guilt. The person may have poor concentration and suffer from insomnia. Symptoms are often persistent, severe, and impact the person's day-to-day life. Sam's case was complex in relation to the violence (stabbing the victim with a knife or other object) being committed against the person who Sam alleged had previously abused him. My role was to assist the Court by completing a comprehensive assessment of Sam to be able to provide an expert opinion on the impact of Sam's PTSD on his alleged offence.

The degree to which mental illness results in interpersonal violence tends to be exaggerated in the media/press, and mental illness can be subject to stigma by the public (see Varshney et al., 2016). Those with mental illness make up only a small proportion of violent offenders, and although a statistical relationship between some serious mental disorders and violence has been found, only a small proportion of violence in wider society can be attributed to people with psychiatric diagnoses (Hodgkins, 2008). Whilst there are some identified links between mental illness and violence, there is the difficulty of identifying direct causation, and some research has disputed a direct causation between serious mental illness and violence (Elbogen, Dennis & Johnson, 2016). Mental health may serve as a disinhibiting factor for violent behaviour, meaning that it may contaminate the thinking process involved in making a violent or non-violent decision.

Research into mental health and violence has largely focused on psychotic-type illnesses such as schizophrenia (Douglas, Guy & Hart, 2009; Fazel et al., 2009). To a lesser degree, the links between PTSD and violence have been explored in the empirical research; however, the available research has tended to focus on those with military-related PTSD. Studies that have explored non-military PTSD and violence have found a link between the two (e.g. Blakey et al., 2016). However, the specific consequences or symptoms of the disorder are theorised to have more of a direct impact on violent behaviour rather than having a diagnosis in itself. This chapter presents Sam's case where mental illness, specifically PTSD, was being assessed to help determine if there was a functional link between this and Sam's alleged serious violent offence. PTSD needs careful consideration in the forensic context, because verdicts associated with this can include the person being considered as not criminally responsible, having acted with automatism, or found responsible for their offence but with 'diminished responsibility', meaning that they have partial responsibility (see Bourget, Gagné & Wood, 2017). This can have a significant impact on the sentence imposed by the Court where the offence is proven to have been committed.

Patient history

Childhood and education

Sam was aged around 19 at the time of assessment. He was born in Syria. When he was aged under ten, his mother died. His father, prior to this, was unaffectionate and would beat Sam if he misbehaved or to maintain discipline, often using a cable. He and his brother were subsequently abandoned by their father, who moved back to his home town and remarried, and they were brought up by their grandmother. His grandmother was more emotionally caring, but without a father, Sam was teased and bullied at school and in the community, where he was beaten up and called a "*bastard*".

Sam attended school in Syria from the age of six to eight, after which time he left to help his brother make money. The two would work as tour guides and sell tourist accessories, giving the money to their grandmother. Sam would go to the Mosque on Fridays and then Church on Saturday and Sunday, where he was given clothes, food, and some basic education. The revolution began in Syria when Sam was a teenager, from which point he had to remain at home with his grandmother to protect his safety. He had been distressed by the loss of his mother and his father no longer being there for him, but he recognised that his grandmother provided some emotional care for him. However, following the region becoming unsettled, he found witnessing death, bombing, and being harassed by the Police as distressing. As is described below, Sam and his brother eventually travelled to Europe, with Sam reaching the UK without his brother. He had spent time homeless and alone in Europe, but when he reached the UK, he was housed with a foster carer whom he lived with for four years (the complainant also lived there for some of this time).

One issue from the reviewed documents was of note. This involved a knife that had been seen in Sam's bedroom in his foster home. He explained this to me as the knife he used to self-harm (he had a well-documented history of self-harming by cutting).

Employment

Sam engaged in some child work in Syria, but in the UK, he had been unable to work due to his visa. He was unable to accept a football contract with a local professional football team for this reason. Sam had instead engaged in education during his time in the UK. His English was very good and of a level that allowed him to successfully study at college. Other than a dip in his attendance linked to problems outside of college, specifically linked to the abuse he was experiencing from the complainant, his attendance and achievement were good. Sam reported that education and learning equate to success for him. He said that when he was homeless in Europe, he was unclean from his living situation and would eat dirty food from bins to stay alive. At this time, he would see the children going to school and strongly desire an education and to be able to learn like they were able to. Sam described great pride in his studies and football abilities and reported that he used his past negative experiences to motivate himself to do well in the future. He described a definition of success as being successful in study and work, as well as hoping for success in relationships and having his own family in the future. Sam went to extreme lengths to attend college when temporarily residing far away from his college for his safety, including getting up very early and making various public transport journeys taking several hours in order to get to college on time. He said that he was proud of this achievement despite the problems he faced at the time. Sam wished to engage in further studies, including international relations studies, and he reported that he spoke four languages.

Relationships

Sam had experienced a couple of intimate relationships in his life. At the time of assessing Sam, he was in a relationship with a female whom he had been dating for around one month prior to the alleged offence, although he had known her for over a year. Sam had no children but reported that he would like a family of his own in the long term. Sam's brother did not come to the UK, and Sam believed that he was in Europe, but he was unsure.

Mental health

There were no identified problems with drugs and alcohol in Sam's history. Sam had previously described being frightened and distressed by the events in Syria, and he suffered from insomnia. He was constantly worried about a bomb strike hitting his home, as had happened to surrounding homes, and he became apathetic, tired, and lacked energy. He was often tearful, paid less attention to personal hygiene, and lost weight through loss of appetite. After his brother left the home to be involved in the revolution, the Police/Soldiers would visit the house regularly, trashing the home. It seems that hypervigilance was a problem at this time, as whenever footsteps were heard, Sam would fear that it was the Police coming to the home. On a subsequent occasion, they did come to the home, out of uniform, and they took Sam, then aged 13, by force to a Police Station. They wanted to know where his brother was. They verbally and physically abused him and also humiliated him in things they made him say about God. He was placed in a cell with adults for two weeks, within which time he was in fear for his life, as he would see the beatings and level of violence used against the adults he was imprisoned with. These adult prisoners would also humiliate him. Sam was released after two weeks; his grandmother had paid money for him to be released. After release, his mental health continued to be poor, and the Police continued to visit his home, searching for his brother. His brother at this point came home and told Sam and his grandmother that they had to leave because of the conflict. His grandmother was too old to travel, but Sam and his brother (who did not make the journey all the way to the UK) set off for Europe.

It is documented in a psychiatric report prepared around 18 months prior to my assessment of Sam that he disclosed the physical abusive behaviour of the complainant to the assessing psychiatrist. Sam also disclosed the abuse to others including his carer and his college counsellor prior to the alleged offence. Sam said that he and his carer told social services of his injuries that the complainant had perpetrated but that no action was taken. The psychiatric report summarises what Sam told the psychiatrist as follows: a Syrian man aged several years older than Sam was violent to him, treated him like a slave, and tried to get him to say that he was his brother or cousin in relation to immigration to the UK. Sam said that this was so that the older male would be offered care and lodgings with Sam, who was a child at the time. Sam reported that the complainant knew that this meant that he would be offered care with Sam despite not being as young. Sam estimated the complainant's age as around 19, and after some immigration-related processes, after being assessed by authorities as being 17 years old, on appeal the male was relabelled as being 16 years old. Sam reported to me that the male pressured him to say that he needed his relative to be with him in his care setting so he would not be scared, when in fact he was scared of this male. It is documented in the aforementioned psychiatric report that Sam reported that he was victimised by the violent and domineering male, and that after a period, he told his carers and the male was removed from the foster placement. There was an incident whereby Sam was treated at hospital and received what the notes term 'complex sutures' after an alleged assault by the complainant. Sam said that the complainant's anger towards him persisted even after he had left the home because he blamed Sam for him having to leave. Sam persisted in being afraid of him and had been told by other peers that the male was threatening him and was out to get him. Sam alleged that the complainant left dead animals outside the home of their carer in order to threaten him/them. He said that the complainant made it clear directly to him and his carer that he had left these items to threaten them, rather than this being an assumption that it was the complainant. Alice, Sam's foster carer, reported this event in the same terms to me. She added that on the same day, threats had been made to her, including threats to rape her, and although the complainant was arrested, no charges were brought. Alice said that she believed that the complainant was threatening her as he thought that she was hiding Sam from him and he wished to harm Sam.

Sam has disclosed that the abuse perpetrated by this male in the home also included sexual abuse and humiliation of him, as well as generally psychological bullying to the point where Sam decided that when with the male it was better not to speak, as he would either be humiliated or hurt. The alleged sexual abuse is described as forced oral sex. Sam said that during the abuse, the complainant would make humiliating statements such as calling Sam a dog. Sam was too scared to report this initially and felt ashamed about being sexually abused. He presented as upset during interview when discussing this. After seeing that they were not supported when they complained to social services, Alice said that the complainant could no longer reside with her and so he moved out.

When in the UK, which followed a highly stressful journey through Europe for Sam, who was still a child, Sam continued to experience nightmares and flashbacks involving the Syrian Police. He also experienced emotional dysregulation linked to his experiences of trauma. He began to self-harm and lose weight and had been close to taking his life on several occasions. It is noted that his problems at home in relation to alleged abuse by the complainant coincided with reduced college attendance and with Sam's increased suicidality. Sam has attended accident and emergency departments on several occasions with incidents involving stitches.

Sam formed a trusting relationship with a counsellor at college. He was diagnosed with **PTSD**, **anxiety**, and **depression** about 18 months prior to my assessment of him (and prior to the index offence). The psychiatric assessment took place in relation to his immigration case. He credited the support he has had from his carer to him being alive still. In the psychiatric assessment, he described hypervigilance and a startle response to noises. The following diagnoses were made: severe depressive episode having improved to become mild at one point, but at the time of the 2016 assessment it was moderate; and PTSD with delayed onset. Fleeting psychotic experiences were noted, although these were deemed to link to trauma as opposed to a diagnosable psychotic illness.

Sam said that he met with a counsellor weekly whilst in prison on remand for the index offence, and he described what he had learned, including breathing exercises and grounding techniques, which are skills taught to help manage anxiety. Sam, aged 19 at the time of the assessment, said that he settled well into his first prison but was moved from the young offender site (which holds prisoners aged between 18 and 21 years of age) to an adult prison so that he could attend Court, and at the adult prison, he had been assaulted by a prisoner. Sam had learned not to wear trainers that may be desirable to antisocial others and gave this as an example of how to unofficially stay safe in prison. He also reportedly learned not to play football in prison despite wanting to; he was skilled and was once purposefully injured by another prisoner on an opposing team because of the other prisoner's resentment of his skills. In an adult prison, Sam was in my view vulnerable because of his age, stature, lack of prison experience (naiveté to risky situations and understanding gang and street words), and mental health. Sam had been seeing a mental health worker in the adult prison and reported that the worker was referring him to the psychiatrist for review.

Sam had been subject to self-harm monitoring whilst in prison, where he was found attempting to make a noose to commit suicide. He had a history of self-harm by cutting whilst in the community in the UK and once travelled to a city away from where his foster home was with the intention of setting himself on fire as a means of committing suicide. Positively, at the time of assessing Sam, self-harm monitoring was not needed, and Sam was working in a trusted job where he was around staff from 9 am to 11 am and 2 pm to 9 pm on a usual day. He reported finding that this job kept him busy and that he enjoyed working with others. This also resulted in Sam being less at risk of harm from other prisoners because he was monitored by staff in the role.

Sam described physiological symptoms of anxiety when coming out of his prison cell, whereby his heart would pound and he would become hot and sweaty. He did not understand that this could be a symptom of anxiety and was keen to learn about such symptoms. Prior to his recent discussion with another prisoner, Sam did not realise that not everyone experiences the things he thought about at times, such as suicidal thoughts. He seemed keen to engage in self-help and taught strategies and he seemed amenable to mental health and psychological treatment. He described ongoing symptoms of trauma and PTSD. He sought reassurance that he was not "*crazy*" and worried that if his thinking did not get better, this may stop his plans to study, have a job, and have family in the future. Sam presented with a fear of not being believed, whether about his past experiences more generally, but also about the abuse that he alleged the complainant perpetrated against him. This fear seemed to stem from his experiences in life so far. For example, Sam had experienced having to gain the belief of others when seeking residence as a lone child in a new country, as well as his fear regarding people viewing him negatively and thinking he had fabricated allegations of abuse against the victim to excuse his alleged offending. In my view, this fear of not being believed, which is not uncommon in victims of abuse and trauma, was likely to persist and contributed to feelings of low self-esteem for Sam.

From my own interactions with Sam, there were no observable signs of him experiencing psychotic symptoms, and there was no indication of learning disability. He was emotional at times in the assessment sessions, but this was context-appropriate, given his experience of trauma and situation of being in an adult prison where there is reason, at times, to feel unsafe on top of existing hypervigilance linked to PTSD. It is important to note that some symptoms of trauma/PTSD can be mistaken for signs of **personality disorder**. There was no evidence of an emerging **antisocial personality disorder**, nor was there evidence for me to suggest that personality disorder assessment was required (alongside Sam's relatively young age meaning that any such assessment would be of limited value).

Offending history

Index offence

Sam had been charged with one count of grievous bodily harm with intent (GBH, Section 18) against an adult male victim. The complainant was known to Sam, as they resided together with the same foster carer, Alice, for a period of time following their entry to the UK. The complainant was not residing with the foster carer or Sam at the time of the alleged offence. This offence involved Sam visiting a shop with friends and finding that the complainant worked there. The complainant was seen on security tapes hitting Sam, who then engaged in an altercation with the complainant. The complainant received serious stab wounds during the altercation, which resulted from the use of an improvised weapon which had been at the scene of the offence.

Previous convictions

Sam had no previous criminal convictions of any kind prior to the alleged offence.

Assessment

Several sessions were held with Sam to inform the assessment. This included interview time and assessment using psychometric tests. Sam's English was good and he appeared to understand the tests. He became emotional (teary-eyed, and cried) at some points during the assessment, in appropriate contexts. He sought reassurance at times regarding his anxiety and general mental health considerations, but he worked well with me as a therapeutic figure and seemed to respond well to encouragement.

Deception

I often apply the Paulhus Deception Scales (PDS; Paulhus, 1998) in a forensic context because psychometric assessment of socially desirable responding is useful to supplement clinical opinions. Given that forensic assessments can influence outcomes for patients in these contexts, deception and 'faking good' is a presentation I often come across. However, I deemed that some of the items in the tool were culturally and situationally inappropriate in Sam's case. I therefore considered that the outcomes of this assessment would have been invalid and so I did not apply this tool.

Depression and anxiety

I applied the Beck Depression Inventory (BDI-II; Beck & Steer, 1990) and Beck Anxiety Inventory (BAI; Beck, Steer & Brown, 1991) to assess the intensity and breadth of symptoms of these conditions. Both assessments measured revealed symptoms to be in the 'severe' ranges, and I considered that there were symptoms overlapping with Sam's PTSD as well as symptoms likely to have been magnified by Sam's current legal situation. Although he was reluctant to see a doctor to discuss medication, Sam reported that he had learned some anxiety-reduction strategies through the counselling he received prior to prison and in the young offender prison. He reported that some of these skills and techniques were effective for him, and he was encouraged to continue with these, as well as to access any counselling or mental health support that he could within the prison setting. As he enjoyed learning, he was also encouraged to access self-help books at the library in the prison or through the prison healthcare department.

Trauma

I applied the **Trauma and Attachment Belief Scale** (TABS; Pearlman, 2003) to help consider the level of trauma-related problems Sam had. This is a psychometric scale designed to assess cognitive **schemas** (beliefs about oneself and about others). Specifically, it is designed to measure beliefs related to five areas of need that are sensitive to the effects of traumatic experiences: *safety*, *trust*, *esteem*, *intimacy*, and *control*. Patients are asked to rate their level of agreement with 84 statements, which are rated on a six-point scale from 'disagree strongly' to 'agree strongly'. There are eight subscales and a total score is calculated. Sam's assessment revealed a high level of disturbance in several areas, as well as in total, as is displayed in Table 8.1 below.

Table 8.1 TABS outcomes

Scale	Score ranges
Self-safety	Extremely high disturbance
Other safety	Extremely high disturbance
Self-trust	High average disturbance
Other trust	Extremely high disturbance
Self-esteem	Extremely high disturbance
Other esteem	Average
Self-intimacy	Extremely high disturbance
Other intimacy	Very high disturbance
Self-control	Very high disturbance
Other control	Extremely high disturbance
Total score	Extremely high disturbance

Elevated scores on the *safety* subscales, as seen in Sam's profile, reflect heightened concerns about the general security of the world as well as for one's own safety and that of others. Affect regulation can be difficult for trauma survivors, and they may at times be overwhelmed with strong feelings like rage, terror, or grief. If the person lacks internal means for managing strong feelings, then they may act on these, rather than being able to tolerate or modulate them. Impulse control can therefore be more challenging. People with elevated *self-safety* scores struggle with feelings about their own safety, and the elevated *other safety* scale represents concern for the safety of others. They may worry about victimisation or harm from others, and this could be a preoccupation due to the reality that within their trauma they were unable to protect themselves from harm.

Shattered trust can be an inevitable fallout from traumatic interpersonal experiences. High scores on the *trust* subscales can indicate that the person is having difficulty in trusting their own judgment and perceptions and they may doubt their own decision-making. This was consistent with Sam's presentation whereby he sought reassurance and support within conversation. However, an elevated score on the *other trust* subscale indicates problems in trusting or relying on others, with the person usually being cautious and suspicious of others' motivations. Despite this, Sam was able to form an appropriate professional relationship with me as assessor, and from his self-report, he was also able to do this with his counsellor at his previous prison. During discussion, it became clear that trusting others who are non-professionals was difficult for Sam, although he does trust his foster carer.

Sam's *self-esteem* subscale score was disturbed, meaning that he had problems with his self-worth and may have blamed himself for the traumas that he has experienced. People scoring high on this scale often feel undeserving of praise or positive regard from others. Sam's *other esteem* score was average. High scorers on this subscale often view others with disdain and disrespect, which was not the case for Sam, and which was likely to be protective for him given the high levels of disturbance in other areas.

Trauma often gives rise to intimacy disruptions including feelings of alienation and loss of community. Sam's high score on the *self-intimacy* scale indicated that he found it challenging to spend time alone and he may avoid it altogether. Again, this is highly consistent of his life in prison, where he worked in a job where he was out of his cell for longer than other prisoners so that he could be around staff for most of the day. It seemed that this was a strategy led in part by the response of the prison to Sam's self-harm or suicide risk, and therefore this approach was in my view sensible and well-targeted at managing this risk. Those scoring highly on the *other intimacy* subscale can be disconnected and isolated from others, and they may avoid interpersonal situations. Although there was an elevation on this scale, this was lower than the self-intimacy score, which may have been protecting Sam from acting on a desire to isolate himself, which he reported he did in the past when being abused.

Disruptions in the need for *control* are often linked to traumatic experiences in which one lacked control when seeing abuse around them. This is linked with Sam's description of his childhood, and often those who have a disruption in this area place themselves in dangerous situations or engage in high-risk behaviours in order to compensate for their inability to make decisions or act without inhibitions or restrictions imposed by others. This finding helped contextualise Sam's trip from his foster home to a different city in the UK, when he had intended to set himself on fire in order to die. He said that this act would also have been a means of highlighting his distress to others. Those scoring highly on *other control* may feel uncomfortable when not in charge, and Sam was encouraged to reflect on this if his behaviours in interpersonal relationships began to reflect an underlying need for control.

Sam's overall level of trauma-linked disturbance was assessed as being extremely high using the TABS. This was not unexpected given his life history, and the profile discussed above helped to formulate his behaviour in the context of the impact that trauma had on him.

Discussion

PTSD and the alleged offending

Sam was alleged to have stabbed a known adult male, who received serious injuries. For the purpose of the assessment detailed within this chapter, I had read the interview transcripts which detail the initial account of the alleged offence that Sam had given to the Police when formally interviewed. I also asked him about his subjective experience during the alleged offence, which informed my opinions. I also read the witness statements and viewed the security surveillance videos which showed some of the incident from two angles. All of the information combined informed my viewpoint, and in a forensic assessment where public safety and potential long-term imprisonment are being considered, accessing a wide range of information is essential.

It was my view that Sam's description of his perceptions at the time of the offence was consistent with **dissociation**, which is a phenomenon associated with PTSD. Dissociation involves a state of altered consciousness, which is often reported as dissociative flashbacks, amnesia for some aspects of the trauma, and emotional numbing (see Bourget et al., 2017). Although PTSD is classed as an anxiety disorder, it is also associated with an increased rate of dissociative symptoms. There was even discussion as to whether PTSD should be listed as a dissociative disorder rather than an anxiety disorder in the diagnostic manuals used by psychiatrists and psychologists (see Brett, 1993). Clinical and neurobiological evidence of dissociative symptoms lend support to a dissociative subtype of PTSD (Ginzburg, Koopman & Butler, 2006; Steuwe, Lanius & Frewen, 2012; Wolf, Miller & Reardon, 2012), which is now listed in the **Diagnostic and Statistical Manual of Mental Disorders (DSM-5; APA, 2013)**. Dissociation involves partial or complete loss of the normal integration between memories of the past, awareness of identity and immediate sensations, and control of bodily movements. It can be summarised as a splitting of awareness. Sam also had a history of hyperarousal, which is likely to have impacted his behaviour within the incident. I did consider the possibility that he could have be feigning his condition given the context of this assessment, but considering the wider information, I formed the opinion that this was likely to be a genuine account of psychological trauma for several reasons. First, the PTSD diagnosis was established prior to the alleged offence, and there is documented evidence of two likely formative traumatic themes: Sam's experiences in Syria and in Europe as a child, and his experiences of alleged abuse perpetrated by the victim, about which disclosures were made prior to the alleged index offence. His PTSD was in my view not straightforward, as there was more than one distinctive source. His experiences in Syria came first, and later Sam's reported experiences of being harmed by the victim of his alleged offence. Furthermore, there was an identifiable trigger for the trauma response in the direct short-term lead up to the alleged offence, in that Sam was assaulted first by the complainant (this is clear from witness statements as well as Sam's self-reported memory of the event). It was my view that any assault on Sam (i.e. a real threat, even without the past relationship between the two involved) could have triggered a response influenced by PTSD. It was also my view that such a response was especially sensitive to the real threat posed by a previous abuser. This was also consistent with the themes that have emerged through psychometric and clinical examination of Sam's case.

The most characteristic symptoms of PTSD are re-experiencing symptoms. Sufferers involuntarily re-experience aspects of the traumatic event in a vivid and distressing way. This includes flashbacks, nightmares, and repetitive and disturbing intrusive images or other sensory impressions from the event. Those with PTSD can often try to avoid reminders of the trauma, including people, situations, or circumstances resembling or associated with the event. They may also try to push the memory out of their thoughts and avoid speaking about it.

On the other hand, the person may excessively ruminate about questions that stop them from coming to terms with the event, for example, why it happened. Those with PTSD also describe symptoms of emotional numbing, for example, not experiencing feelings, feeling detached from others, and giving up their previously important activities, and they may report some level of memory loss from the disturbing event. Other associated symptoms include depression, generalised anxiety, shame, guilt, and reduced interest in sex. These symptoms can contribute to the person's distress. Sleep problems, anger outbursts, irritability, difficulties concentrating, hypervigilance, and an exaggerated startle response are symptoms that are considered when diagnosing PTSD using the **International Classification of Diseases, 10th Version** (ICD-10; WHO, 2016 version) guidance.

Dissociation, as discussed above, involves partial or complete loss of the normal integration between memories of the past, awareness of identity and immediate sensations, and control of bodily movements. Sam had a history of some level of dissociative symptoms as cited in the psychiatric report. His description of his memories of the immediate lead up to the alleged offence after the complainant came into close proximity with him and hit him contributed to me forming the opinion that dissociative symptoms were present for at least some of the period of his own violent response to the complainant. My summary of his description of his subjective experience of the event, when elicited from him carefully, is that he described observing what happened from outside of his body. The difficulty with dissociation is that it is extremely difficult to determine with any confidence for how long the person was experiencing dissociation. Dissociation can result in 'freezing', which did not seem to occur in some of the incident as seen in the security footage.

The 'fight or flight' response is part of the limbic system (autonomic nervous system) which is concerned with survival. PTSD can result in a person being hypervigilant to threat. Hypervigilance is part of the 'fight or flight' response. This ongoing state of anxiety differs from paranoia and is very emotionally and physically draining for those with the disorder. In PTSD, therefore, the limbic system is active and sensitive to threat even in the absence of immediate threat. Sam has described various signs of hyperarousal as part of his PTSD. It was my view that this existing hyperarousal, combined with being confronted with an actual threat from a person who had caused him harm, is likely to have significantly influenced Sam's behaviour in the incident. It was reasonable to conclude that in this situation, Sam was in fear of significant harm, contributed to by his PTSD, and that in the situation, his 'fight or flight' response, which was already more prominent than that of others without PTSD, was triggered and resulted in the harmful outburst. Although part of PTSD can involve anger outbursts that for some can result in perpetrating violence, a response driven by self-preservation (the 'fight' of the 'fight or flight') can be seen as distinct from an irritability/anger outburst. It was my view that Sam, at least in part, described his actions as a 'fight' response over and above an anger response. His description of this being a result of something inside him was not as I would have expected when describing anger; in my view, this was more like a description of the result of constant vigilance, with the need to protect triggered by the real threat. Increased arousal resulting from anger was not a process described or which I could pick out of Sam's account of the incident. He also had no recorded or reported history of anger outbursts resulting in violence towards others; indeed, he had previously internalised anger, including self-harm, and threatened to kill himself when he was in the community.

It was my overall view that Sam's mental health, specifically his PTSD, had a significant impact on the alleged offending. The events leading up to the offence were, in my view, highly likely to have served as a trigger for PTSD symptoms for Sam. In my opinion, some level of dissociative experience was described by him. However, for Sam, probably more prominent was the exaggerated 'fight or flight' response in the situation, which notably was triggered by a real threat from the person that his existing hypervigilance (perceived threat where no such threat is present) focused on. The PTSD and threat from the feared person were likely to have exaggerated what for him was his perceived self-defence ('fight' response) in a threatening situation. It was not possible to assign any form of percentage or rating to how much of the behaviour this accounted for, or if this accounted for his behaviour in its entirety. However, it could be concluded that this was a possibility.

Regardless of the prosecution and outcome of this case, Sam, in my view, required psychological treatment in relation to his PTSD and complex history. He was awaiting an appointment with the psychiatrist at the prison at the time of the assessment. Sam in my view presented as being amenable to psychological treatment, having already benefited to some degree from the intervention in a previous prison. I was of the view that if specialist treatment was provided at this critical time in Sam's life, the prognosis in relation to his PTSD could be fairly positive. I recommended that access to appropriate psychiatric/psychological treatment be expedited, whether in prison or in the community.

I also had a duty as a healthcare professional to highlight that Sam was in my view a **vulnerable prisoner** as a young person aged only 19 years residing in what was mainly an adult prison (housing prisoners over the age of 21 years), alongside his PTSD symptoms. Sam had been violently victimised on more than one occasion in the prison, with staff not being fully aware of the incidents due to Sam not wishing to be further victimised because of then being considered what in prison is termed 'a grass' (i.e. being considered to be telling on other prisoners). I recommended that appropriate attention be given to this vulnerability, as well as the potential for suicidal/self-harm intent should he be convicted of the alleged offence and therefore imprisoned for a longer term. I concluded that Sam should access PTSD treatment as a means of risk reduction as opposed to there being a high need to address antisocial attitudes or violence-supportive views. This was because, in my view, general antisocial/pro-violence or poor thinking skills were not critical **risk factors** influencing the offence, and so a typical 'offending behaviour programmes' treatment pathway was much less relevant to Sam than him receiving an appropriate type of, and intensity of, psychological treatment for his PTSD. Treatment such as Eye Movement Desensitisation and Reprocessing (EMDR; Shapiro, 1989, 1990) would in my view be appropriately targeted in this case, alongside peer support and self-help. EMDR is included in the British national healthcare guidelines (NICE, 2005) for treating PTSD. EMDR is theorised to work on the basis that the unprocessed memories of traumatic experiences cause many of the symptoms of PTSD. EMDR does not focus on describing the distressing event in detail and works via a number of phases to help process the traumatic memories, with the aim of reducing distressing symptoms. I recommended this as being important for Sam to access through the prison mental health team.

Outcome of the case

As Sam's PTSD was assessed as a contributing factor to his case rather than a full causal factor, his PTSD could not be used in the law of England and Wales as a full defence for his actions. Therefore, the assessment was used in mitigation and presented to give the Court an understanding of Sam's actions. Sam received a custodial prison sentence, and it was hoped that he would share the report with prison staff so that he could get the psychological therapy and support recommended, in order to reduce future violence risk and to aid his well-being.

Conclusions

This case has highlighted the importance of consideration of mental health problems within forensic psychological assessment and Court proceedings. In England and Wales, people with acute mental health needs whose offending links to those needs can be ordered by the Court to be detained in a secure psychiatric facility instead of prison. This was clearly not necessary in the present case in that Sam was not so unwell to not be legally responsible for his offence, and the psychological treatment required for his PTSD was available in the prison setting, where he was able (with support) to cope with prison life. Instead, the forensic assessment and consideration of mental health aided the Court in fully understanding the background to the case, which enabled justice through the sharing of information and expert opinion with the Court. Having completed many assessments to aid the Court, it is my experience that each case is very different, and bespoke assessment is required based on the client presentation and background to the case. A 'one size fits all' approach to assessment, such as by using the same psychometric tests and modes of assessment for each case, would be impossible and inappropriate to apply in practice. PTSD is complex as a disorder, and the assessment of symptoms does require significant expertise on the part of the assessor. It is also important to consider that the current state of knowledge in this area is limited in various ways, but especially because the nature of the disorder is such that diagnosis is made based on self-report and the subjective experience of the patient (Bourget et al., 2017). Although this is not dissimilar to the nature of other psychiatric and psychological conditions, there is a need for further research into PTSD to be undertaken, using rigorous methodology and examining the links between PTSD and violence.

References

Beck, A. T., & Steer, R. A. (1990). *Beck Anxiety Inventory manual*. San Antonio, TX: The Psychological Corporation.

Beck, A. T., Steer, R. A., & Brown, G. K. (1990). *Beck Depression Inventory-II manual*. San Antonio, TX: The Psychological Corporation.

Blakey, S. M., Love, H., Lindquist, L., Beckham, J. C., & Elbogen, E. B. (2018). Disentangling the link between posttraumatic stress disorder and violent behavior: Findings from a nationally representative sample. *Journal of Consulting and Clinical Psychology, 86*(2), 169–178. doi:10.1037/ccp0000253

Bourget, D. M., Gagné, P., & Wood, S. F. (2017). Dissociation: Defining the concept in criminal forensic psychiatry. *Journal of American Academic Psychiatry Law, 45*, 147–160.

Brett, E. (1993). Classifications of post-traumatic stress disorder in DSM-IV: Anxiety disorder, dissociative disorder, or stress disorder? In J. R. T. Davidson & E. B. Foa (Eds.), *Post-traumatic stress disorder: DSM-IV and beyond* (pp. 191–204). Washington, DC: APA.

Douglas, K. S., Guy, L. S., & Hart, S. D. (2009). Psychosis as a risk factor for violence to others: A meta-analysis. *Psychological Bulletin, 135*(5), 679–706.

Elbogen, E. B., Dennis, P. A., & Johnson, S. C. (2016). Beyond mental illness: Targeting stronger and more direct pathways to violence. *Clinical Psychological Science, 4*(5), 747–459.

Fazel, S., Gautam, G., Linsell, L., Geddes, J. R., & Grann, M. (2009). Schizophrenia and violence: Systematic review and meta-analysis. *PLoS Med, 6*(8), e1000120. doi:10.1371/journal.pmed.1000120

Ginzburg, K., Koopman, C., & Butler, L. D. (2006). Evidence for a dissociative subtype of post-traumatic stress disorder among help-seeking childhood sexual abuse survivors. *Journal of Trauma Dissociation, 7*, 7–27.

Hodgkins, S. (2008). Violent behaviour among people with schizophrenia: A framework for investigators of causes, and effective treatment, and prevention. *Philosophical Transactions of the Royal Society of Biological Sciences, 363*(1503), 2505–2518. doi:10.1098/rstb.2008.0034

NICE (2005). *CG26: Post-traumatic stress disorder (PTSD): The management of PTSD in adults and children in primary and secondary care*. London, UK: NICE.

Paulhus, D. L. (1998). *Paulhus Deception Scales (PDS): The balanced inventory of desirable responding-7*. North Tonawanda, NY: Multi-Health Systems Inc.

Pearlman, L. A. (2003). *Trauma and Attachment Belief Scale (TABS)*. Los Angeles, CA: WPS.

Shapiro, F. (1989). Efficacy of the eye movement desensitization procedure in the treatment of traumatic memories. *Journal of Trauma and Stress, 2*(2), 199–223.

Shapiro, F. (1990). *The EMDR approach to psychotherapy.* Watsonville, CA: EMDR Institute.

Steuwe, C., Lanius, R. A., & Frewen, P. A. (2012). Evidence for a dissociative subtype of PTSD by latent profile and confirmatory factor analyses in a civilian sample. *Depression and Anxiety, 29,* 689–700.

Varshney, M., Mahapatra, A., Krishnan, V., Gupts, R., & Deb, K. S. (2016). Violence and mental illness: What is the true story? *Journal of Epidemiology Community Health, 70*(3), 223–225.

Wolf, E. J., Miller, W., & Reardon, A. F. (2012). A latent class analysis of dissociation and posttraumatic stress disorder. *Archives of General Psychiatry, 69,* 698–705.

World Health Organisation (2016 version). *International Classification of Diseases 10th Version.* Author. Available from http://apps.who.int/classifications/icd10/browse/2016/en

Chapter 9

Conclusion

Ruth J. Tully and Jennifer Bamford

Why case studies?

Very often in academic study, it is the large-scale studies of populations that receive the most attention and weight, quite appropriately due to the reliability of conclusions incorporating a high number of individuals under testing. However, as practitioners in the field, what we have often found is that the various idiosyncrasies of our clients can offer us a real opportunity to expand our understanding of what works with people who might not fit the more mainstream clinical 'mould'. You will notice that all of the chapters within this book took an individualised approach, or at least recommended one, to working with the client. There are many advantages of group-based interventions for forensic clients, including the opportunity to learn from others and to feel supported by those with similar difficulties (Brabender, Smolar & Fallon, 2004; Yalom & Leszcz, 2005). Group-based interventions are also, from a service perspective, a more cost-effective way of delivering treatment. However, where the responsivity needs of the individual outweigh the benefits of these group-based interventions, it may become necessary for additional expenditure to be directed towards these more complex individuals.

In some of the chapters, we have seen how individualised approaches were especially important for clients with needs that were less common. For instance, a violent female offender with an interest in sexual sadism has been described in Chapter 7, a notoriously rare and complex population making up between 2% and 12% of all perpetrators of sexual offences (Miller & Marshall, 2018). Other times, individualised intervention may become necessary due to timing. For example, in Chapter 2, the author describes a brief period of individualised intervention with a young person working under the time restraints associated with his impending trial and sentencing.

In writing a book using clinical case studies, we have endeavoured to offer an insight into the real-life applicability of forensic psychology by amalgamating our understanding of best practice, the practical constraints of organisations and resources, and consideration of the heterogeneous nature of our clients.

Formulation

It is beyond the scope of this concluding chapter to offer a full discussion of the history and study of psychological formulation, especially as this is an area that has attracted decades of discussion and argument (Sturmey & McMurran, 2011). What we have aimed to demonstrate within this book is that there is no single prescriptive way to formulate a case, but that all of the authors have derived their formulations through a comprehensive process of interviewing each client, reviewing their background history, and incorporating the use of psychometric assessment measures where appropriate. Formulation is, as we hope to demonstrate, at the heart of understanding the client, assessing their presenting problems, and from there, designing effective treatments to help them change their unhelpful thinking patterns or behaviour. Formulation is therefore crucial, as the process is open-ended. Formulations can be dynamic and change as the client develops, as is often the case with young people, or as the person's circumstances change. Additionally, what we initially consider as the problem may come, over time, to represent a symptom of a different problem altogether. We, as clinicians, therefore need to be flexible to the idea that our understanding of clients may change over time if indeed we have the opportunity to remain involved with clients over a period of time. In Chapter 4, we saw the application of long-term schema therapy within a secure hospital setting, offering the opportunity to revisit the formulation and refine it over time. This is not always possible, and as evidenced in Chapter 3 regarding a Court referral, sometimes formulations are generated and never revisited by that clinician because of the short-term nature of the assessment.

Formulation is also important when contributing to decisions regarding risk management. For example, in Chapter 3 we saw how the author utilised the Risk for Sexual Violence Protocol (RSVP; Hart et al., 2003) to derive scenario plans for future sexual violence and areas for future risk management, and also how this risk assessment tool contributed to their understanding of the client's primary areas of treatment need. Formulations, in this sense, can guide our understanding of Offence Paralleling Behaviours (OBPs; Jones, 2004, 2010), which are behaviours that closely relate to (or mirror) the identified problem behaviours, and which may indicate that risk is still manifesting, or in some cases that risk is imminent.

However, as we saw in Chapter 6, sometimes case formulation is complicated by co-morbid diagnoses, such as learning disability and Autism Spectrum Disorder (ASD). In these cases, it can be difficult to separate out the aetiology of presenting problems, which may have overlapping relevance. Further compounding the reliability of formulation is the problem of information decay, that is, the degree to which accurate information about the client is either difficult to get, has been lost over time (especially relevant for clients with long forensic histories), or the degree to which the client and their file information show gross inconsistencies. This can lead clinicians to become investigators whereby they have to seek all relevant information or risk relying on incomplete information, which may result in risk being under- or overestimated.

Some clients will, understandably, not enjoy having their life mapped out and inferences made, which they often perceive as judgments, about how their experiences have shaped them. This can feel intrusive and, if lacking insight or if they deny having committed offences that they are convicted of, can feel mis-representative of them. This has brought about a surge in awareness regarding the value of shared formulations with clients, this being a process by which the client has engaged in a collaboration with the clinician to uncover the reasons for their behaviour (Weerasekera, 1996). Another important, and emerging, element to case formulation and risk assessment is the importance of including 'protective factors', which have their roots in the positive psychology movement (Seligman & Csikszentmihalyi, 2000). In a number of the enclosed chapters, you will have seen consideration of the Structured Assessment of Protective Factors (SAPROF; de Vogel et al., 2012), which is a protective factors tool that offers a strengths-based approach to formulation. The application of such tools offers a greater balance to the prognosis of the client's ability to refrain from returning to the presenting problems.

Complications

The collection of case studies in this book highlights the various settings within which clients can be assessed and offered treatment. Chapters 7 and 8 refer to prison settings, Chapters 2 and 3 refer to community-based clients, and Chapters 4–6 refer to inpatient settings. Within each of these settings, there are differing resources available to practitioners and patients, but the environment itself is also worthy of note here, in particular, the specific nature of the prison environment. Whilst some may argue that the structural conditions of prison fail to show consistent damaging effects on the well-being of prisoners (Bonta & Gendreau, 1990), others have argued that prison impacts levels of distress, vulnerability, and suicide (see Liebling & Maruna, 2005, for an extensive contribution to this area). So what impact do these environments have on our formulation of difficulties? It may be reasonably straightforward to formulate that an increase in anxiety from a prisoner may be, at least in part, due to being in a custodial setting where their rights have been taken away, they struggle with low self-efficacy, and may be fearful for their safety amongst others whom they view as violent and volatile. This needs careful consideration, as although as practitioners we cannot change the environment, we can do our best to ensure we are responsive to the individual's needs, which are impacted by context.

However, it is less straightforward to consider the degree to which this environment might impact the interventions we are delivering to our clients away from the prison wing. For example, if we are teaching men in prison to negotiate their needs with others through assertive communication, how does that assist them when faced with a situation where they are attacked by a prisoner under the influence of illicit substances and armed with a makeshift weapon? In a very early study conducted in the USA, which has continued application and relevance today, Sykes (1958) referred to prisoners engaging in a game of dominance where their willingness to defend themselves was tested, usually by the prisoner being required to demonstrate a willingness to use violence or aggression. Those working in prison environments will know all too well the power dynamics and imbalances that exist in these environments between prisoners, and also between prisoners and staff. This is one of the complications with interventions delivered in secure environments; the culture of that environment, and the secrecy around that culture, is difficult to understand by those outside of it. It is therefore difficult to appreciate the extent to which learning from interventions is as easily applied as one might expect it to be if the patient were living in the community. Whilst these difficulties exist in custody, others also argue that prisoners require specific psychological support in making the transition from custody to the community (Haney, 2002). Psychological assessments and interventions therefore need to be responsive to the individual, as well as their needs arising from the specific forensic setting in which they have resided.

Another complication endemic to the role of a psychologist is the degree to which what we *want* to do, and what is considered good practice, is mediated by what we *can* do. Sometimes we work in services where we are fortunate enough to make our own decisions on how to assess, formulate, and treat a case, and other times we have to adapt to the prescriptive nature of what our service has to offer in terms of our time and resources. Psychologists often have to navigate the complex world of budget cuts, restricted resources, and impossible time limitations. They therefore have to be adept at not only working with clients but also negotiating their needs with other professionals when time and resources are limited and expectations are high. Psychologists therefore have to do their best to maintain professional integrity and resiliency in the face of organisational demands. These are the things that remain unsaid in chapters such as those enclosed but which require some appreciation.

Good practice in forensic settings

In each chapter, we offer examples of good practice, whether this relates to the therapy approach, the methods of assessment, or the responsivity considerations. In Chapter 4 we saw the value of a multidisciplinary team approach to the assessment and treatment of a patient, as well as their longer-term assessment by a team who understood the client's difficulties. In Chapter 5, the author highlighted the difficulties of working with clients with fluctuating levels of motivation and openness, and how we need to be responsive to this within treatment. In Chapter 6, the author highlighted the importance of adhering to a complex range of interplaying responsivity needs to maximise treatment gains for the client. Underlying many of these interventions is the importance of working towards a therapeutic alliance, achieved through a combination of the personal attributes of the therapist (honesty, confidence, warmth, etc.) and therapist techniques (reflection, noting past success, and facilitating the expression of affect; Ackerman & Hilsenroth, 2003). We hope that by sharing some of our clinical experiences in this book, we have contributed to the literature available on sharing good practice and effective treatments with a complex client group.

Not made overtly obvious in the enclosed chapters are various everyday demonstrations of good practice, which those working in forensic fields will be familiar with, but which are not always discussed. Examples may include:

- having to contravene confidentiality with a client in order to communicate imminent risk to self/others when the individual discloses suicidality or violent plans;
- having to navigate through interview sessions with difficult, manipulative, or sometimes subtly aggressive clients using an empathic approach and robust self-awareness to reduce the impact of this upon an assessment;
- remaining aware of our personal feelings about clients and utilising supervision to discuss those cases which stay with us;
- supporting colleagues with the demands of working in forensic environments; and
- managing the impact of staff who, despite not meaning harm, may demonstrate inappropriate or harmful ways of managing clients.

Good practice can go beyond the client and extend to how we treat our colleagues, how we communicate and work with external services, right the way down to how we manage data protection and administrative duties. It is the responsibility of every psychologist to know what good practice means and to abide by their code of conduct to maintain high standards of practice. At the end of the day, we are people working with (often vulnerable) other people, and irrespective of their offending behaviour, all of them require the basics of care and respect if we are to have any chance of promoting that they demonstrate these same qualities and desist from offending on release/discharge into the community.

Conclusions

In the opening chapter of this book, we set out our aim to provide a set of case studies which would offer the reader an insight into the idiosyncratic nature of the assessment, formulation, and treatment of a range of service users from a breadth of forensic settings. We have discussed sexual deviancy, personality disorder, neurodevelopmental disorder, ASD, sexual sadism, and trauma within a range of settings, including the community, prison, and psychiatric hospitals. These few topics are just some of the very varied cases that we, as psychologists, work with. Whilst each individual author may have an area of specialism, it is generally accepted that psychologists are able, with sufficient experience and training, to work with a vast array of people, 'disorders', and populations. The varied work of a psychologist is often, in our experience, what keeps practitioners interested in the field, and we hope this book offers an example of that diversity. We have argued for the importance of balancing good practice and consideration of 'what works' with an individualised approach to the treatment of those with complex presenting problems and diagnoses, and we would invite the opportunity for more texts of this kind.

References

Ackerman, S. J., & Hilsenroth, M. J. (2003). A review of therapist characteristics and techniques positively impacting the therapeutic alliance. *Clinical psychology Review, 23*, 1–33.

Bonta, J., & Gendreau, P. (1990). Re-examining the cruel and unusual punishment of prison life. *Law & Human behaviour, 14*, 347–372.

Brabender, V., Smolar, A. I., & Fallon, A. E. (2004). *Essentials of group therapy.* Hoboken, NJ: Wiley.

de Vogel, V., de Ruiter, C., Bouman, Y., & de Vries Robbé, M. (2012). *SAPROF: Structured assessment of PROtective factors.* Utrecht, The Netherlands: Van Der Hoeven Stichting.

Haney, C. (2002). *The psychological impact of incarceration: Implications for post-prison adjustment.* Paper prepared for the "From Prison to Home" conference, January 30–31, Bethesda, Maryland, USA.

Hart, S. D., Kropp, P. R., Laws, D. R., Klavern, J., Logan, C., & Watt, K. A. (2003). *The Risk for Sexual Violence Protocol (RSVP).* Burnaby, BC: The Mental Health, Law, and Policy Institute of Simon Fraser University.

Jones, L. (2004). Offence Paralleling Behaviour (OPB) as a framework for assessment and interventions with offenders. In A. Needs & G. Towl (Eds.), *Applying psychology to forensic practice* (pp. 34–63). Oxford, UK: Blackwell.

Jones, L. (2010). Case formulation with personality disordered offenders. In A. Tennant & K. Howells (Eds.), *Using time, not doing time* (pp. 45–62). Chichester, UK: Wiley-Blackwell.

Liebling, A., & Maruna, S. (2005). *The effects of imprisonment.* Cullompton, Devon: Willan Publishing.

Miller, H. A., & Marshall, E. A. (2018). Comparing solo- and co-offending female sex offenders on variables of pathology, offense characteristics, and recidivism. *Sexual Abuse.* Published online. doi:10.1177%2F1079063218791179

Seligman, M. E. P., & Csikszentmihalyi, M. (2000). Positive psychology: An introduction. *American Psychologist, 55*, 1–5.

Sturmey, P., & McMurran, M. (2011). Forensic case formulation: Emerging issues. In P. Sturmey & M. McMurran (Eds.), *Forensic case formulation* (pp. 283–304). Chichester, UK: John Wiley & Sons.

Sykes, G. (1958). *The society of captives: A study of maximum-security prison.* Princeton, NJ: Princeton University Press.

Weerasekera, P. (1996). *Multiperspective case formulation: A step toward treatment integration.* Malabar, FL: Krieger.

Yalom, I. D., & Leszcz, M. (2005). *Theory and practice of group psychotherapy* (5th ed.). New York, NY: Basic Books.

Glossary of terms

Antisocial Personality Disorder   is characterised by pervasive impulsive, reckless, irresponsible, and often criminal behaviour. **Dissocial Personality Disorder** can be seen as the ICD-10 equivalent, although these have some differences.

Attachment   is defined by Bowlby (1969) as a *'lasting psychological connectedness between human beings'.* Childhood, he suggested, played a critical role in the formation of attachments, and early experiences could have an impact on the relationships people form later in life. Attachments tend to be enduring, meaning they may last a very long time.

Autism Spectrum Condition (ASC) or Autism Spectrum Disorder (ASD)   affects social interaction, communication, interests, and behaviour. It includes Asperger syndrome and childhood autism. Some people also use the term 'neurodiverse' (as opposed to people without autism being 'neurotypical'). The main features of ASC typically start to develop in childhood, although the impact of these may not be apparent until there is a significant change in the person's life, such as a change of school. In the UK, it is estimated that about 1 in every 100 people has ASC.

Avoidant-Fearful Attachment Style   is characterised by a negative view of self and others. Those who fall into this category view themselves as unworthy and undeserving of love. Additionally, they feel that others are unworthy of their love and trust because they expect that others will reject or hurt them. Given their negative view of self and that others are bound to hurt them, those with an avoidant-fearful attachment style tend to avoid close involvement with others in order to protect themselves from anticipated rejection.

Borderline Personality Disorder   is otherwise known as **Emotionally Unstable Personality Disorder** and is a disorder characterised by attachment difficulties, unpredictable and fluctuating mood states, and emotional impulsivity.

Cognitive Analytic Therapy (CAT)   is a type of therapy that brings together ideas from analytic psychology with those from cognitive therapy (Ryle, 1997). Looking at past events and experiences, the therapy aims to understand why a person feels/thinks/behaves the way they do, before helping them problem-solve and develop new ways of coping. Each programme of therapy is tailored to the individual's needs, taking into account their current situation and problems they are dealing with. Considered a time-limited therapy, CAT can last between 4 and 24 weeks depending on the nature of the problem being explored, but an average of 16 weeks is considered the norm.

Cognitive Behavioural Therapy (CBT)   is a talking therapy that can help individuals manage problems by changing the way they think and behave, and learning about the relationship between thoughts, emotions, and behaviours. It is commonly used to help treat anxiety and depression.

Community Mental Health Team (CMHT)   is a team of mental health specialists who work with people in the community who have mental health difficulties, such as schizophrenia. CMHTs often include mental health nurses, psychiatrists, and psychologists.

Co-morbidity   is the presence of one or more additional diagnoses or disorders co-occurring with (that is, concomitant or concurrent with) a primary disorder; in the countable sense of the term, a co-morbidity (plural co-morbidities) is each additional disorder.

Confabulation   is where imaginary experiences are believed to have happened by the person, often as compensation for loss of memory.

Confidence Intervals (CI)   provide a way of expressing score precision of psychological tests and serve as a reminder that measurement error is inherent in all test scores. Measurement error relates to the fact that a test may not accurately measure the construct that it intends to. Psychological tests such as cognitive tests encourage practitioners to report the CI around the obtained scores and to use this information to ensure greater accuracy when interpreting test scores.

Depression   is more than simply feeling unhappy or fed up for a few days. Most people go through periods of feeling down, but depression involves persistent sadness for weeks or months rather than just a few days. Symptoms vary but can include continuous low mood and sadness, hopelessness, low self-esteem, tearfulness, loss of motivation, problems making decisions, or having thoughts of self-harm or suicide.

Dialectical Behaviour Therapy (DBT)   is a form of cognitive behavioural psychotherapy developed in the late 1980s to help better treat those with borderline personality disorder and other mental health disorders. The core DBT treatment areas are *mindfulness, emotion regulation, distress tolerance,* and *interpersonal effectiveness.* DBT treatment manuals, such as Linehan (2014), are available to help practitioners adhere to the treatment model.

Dismissive Attachment Style   is characterised by a positive view of self and a negative view of others. Those who fall into this category view themselves as worthy and deserving of love but feel that others are not worth trusting. They often feel that they are capable of loving but that potential partners are not trustworthy, are not supportive, and are likely to disappoint them. Given that they are fearful to open up and be vulnerable with others, they become avoidant of intimate relationships. They may claim to be overly independent, claim that they do not need others, and act as though their relationships are not a priority to them.

Dissociation associated with Post-Traumatic Stress Disorder (PTSD) involves a state of altered consciousness which is often reported as dissociative flashbacks, amnesia for some aspects of the trauma, and emotional numbing. Although PTSD is classed as an anxiety disorder, PTSD is also associated with an increased rate of dissociative symptoms.

Diagnostic and Statistical Manual of Mental Disorders-IV (DSM-IV) and International Statistical Classification of Diseases and Related Health Problems, 10th Version (ICD-10) are two different diagnostic manuals used to assess mental and personality disorders. Dissocial (ICD-10) and antisocial (DSM-IV) personality disorders can be considered as similar across the two manuals, as can emotionally unstable (ICD-10) and borderline (DSM-IV) personality disorders. The newest version of the DSM is **DSM-5**.

Dysexecutive Syndrome consists of a group of symptoms, usually resulting from brain damage, that fall into cognitive, behavioural, and emotional categories and tend to occur together.

EMDR is an abbreviation for 'Eye Movement Desensitisation and Reprocessing'. EMDR is included in the British NICE (2005) guidelines (CG26) for treating PTSD. EMDR is a powerful psychological treatment method that was developed by an American psychologist, Dr Francine Shapiro, in the 1980s. Since then a wealth of research has been conducted demonstrating its benefits in treating psychological trauma arising from experiences as diverse as war-related experiences, childhood sexual and/or physical abuse or neglect, natural disaster, assault, surgical trauma, road traffic accidents, and workplace accidents.

Epilepsy is a common condition that affects the brain and causes frequent seizures. Seizures are bursts of electrical activity in the brain that temporarily affect how it works. They can cause a wide range of symptoms.

Foetal Alcohol Syndrome is a type of Foetal Alcohol Spectrum Disorder (FASD), the name for all the various problems that can affect children if their mother drinks alcohol in pregnancy.

Formulation in psychology is the process of analysing why a particular behaviour occurred. In forensic psychology, the presenting problem can be a form of offending or other maladaptive, harmful behaviour. There are various ways of formulating, and many models support this approach to understanding behaviour.

Functional Family Therapy (FFT) is a short-term intervention program with an average of 12–14 sessions over three to five months

(Alexander et al., 2013). FFT works primarily with 11- to 18-year-old youths who have been referred for behavioural or emotional problems by the juvenile justice, mental health, school, or child welfare systems. Services are conducted in both clinic and home settings and can also be provided in schools, child welfare facilities, probation and parole offices / aftercare systems, and mental health facilities.

Generalised Anxiety Disorder (GAD)   is a condition that causes anxiety in relation to a wide range of issues rather than in relation to a specific event. People who have this condition feel anxious most days, and they struggle to feel relaxed. The condition has a range of psychological and physiological symptoms.

Institutionalisation   in a forensic context refers to when a person has been detained in a residential institution (prison, children's homes, hospitals, etc.) for a prolonged period of time, and as a result, they have come to fear (or possibly struggle with) having their own independence reinstated.

Learning Disability (LD)   is diagnosed when a person has significant problems with learning new skills/information (impaired intelligence) and a reduced ability to cope independently (impaired social functioning). It must have started before adulthood and have a lasting effect on the person. This is also referred to as Intellectual Disability within the literature on the topic.

Mental Health Act 2003   enables medical professionals to detain and treat people, even where this is against their will, on grounds of them having a diagnosable mental disorder considered to be severe. In the UK, detention under this Act this is sometimes informally referred to by people as 'sectioning', because the person is detained according to a 'section' of the legislation.

Meta-analysis   uses a statistical approach to combine the results from multiple studies in an effort to estimate the size of the effect being considered and/or to resolve uncertainty when different research projects have resulted in varied findings.

Mindfulness   is a practice that can help general well-being by helping the person reconnect with what is going on around them in the here and now rather than their thoughts wandering to the future or the past. It can help them notice the present moment and help them understand themselves better and avoid judgmental thoughts about themselves and/or other people.

Narcissistic Personality Disorder   is where an individual has a distorted self-image and unstable and intense emotions, is overly preoccupied with vanity, prestige, power, and personal adequacy, lacks empathy, and has an exaggerated sense of superiority.

Neurodevelopmental Disorders   are differences in the growth and development of the brain or central nervous system which usually become apparent when a person is a child. Examples include autism spectrum disorder and attention-deficit hyperactivity disorder.

NICE (the National Institute for Health and Care Excellence)   is an executive non-departmental public body of the Department of Health in the UK, which publishes guidelines for clinical practice.

Obsessive Compulsive Disorder (OCD)   is a mental health condition where a person has obsessive thoughts and compulsive activity.

Occupational Therapy   is the practice of providing practical support and skills training to help those with mental, physical, social, or learning difficulties. The aim is to help them to be able to carry out everyday tasks with confidence and independence.

Offence Paralleling Behaviour (OBP)   can be defined as any form of offence-related behavioural pattern that emerges at any point before or after an offence. It does not have to result in an offence but significantly resembles the sequence of behaviours that led to an offence (Jones, 2004).

Paranoid Personality Disorder   is characterised by paranoia and a pervasive suspiciousness of others. Individuals with this personality disorder may be hypersensitive and easily influenced, and may anticipate harm or ridicule from others.

Paraphilias   is described by the DSM-IV-TR (a mental health diagnostic manual) as *'recurrent, intense sexually arousing fantasies, sexual urges or behaviors generally involving nonhuman objects, the suffering or humiliation of oneself or one's partner, or children or other nonconsenting persons that occur over a period of six months'* (criterion A), which *'cause clinically significant distress or impairment in social, occupational, or other important areas of functioning'* (criterion B). DSM-IV-TR names eight specific paraphilic disorders (exhibitionism, fetishism, frotteurism, paedophilia, masochism, sexual sadism, voyeurism and transvestic fetishism plus a residual category, and paraphilia – not otherwise specified). Criterion B differs for exhibitionism, frotteurism, and paedophilia to include acting on these urges, and for sadism, acting on these urges with a non-consenting person.

Penile Plethysmography (PPG)   is a measure of blood flow to the penis, used as a proxy measure of sexual arousal.

Percentile ranks   in relation to psychological tests indicate an individual's performance when compared to the general population.

Personal Construct Theory   suggests that people develop personal constructs about how the world works. People then use these constructs to make sense of their observations and experiences.

Personality Disorders   are pervasive conditions that can cause a range of distressing symptoms and patterns of behaviour.

PIPE (Psychologically Informed Planned Environments)   residences are those designed in partnership between the criminal justice and health services in the UK to aid those who have personality disorder/difficulties or who may be otherwise resistant to treatment, resettling, and engaging with supervision. Staff within PIPEs have specialist psychologically informed training in order to aid them in supporting residents. These units offer close monitoring opportunities.

Post-Traumatic Stress Disorder (PTSD)   is an anxiety disorder caused by very stressful, frightening, or distressing events. Someone with PTSD often relives the traumatic event through nightmares and flashbacks and may experience feelings of isolation, irritability, and guilt.

Protective Factors   in the context of risk assessment are factors that may reduce the risk of an offence occurring. Protective factors are considered within risk assessment, and common protective factors include positive motivation for change, having a supportive social support, or developing good self-control. These factors can be internal (like self-control) or external (like having restrictions imposed on the person).

Psychosis   is characterised by an impaired relationship with reality. It is a symptom of serious mental disorders, such as schizophrenia. People who are experiencing psychosis   may have either hallucinations or delusions.

Psychoeducation   refers to the process of providing education and information to those seeking or receiving mental health/psychological services to aid their understanding of their condition.

Psychopathic Personality Disorder   is characterised by a constellation of interpersonal, affective, and behavioural characteristics. Psychopathic traits overlap with antisocial/dissocial personality traits. Traditionally, psychopathy is seen to comprise of an interpersonal/affective element (factor 1) and a social deviance (factor 2) (Hare, 1998).

Risk Factors   are a set of factors that can increase the risk of an event occurring. In forensic psychology, risk factors for offending would be factors that research has demonstrated increase the chances of an offence taking place. For example, factors include substance misuse, attitudes that permit violence, or problems with supervision.

Schizophrenia   is a mental health condition that is characterised often by hallucinations and delusions. The paranoid subtype of schizophrenia includes paranoid beliefs about others, usually self-referential fears that others are out to do the sufferer harm.

Schema   is a cognitive framework that a person uses to interpret themselves and the world around them. In schema therapy, these are the self-defeating life patterns of perception, emotion, and physical sensation (Young, 1990)

Schema Therapy (ST)   is a treatment for complex psychological problems that has developed over a period of some 25 years. Founded by Jeffrey Young (1990; Young et al., 2003), it combines aspects of cognitive-behavioural, interpersonal, psychodynamic, and experiential techniques. In comparison to CBT, ST places a more intensive focus upon an individual's problematic emotions, childhood difficulties, and the therapeutic relationship. ST has been adapted for effective use with forensic patients within secure mental health settings (Bernstein et al, 2007, 2012), and for use with individuals with personality disorders (Bamelis et al., 2015).

Schizoaffective Disorder   is a mental health condition in which a person experiences a combination of schizophrenia symptoms, such as hallucinations or delusions, and mood disorder symptoms, such as depression or mania.

Sex Offender Treatment Programme (SOTP) is one of a range of therapeutic programmes available for sexual offenders, providing a menu of interventions that are offered according to the level of risk and need of the offender.

Sexual Sadism Disorder is the condition of experiencing sexual arousal in response to the extreme pain, suffering, or humiliation of others.

Social Learning Theory is a theory of learning and social behaviour which proposes that new behaviours can be acquired by observing and imitating others (Bandura, 1977). It states that learning is a cognitive process that takes place in a social context and can occur purely through observation or direct instruction, even in the absence of motor reproduction or direct reinforcement. In addition to the observation of behaviour, learning also occurs through the observation of rewards and punishments, a process known as reinforcement. When a particular behaviour is rewarded regularly, it will most likely persist; conversely, if a particular behaviour is constantly punished, it will most likely desist.

Structured Professional Judgement (SPJ) risk assessment tools, unlike actuarial (statistical) methods of assessing risk, encourage assessors to consider the risk factors defined within the tool, but they allow the assessor the freedom to 'label' risk level depending on the factors present.

Therapeutic Community (TC), in prisons, is a democratic space that provides a residential, offending behaviour intervention for prisoners who have a range of complex offending behaviour risk areas, including emotional and psychological needs and personality disorders. TCs provide a 24/7 living-learning intervention for offenders whose primary criminogenic risk factors need to be targeted, whilst simultaneously addressing psychological and emotional disturbance.

Vulnerable Prisoner (VP) Wing is a special wing within a prison where vulnerable prisoners reside. They may be classed as vulnerable due to their offence type, meaning that they may be at risk of harm from other prisoners (usually sexual offending), mental health vulnerabilities, or physical health vulnerabilities. The VP wing prisoners are separated from the main population of the prison, often informally referred to by prisoners as 'the mains'.

References

Alexander, J. A., Waldron, H. B., Robbins, M. S., & Neeb, A. (2013). *Functional family therapy for adolescent behavior problems.* Washington, DC: American Psychological Association.

Bandura, A. (1977). *Social learning theory.* Englewood Cliffs, NJ: Prentice Hall.

Bamelis, L. L. M., Arntz, A., Wetzelaer, P., Verdoorn, R., & Evers, S. M. A. A. (2015). Economic evaluation of schema therapy and clarification-oriented psychotherapy for personality disorders: A multicenter, randomized controlled trial. *Journal of Clinical Psychiatry, 76,* 1432–1440.

Bernstein, D. P., Arntz, A., & de Vos, M. E. (2007). Schema-focused therapy in forensic settings: Theoretical model and recommendations for best clinical practice. *International Journal of Forensic Mental Health, 6*(2), 169–183.

Bernstein, D. P., Nijman, H., Karos, K., Keulen-de Vos, M. E., de Vogel, V., & Lucker, T. (2012). Schema Therapy for forensic patients with personality disorders: Design and preliminary findings of a multicenter randomized clinical trial in the Netherlands. *International Journal of Forensic Mental Health, 11*(4), S312–S324.

Bowlby J. (1969). *Attachment. Attachment and loss. Vol. 1: Loss.* New York, NY: Basic Books.

Hare, R. D. (1998). Psychopathy, affect and behaviour. In D. Cooke, A. Forth, & R. Hare (Eds.), *Psychopathy: Theory, research and implications for society* (pp. 105–139). Dordrecht: Kluwer.

Jones, L. (2004). Offence paralleling behaviour (OPB) as a framework for assessment and interventions with offenders. In A. Needs & G. Towl (Eds.), *Applying psychology to forensic practice* (pp. 34–63). Malden, MA, UK: Blackwell Publishing.

Linehan, M. M. (2014). *DBT skills training manual* (2nd ed.). New York, NY: Guilford Press.

NICE (2005). CG26: *Post-traumatic stress disorder (PTSD): The management of PTSD in adults and children in primary and secondary care.* London, UK: Author.

Ryle, A. (1997). The structure and development of borderline personality disorder: A proposed model. *British Journal of Psychiatry, 170,* 82–87.

Young, J. E. (1990). *Cognitive therapy for personality disorders: A schema-focussed approach.* Sarasota, FL: Professional Resource Press.

Young, J. E., Klosko, J., & Weishaar, M. (2003). *Schema therapy: A practitioner's guide.* New York, NY: Guilford.

Index